W9-COO-795

come walk

with Theo

look over

his shoulder

let him

reveal

a loving way

to see life

on earth

—Mickey Melragon

Maywood Public Library
121 S. 5th Ave.
Maywood, IL 60153

Thinking Wild:
Its Gifts of Insight

A Way to Make Peace with My Shadow

THEO GRUTTER

TURNING
STONE
PRESS

First published in 2013 by
Turning Stone Press, an imprint of
Red Wheel/Weiser, LLC
With offices at:
665 Third Street, Suite 400
San Francisco, CA 94107
www.redwheelweiser.com

Copyright © 2013 by Theo Grutter

All rights reserved. No part of this publication may be reproduced
or transmitted in any form or by any means, electronic or mechani-
cal, including photocopying, recording, or by any information storage
and retrieval system, without permission in writing from Red Wheel/
Weiser, LLC. Reviewers may quote brief passages.

ISBN: 978-1-61852-031-9

Cover design by Jim Warner
Cover image: Theo Grutter

Printed in the United States of America
IBT
10 9 8 7 6 5 4 3 2 1

*How can I love the wildness of Life if I cannot
jump the garden fence around my domesticated mind
and get a taste of that wild thinking outside?*

Acknowledgments

Thank you Taft Perry and Addie Johnson Talbott for helping me with the editing. Thank you Mickey Melragon for shining on me your unbreakable enthusiasm for this project. Thank you, Ann Elise Pollnow for the wonderful picture.

Contents

Introduction

Dear adventurer, I wrote this book to tease myself and other adventurous minds to look at our crooked lives and loves from a wider-angle view. This journey will sail us into the wild open sea. Out in that openness, it may at first be a rough ride for indoor minds. I promise to navigate the smoothest tags those waters allow. Welcome to the ride.

A Fruitful Meeting

Fifty years ago, in Paris, a young Swiss executive in the making met a young Belgian concert pianist in the making. Both shared a doubt that they had embarked on the life they were meant to live. There, a wonderfully confused and fruitful season started for us. And, yes, Clara, when I invited you on a lifelong trip, you so generously said, "Wherever you want to go, I want to go."

So, we spent some years as vagabonds, exploring and traveling to regions far and wide, and also to those inside ourselves that we had never visited before. I was writing and questioning myself. Early on, I published some notes I called *Anger and Gentleness*. Yet, I was more angry than gentle then, because Life had not stuck to the morals I had learned to expect and accept.

Nonetheless, this tumult of thoughts started a fortunate adventure for us. Since then we have been migrating, with our troupe of ultimately five children ('till they flew out into their own adventures), between the coast of Alaska in spring and a tropical fishing village in fall, and each year trekking in far-off cultures and lands as we migrated between our two homes. After a few years logging in camps, I have now been fishing alone for a living in the South and in the North for some forty-five years. I have spent maybe five thousand days and nights alone on the ocean, fishing. This helps me to leap out of my society's "orderly" scene. This solitude has also become my drug of choice. We lead a simple life that has been sweeter to us than I was told to expect.

Well-Kept Mysteries

From far below the veneer of my schooled mind, an old, old voice teases me: "Life, not as you want it to be, but Life as it is, with pimples, crimes, do-gooders, scorpion tails, and farts, is the most perfect expression of compassion. Each creature is fully engaged in helping others in a way mostly beyond the scope of your homely imagination. One look at this vision could instantly make you go mad with joy!"

And I answer: "Just a tiny glimpse, please, of this mind-crushing beauty. It makes my world a sweeter world."

With this old, old voice in my heart always charming me to break out of my cocoon, I try to make peace with my shadow— to celebrate Life *as it is*. For this I put my mind to explore what extended functions in Life those rascals and cussed acts have, which our moralists and agronomists demonize as sins, weeds, pests, crimes or simply as evil. Obviously, the evolutionary forces of Life tested those tricksters countless times. And they survived. So, I infer, they also must be forms of Life's joys. Here are the well-kept mysteries of Life's goodness that, solved, could ruin many of our dearest prejudices, closely held angers and ready criticisms. Indeed, strict believers might be less able to indulge in bashing the Creator for being such a curious tinker.

The ways of Life are mostly mysterious. So, compared with our exact science, ever preoccupied with pretended clarity, the fertile, messy science of likenesses is for me a bullet train to wisdom. In my climb to glimpse this vista, to rethink and to create anew my view of how Life's morals work, I like to freely use likenesses from any tribe of Life to solve a problem we share. For this I had to slay that darn arrogance seeing man as from a superior order than the rowdy Life at large. Metaphors have become for me wonderful aids in thinking. They supply me with prefabricated answers that have often been assembled by other species long before our time. Why not try to learn from what others have already figured out? So, expect here some of this creative untidiness. To accept a woman or a man as is, not as my learned morals want her or him to be, has now become the daily mental safari and joy of my thinking. It's time to be born into a more wondrous world!

The Wisdom in a Thorn

My project here is to dismantle my negative feelings: guilt, fear, foul mouth, or that darn notion of evil, and to instead create positive feelings by adding new viewpoints to those hazy old vistas. When Life lines up some creative mischief for me, it starts by whirling around my good old common sense, puzzling it with a new hint, teasing it until it blinks—and I look yet again. A stagnant mind stirs into fresh action.

Dark events, when spotlighted from another viewpoint, instill less fear. Sad happenings might tease out a smile when I am introduced to their lovely side effects. They may brighten up and get me to love, a little, my own ugly ducklings and ghosts. How do I get the wisdom in a thorn? Monks may sit and meditate on theoretical constructs. Scientists may test hypotheses. I try to step outside the garden fence through a gateway of metaphorical pictures. This greater mosaic beyond the manmade world shows me how other species solve the problems we all share. It teases out in me these deeper insights I need.

For instance, I mull over the wisdom in anger. Sometimes, deep anger is the only way to get things done. Anger with tears in the eyes, clean as mountain water with no sugar added, can clearly speak unspeakable truths. Such anger gave Jesus the steam to chase the merchants from the temple. The adrenaline rush of anger can focus our vision and power. Bless your anger. Give this unwanted child a benediction of your own. Hang on! Here starts the adventure into thinking dangerously wild.

Conservation of the Inner Rainforest

Here is an example of how thinking in likenesses can help to better see our world. I compare intense agriculture with a school's intensive cultivation of a child's inner rainforests. I see similarities in the side effects that occur when a merry land that is filthy rich in options is forced into a monoculture of oil palms, just as a young man's merry soul is clear-cut, weeded, traversed with roads, and made to sit down and stay level for a cash crop of some marketable expertise. "Smart" drugs like Ritalin and Adderall can focus that mind that was born so darn poetic, and make it more focused and practical.

In the Sumatra palm plantations, many species of Life's joys, which give this green community the gift of self-maintenance, start to disappear. With just oil palms to eat, what bird wants to live here? The lemon butterflies are losing their red berry bushes, from which they hang their love nests. The Sumatra boys lose the bark trees where they would carve in their lover's name. In brief, a drastic loss of sounds, perfumes, genes, forms of lovemaking, species, ideas, and colors. Yet our big rigs are happy. They get an extra serving of bio-diesel to eat up the miles on our speedways.

Transplant a youngster's ecstatic mind into a hothouse for schooling, and the deep nutrients, the deep love from Life at large, may fail to reach that little lover. Her magic talents and innate trace elements are shy tricksters, and may be crowded out of her mind altogether. We might together wonder, what inner songbirds go silent in highly structured schooling? Where are the teaching-stories for solving problems, or the options for cooking fish, or the ways for getting rid of fleas, that get forgotten in such a simplistic approach? What are the rare passions, the lightamines (environmental messages of awesome complexity) and the vitamins in a young exuberant mind that disappear? In such indoor lecturing, whole species of thoughts, restorative metaphors for fighting gloom or anger or fear, may go dark. How does a young mind learn to enjoy juicy, fertile intercourse with Life at large in a world reduced to words?

The Key to Serenity

In such an impoverished mindscape, impoverished souls may rise, with terrible droughts of rich, caring love, and with fearful wildfires of egotism. We can see here in action the rule for any creature's capacities: use it or lose it. Use our capacity for love and connection, or lose it. Yet when we lose it, our tipsy goddess on high heels, the economy, celebrates. So I have to keep thinking about how to preserve a sound ecology in my deeper mind—this is the key to serenity.

The quest for this larger vision is not so far off. It is not superhuman, or beyond our natural capacities. It is not amoral, or blasphemous, even when our wilder thoughts might lead us into territory not within our familiar societal turf. It's like seeing the wonderful color feast of the maple leaves being "killed" by fall and applauding the "killer" for doing her good work. Or meeting a gay couple in love and truly feeling their joy. Any modest mental adventure can be a start. This leap of imagination can be ours.

Just because there are awesome fancies of Life that seem quite beyond my mental capacity to digest, there's no reason not to try. Repeatedly hammering my mean, impenetrable convictions with ever more viewpoints may slowly soften and open them to new guests.

I think that the day a woman or a man dares to take off into thinking wild, to scout for likenesses outside humanism with its man-centered worldview (which is intent to traverse the great jungle of Life with its neat little ballroom steps), to commit their love to the Earth, this is a lucky day. On that day all birds will sing. No, this step beyond does not make monsters of us. How do I know? For I do it—and I can barely remember when I haggled with somebody mean-heartedly. It beats preaching the duty to be tolerant and forgiving. It ultimately distills these duties into sweet natural needs.

Rascal Theo and Thinking Wild

So many good happenings have visited me in my seventy-eight years. I know of no other man's life I would trade mine with. (Ah, Clara will catch me with this splendid piece of bragging.) And one of the best happenings: to bring here some light to these tracts of my dark inner Amazon by way of the many new catalyst-thoughts with which they acquaint me.

Among adventurous lovers, we can take off our niceness masks. That's how we help each other to better physical and emotional health. That's how we do our spiritual fitness courses. I used to be angry with many people and happenings because they did not perform according to the steps I learned to dance growing up. Had I read this book in my twenties, I would have given its rascal author hell. I am now a more cheerful man. I am even treated, at times, to a morsel of serenity. So, please don't cock your gun, not just yet, when Theo scales a wall of your fortress. He might bring you news from the outside.

About ten years ago, I published *Dancing with Mosquitoes: To Liberate the Mind from Humanism*. Now, in the journey of this book, I spread wide my arms and beg, "Help me to embrace my reader with love, and share some more mischievous thoughts that have come up." I offer them in this freshly baked collection of more than a hundred short "try-me-outs."

Are you ready to stretch your imagination a little more than from the broom handle to the broom? I love to track down Life's incredible connectedness. For this I let the forms of ideas remain complex, and give their expression free range. I hope they will break the rules of traditional writing. May they trespass where they should not, so wisdom may run loose to do its very large and unfocused loving. But please, bring your own observations on this safari into our deeper selves.

These stories are for people on the move with a continual unfolding of vistas. There is no way to guess the result, and so the result is of no importance. People eager to settle down on perfectly cooked and rounded conclusions are not invited to this outdoor storytelling. Read slowly or quickly, a page at a time, or all the way through once and again. A little snack of it a day keeps boredom as well as indigestion away. No need to read from beginning to end. Just open this book wherever, whenever you need an energy bar to chew on.

The good, old hat common sense is the loudest loudspeaker in town, so there might be profit in reading some of it twice. This is meant to be an organic process, delving into a wider worldview, exploring new ways to say new things, beyond fake clarity. A workshop. It's far from being a result. So please do not judge these writings sentence by sentence. Here there are things so deeply felt, they can only be said without elegance. And please forgive me and ignore me when I slip into preaching. I learned English only as an adult. This may be good for the reader as I am less tempted to play with words, but I do use words in unusual ways. Your willingness to travel into these wilds with me gladdens my heart, more so than having hooked another boatload of fish.

Theo Grutter

1. To what would I amount, were I only born once?

I can keep on giving birth to Theo in a thousand different ways.

Welcoming Troubles

My goofs, my pains, my shadow that follows me so lovingly, these are my midwives.

Take a specialized cell. Not many birth pains here. Yet the geneticists starve it, give it hell, and lo! That little couch potato is forced to wake up to become a stem cell, a general practitioner again, and to bring to light all its muted memories. Troubles? I do not kill them, but instead welcome them to do the same to me.

Look at some of the tundra grasses. Only those tufts that get vigorously nibbled on by an exploding arctic hare population keep birthing, bringing forth their hidden talents. Only these battered tufts give light to their dormant capacity to produce toxins against these deadly nibblers in their grass and fireweed fields.

Take a man who risks discomfort, deprivation, fasting, low-level contamination, exposure to unusual customs, religions, and radiations. Being caught in a bind or in ripped pants. Take a woman who cradles in her arms the biggest bundle of curious uncertainties she can swim with, a man who dares to be alone to the limit of not being sunk by loneliness. These provocations can *Rocks that roll do not get loaded down with muck and moss.* give birth to their souls' unborn capacity for immunities beyond their regular system of immunity: immunity against fear, guilt, blaming, hate, foul mouth—immunities that, even caught in a

1

mess, can render her serene! Think of a shaman. He begs the tough, wild environment to give birth to his inherited, wild capacities that a practical commonsense life never intends to fertilize. He begs God to put more of His looks in his eyes.

Are We Not All Walking Torches?

Take a poet. You meet an extraordinary man who, against all the prizes offered, fought off to become specialized, so to remain a stem cell of Society for life. You meet an extraordinary woman who could hold on to her embryonic innocence and to the wealth of all her inherited options, against all the economy's siren songs. Likewise, watch how richly I dance when I am a little tipsy from a drink and my internal editor fell asleep.

A rather monogamous sex life can anchor a man more in routine than anything else. To settle us in a routine sweet to our kids, is that not what our sex's wonderfully bonding ecstasy is now mostly about? Yet life may for instance choose a special man and impose sexual abstinence on him. With this "quake" Life may seek to wake the seer and healer in this special woman or man. Think also of the surge of energy the mountain stream builds up behind the dam we put in its way!

Every critter is the temporary solution to a difficulty. And, thank God, Life never tires to shovel new trouble in its own path.

Three times thanks for a life that is not dumbed down with ease and comfort!

Take a creek. The beaver, that devil, forks a dam into its flow. Among the drowned trees, up stands next spring a new wetland flower gloriously shouting, "Hello!"

There are those troublemakers among us who are after more than what niceness can offer us. Are we not all walking torches soaked with different flammables all itching to be lit, some to burst into kilowatts, others into watts? There are seeds that need a forest fire to sprout!

Do You Want to Be Safe?

To see and understand the unknown things, some of our helper spirits want to be treated to a sickness, a physical abnormality, a shipwreck, a handicap, a persecution, a sandstorm, a depression, an obsession or a hurricane to be teased out into the light and give their insights. Name here any breakup of a dear routine. Others of our great "ghosts" are Sleeping Beauties. They cannot stir in a climate of niceness and of being polite. What can the fear of not finding a bed do to a tired man who has slept on a pile of hay in the past? Some good patriarch wants the goat grazing tied to a stake, promising, "You will be safe!" Dear adventurer, do you want to be safe?

A woman learns from a molting crab. Bursting with vitality, she breaks the promises she made as an adolescent. Unlocked, she opens her arms wide to a larger world. And zap! A seam in her conventional wisdom cracks. Careful Theo, with your promises— they can slow your growth!

A man dares to venture outside the fortress of his system of beliefs that society has tattooed into his mind. Oh, the terror of all the thousand voices of the wild! Single-mindedly, he battles the confusing sea of unlimited options he plunged into. High from that cocktail of dangers, a talent sunk in him long ago may resurface again. He ventures off the highway and stumbles into beautiful and helpful likenesses the fainthearted have given up for lost.

Full Exposure

The effect of a fuller exposure, not only to germs but to the torrent of life at large can create a whole new string of vaccinations that Theo, if nicely bedded down in a life in a padded niche, would never have had the chance to welcome in. "Theo, walk the tightrope of exuberance, braving the abyss of acute mania, to keep lavishly awake! Danger can breathe alive in your body a thousand kinds of dormant helper proteins."

The Kulu River in Kashmir told me: "There are physical pains that can or should not be evicted, but with a change of vision can be halved." Think of a woman's birthing pains that are anesthetized with the exuberant sense of a love affair.

And so, when I enter a stadium, a church, a concert hall, I feel a timid sense of defeat overshadowing my sense of relief. Then the God of creativity encourages me to be brave, to live my share of "disorderly" wild states of mind, to not lightly take refuge in an orderly, predictable mental scene, like that of the sports, the esthetic and anesthetic arts, music, rituals, games, which are all realities reduced and whitewashed of the imponderables so to fit my whimpering, reasoning ego. What a waste of a curious day full of try-me-outs, of things I have never thought, talked about or done; a day I never get up and ask one of those try-me-outs for a dance. Playing the "good boy" makes my creativity yawn.

Fishing Alone

Fishing alone on the oceans, maybe five thousand days and nights by now, is my breakout from society's orderly scene. This bouquet of solitudes has become part of my practice. This magnificent scene of power and beauty is mostly still out of our control, a reality that spices my life with many flavors of anxieties, leaving me never quite sure what gift will unwrap itself in front of me. After a day or two in this untamed environment, my perception and my thinking rearrange themselves, a little like the view of a goldfish does when its bowl is emptied into the lake.

In comfort and abundance, a biological law commands a cell, as well as a man, to specialize and to settle down in a niche. In hostile provocative environments, that same law fosters not only new species of animals and plants, it orders a man or woman to generalize and to give birth to new species of realities from which we can draw new tricks of adaptations and advice. All pain turns into wax for the candle of insights. To adapt our mentality to different life situations, some of us may use also psychoactive plants as a tool. For mind-expanding medicine, I prefer to sometimes drag Theo by the hair out of his comfy routine and into the four winds. And with all his senses stretched out, I make those winds shake that dear old chestnut tree. And, my my, some small tasty fruits start falling down my way.

Our Own Love Song

Here is the dilemma of us parents. I burn to protect our five children from harm. And then I immediately think of the great people in my life who only became great because they were tempered, broken open by fire, setbacks, years of ice age, deprivations and depression, broken love, drunkenness, and you name it. What hammering, ah! And by the terrible risk of going completely to pieces by these initiations. This was the cost of their ticket out of mediocrity.

Are we not all embryos, fantastic grab bags of memories heaped with gifts that are all impatient to be unwrapped and given light? Theo's mind is a new moon that gives itself birth. It took two hundred and seventy days of tender isolation in the womb to give birth to little Theo. Do you want your mind to remain in a placenta of some -ism for life? Socialism, Buddhism, humanism? Or, we can dive into this huge ocean of ideas and find out what this godly engine of creativity can do with us.

May each man play his own tune and love song, and compose it on his cruise on a daily basis. May she be creative and recompose that song a thousand times. May he not hold on to his baby shoes for life. Tomorrow, may he include in his Song the beavers of the Alaska National Wildlife Refuge, the willows and the wolves. How could I weep today for the same reasons as I did fifty years ago? I do not want to waste my life guarding a fence.

From one mysterious seed, I see Life bringing forth this ever more amazing division of labor to better and better care for itself. Creator of ever more options to survive, first in the sea, then a feeble foothold on land, even a tiptoe on the moon. What lust for diversity and leaving

I awaken a sleeping talent. It joins Theo's orchestra. My bag of birthday gifts gets filled.

5

home! You are not alone with your homesickness. No creature is exempt from nostalgia.

Life loves critters, so it stirs them, cooks them, and knocks them about to bring their capacities and flavors out. Modest stress from daring to meet what others avoid seems nature's favorite rejuvenation pill.

2. Dear adventurer, think of an encounter, any encounter. Here is your chance for a work of art.

We are all discreet artists, and the greatest of us, like Clara, simply shine and do not exhibit. It is said we are Life's musical instruments with the most prodigious assortment of pipes, drums, and strings.

Every encounter puts a bundle of ingredients into my mind and hands. Theo, here is your clay; knead something beautiful out of this mess. A rich relationship may slowly appear out of this lump of clay. Streetlights may start to light up in our dark alleys. There is love that finds ways to tunnel out of any dead-end street.

Ah, to be given clay, sounds, a palette of numbers, of colors or insights, and fashion a harmonious something of it. Some work of art may be created, but not of the best, then it breathes not. It is a modest symbol, a whisper at best, of how art should be, how beautiful a piece of art my encounter with you, her, or it could be. My relationships are the most precious wealth I build up in my life.

Golden Pairings

Ah, to be given a loose bundle of encounters we can fashion into something that makes us fly, dance, or that turns into ice cream so finger-licking good, it makes any soul close by salivate! We can visit each other's hearts and dare to be far, far more than nice. We can improvise and dare to reveal ourselves talking the coarse language of the heart. Slowly this way the thought vessels and the blood vessels of a woman and a man grow and root into each other, whereas merely nice people remain constipated with mysteries. Fence poles and border patrols between the *you* and the *me* can be laid off. Fear may blossom into curiosity. Our discussions and our games need no winner anymore.

"Clara, you have been making my life beautiful for forty-nine years. You rubbed off a sliver of your cheerful soul and rubbed it into my skin. And lo, it started to sprout. You amaze me. You know so many ways of making love. You have been the artist who has been kneading our relationship so everything close by may start to sing."

Building Our Sweet Home

If a slab of rock or a bouquet of sounds that one kneaded into some harmonious form can be a work of art, how much more so a compassionate criticism, a conversation, a relationship, an encounter with a stormy soul that is so well done, everything nearby starts to clap in applause.

Did you hear of that daring young woman and man? For their wedding ceremony, they burnt their clothes. Did you hear of that young couple? To marry, they cut open their thumbs and mixed their blood. Thus laid bare, a workbench heaped with hidden tools and shy talents came to light for them. May a woman choose a man of good wood for carving. May a man join in, so together they can carve a relationship that makes a warm stove everybody comes huddling around when cold. Continuously we also build our sweet or not so sweet home with what we speak, and what we do not speak. We speak our work of art. Whereas any fool can blackmail with brute bitchiness to get his or her lonely way. It takes a great heart to mend an offense—a woman or man who in spite of rain and hail knows how to spread true elegance.

Remind me, when I am about to fume, that telling you whatever and planting a tree are much the same. Both happenings shoot roots, and start to grow. My conversations with you are that garden. Here, we grow our sweet potatoes, our thorn bushes, our enmities, our purring feelings, our nettles and stress hormones, our blue lilacs.

In their spring urge, do not a woman and a man marry to plant that garden together? We compose music together that makes our sadness and joy dance together as happily as the seasons make blossom and fruitful the year.

From deep down in me, a voice teases, "Theo, don't remain a baby, content to be spoon-fed mere imitations of that Beauty in some art gallery or concert hall. Stop tiptoeing in the surf foam of that sea. Jump in over your head, splashing, going under, and shooting up triumphantly again. Your loving, your burping, your haggling for a better green pepper price with the market matrons, the visit from the landlord who thrives on foul play, whatever. Here are the raw materials for the symphony you are invited to compose and dance. Great achievements demand great risks.

"Think of a lover who can integrate into The Beauty whatever quality you learned to hide, who brings forth the use of all that you assume to be useless in you, a soul so generous, she knows any character trait you can name as a carving tool of Life. Here forms an orgasm that lasts."

When you present me with a work of art I ask: "Where is the lantern it lights in my heart?" I am not after a soothing pill for my growing pains.

To sit with others is always a challenge to a work of art.

A first-class ticket to our hearts, please, for
she who has the power to open eyes!

3. I train to become an acrobat and walk the tightrope. I train in the art of not taking a side.

Rugged-minded, I sit on a windfall across the Lisa Creek, and watch the meandering waters play underneath. A fabulous wealth of designs and ideas, countless stories on how to live well, virtues and vices holding hands, meander by. For this special moment, I forgo our aesthetic artworks, the bickering of Theo, my ego, our sacred books, so my extra-large mind may fall in step with the extra-large happening out here. I switch from local voice to the Voice of the Earth.

It is fall. The October spirit prepares the elder bushes, the spiders, and the greater leaf trees for the season of the bitter cold. The first frost, that front man of the great executioners, is doing his good work with a beautiful firework of colors. I breathe in the perfumes of fermentation and rot. The rich scent of the brewery is everywhere. One good whiff of this perfume and the logician in me gets drunk—and the poet gets its chance. All my fellow travelers around me, tiny and big, compete to catch my eyes, anxious to show off their deeper meaning beyond my homey common sense. To be with them, not with a fisherman's mind, not with my titles and my complaints—just to be with them; to have this age-old chorus of nature's "psychiatrists" talk me out of my dualism and out of my bad habit of taking a side, these sane companions around me keep my telephone conversation with the Earth going. To let Life's newspaper talk to me without me talking back. To a mind all lusty to conceive—this is the place!

Yesterday, I sat comfy on the couch in the company of my newly painted walls, the manicured lawn, my neat, cultivated thoughts, the pile of structured books and sacred texts with conclusions guaranteed. Neat, inoffensive efficiency kept sexy, messy diversity locked out. I sided with the lawn grass against the daisies, the buttercups, and the moles. I sided with the clear canon of science against the deep mysteries of Life. I sided with the dry-cleaned souls. I was a farmer who sided with his soya field against the countless "naughty" homesteaders on the Earth who love to live it up, yet have no niche in our commodity market's list. How did that feel?

I am also stuck with a heart region that no book reading, no lightweight pains and joys, no tame thinking, no sacred text, no structured love can reach and fertilize. Enough of farming the

Earth, and of farming Theo's soul, for now. Enough is enough. I need to retrieve some of the discarded love stories of Life that I was told to weed out. Time to go after the complete Life cycle that includes charity, infanticides, fertility rites, abortion, tender holding hands, dandelions, terror, betrayal, tulips, mildewed love, and rice. Name any burning spice or brand of honey in the cupboard of Life. My hunch is that they belong to the Creator's garden tools that produce the banquet for my soul. To face the darn mystery of a cataclysmic act or a cataclysmic man without swiftly taking sides for or against it, this requires mental exposure that takes the courage I didn't learn in either the army or in church. To penetrate deeper yet, and search for the meaning of all those hair-raising, heart-trampling happenings, what adventures, what festival of light waits for us. Watch out, Theo, our idea of a better life for us, of a Great Society, of a paradise, will turn out to be an enormous underestimation of the beauty of Life, and will nearly become a blasphemy.

Science is a slowpoke in helping me on to make peace with The Way, and makes the poet in me lose patience. Science is too slow to prove to me the lawfulness of a starving child, or of a soldier's euphoric joy of killing to a victory, or to show me the good intention of my migraines, or how the wolf, the locust swarms, and the hole-in-the-shoe are also protectors of Life.

Imagine what the spilling of all the secrets belonging to Life's goodwill could do. Any "good" deed, any "bad" deed, any side taking could become simply an adventurous little sidestep on the sky-rope soon to be counterbalanced and mended when Life tiptoes to who-knows-where. We could throw away our cocoon of the child's notion of good and evil—be done with it. We could start to read a newspaper as a pure description of Life, absolutely no anger, no frustration, no disappointments, no need for bashing, nothing shocking, no complaints or petitions with God. Imagine, we could listen to the news as a pure lesson in advanced biology. Any newspaper would become a safari for our minds—and for fifty cents! No judgment, no Judgment Day! Nothing less than a sober, realistic description of that most beautiful, most wondrous phenomena of Life would do. The floods and disasters, the polar icing and the steaming heat of other loves, the lovers and the love of the terrorists, the frogs serenading in the pond, the falling rocks, the rain clouds and the locust clouds and, yes, people just as they are—each an instrument in the Song of the Earth. A different man and a different woman for every life situation and for every season. Each a one-handed, applauding clapping sound. *How would that feel?*

This enticing idea is always with me, making fun of the old whiner, basher, and critic in me. I think of it as my future landing on another galaxy.

To make this discovery come true, which seems still so monstrous an idea to my loudmouthed common sense, how many dear assumptions have to go? How many of the sweaters my church, my dear mom, my politicians and educators have knitted for my whimpering mind will I have to pull off so I can soak naked in this overpowering stark naked truth?

One lifetime is a canvas that's just not roomy enough to lay out the beauty of Life. It is merely one step, and so not choreographic enough to play the divine comedy. I need to keep in touch with what is eternal in me, hence my outbreaks into wild land, and sitting on those logs blown down across the Lisa Creek.

I have a hunch that serene women and men have cleansed and cleansed again their minds in just such an ardent steam bath. They have made peace with their shadows with handshakes that take place entirely in the mind. A handshake in my mind, for instance, between the Jews and the Palestinians—any ascent into thin reasoning and big "souling." Is it not this sweet, finger-licking high we are all secretly longing for? Life might just have such a gift for us hiding behind her back.

4. Theo, beware of a teacher who insists that, we, the clan of man, we are superior outsiders in the family of life. That teacher is out to steal something from you.

A man disconnected from his love for the animals, the oceans, the constellations, the trees, from the great laws of the outdoors, might he not become a homesick drifter—a lost son who lost the trail to his home? An indoctrinated arrogance that crowns our species as the darlings of the Creation can make him lose most of his teachers, his guiding spirits, his confidence, his orientation, his omens, and his toolbox for perking metaphors. His telephone conversation with the Earth gets disconnected. He can no longer hear the soothing warmth of the Earth's identification hum, telling him: "Wherever you are, you are home."

Silver-Moon told me, "Beware of anyone who defames your animal soul. It is his first step to neuter your mind, to amputate that intimate guiding voice in you and to take over command. You will become helpless, homeless, confused, a kite without a string, an apple with no stem. You might soon become a willing candidate ready to be invited with promises and gifts into some safe '-ism' in which an ambitious shepherd rounds up his flock."

A frail man who feels not up to living in the world of wild horses and wild love—don't blame him for trying to seduce others into helping him to create a neutered world, a world with no thistles, no cold spells, no hardships, no storms, just some worldwide greenhouse with endless spring. What Starbucks and McDonald's do for our bellies, other enterprises gladly do for our souls. Continuously, we are tested to see whether we are up to the privilege to live without a middleman to our bellies and souls.

Each child is born his own queen or king. Yet rather thoughtlessly we nodded to our culture and let it graft the illusion of our grandeur onto that little lover: "We are apart from common life. We are the exception!" Or: "We are the sweethearts of some god." Generation after generation has tattooed this caste sign on its next generation's forehead. Again and again, the whole rowdy world of metaphors that wants to give that little adventurer courage and guidance is cut off to make room for this graft. That child might never grow up into a man who does not need a middleman to his soul. He or she might end up a puppy for life.

Disorientation is the tamer's old trick. Scold that proud animal soul in a child into numbing confusion and her self-trust, her poetic curiosity, and her gusto to peek under costumes and over fences eventually breaks down. In apathy, that confused young adventurer eventually begs to be let into some safe house for confused souls. A comfy housing complex awaits her where she is graciously offered to be safely tied to a job and a safe manmade network of love.

Elephant trainers know. They mercilessly beat captured wild elephants for days, till these poor souls have completely lost their dream of Hindustan. In that deep spiritual amnesia the whole world of the elephant's wild soul goes under. Broken-in, her disoriented mind recombines into a prodigious smartness of yes and no, of go-left-go-right. It's a kind of mental hypothermia that can serve a society or a master or an army well. A few animals, I was told, are so hardwired, they can only go completely berserk when tamed, and might even die. This tragedy can happen among us too.

Each child is born with a pledge of allegiance to the Dream of the Earth. That fabulous dream voice is born with them. "Look around. Here are your omens; here are your guides and teachers. The trees, the things alive, the streams, the skies, the pods of orcas, and the flocks of Canadian geese, all the locals, they know how to live in this place—ask them! The creeks know the way to the top of the mountain. They head first to the ocean. For your trip, don't ask advice from some ordained travel agent who

The creeks know the way to the top of the mountain. They head first to the ocean.

works in the stress of his heart arranging tickets to retirement in some comfy yonder place—ask the locals."

The Tlingit children here in Sitka, Alaska were forbidden in the missionaries' school to talk in their native tongue, and for "good" reason. Cut off from their native language, which talks to and responds indiscriminately to people, trees, whales, the fleas, the clouds, the ravens, these youngsters soon became outsiders in their own outrageously talkative land that is blessed with innumerable oozy, yeasty, untidy, recklessly fertile ideas. In their haughty new classroom of sensory deprivation, the natives' full bowl of wisdom soup, cooked and distilled by all the critters of the Earth, soon was not so full. The conversation of the Earth became crowded out and rather unintelligible to them. That is what the principle of "use it or lose it" can do. They became ready to work under guidance for some promised better world for man. Gone was the capacity to be schooled outdoors by an ocean exploding in the morning with huge schools of needlefish, the feeding frenzy of humpbacks, fleets of puffins, cormorants, albatrosses flit-fluttering above this breakfast table boiling with food. For a young, free mind, that table is also set with plates and more plates heaped with mind-nourishing metaphors, plates heaped with medicine that can give her immunity against doomsday fever, depression, constipation of the mind, loneliness, critic-itis, arrogance, and foul mouth, fits of bashing, and bangs of shame. In fact, in this openness, each critter seems to reveal itself as medicine for all others, and for this reason is invited to stay on.

Watch now, as the priests of the religion of one world-wide economy do the same disorientation. One language, a highly rationalized, simplified, and sanitized English, is globally enforced, a language for cultured poppies that is disconnected from the local, yeasty, and diverse environment of real people, animals, rivers and plants. A wildly permissive and poetic mind is grounded, focused and tamed.

Dear reader, I infer we are adventurers. No need for us to sneer at and black out this bleeding, flipping, thrashing, boiling, moaning, jubilating, surging and ebbing hunk of ocean scene. It has its teachings for us, morsels of wisdom acted out for those burning to see. Christ, Clara, Buddha, Johnny and John, Mercedes, the orioles, all the green-coats of the Amazons, an ocean serving breakfast to the puffins, and Theo—each is an omen. Each has a different morsel of the teaching, some big, others tiny, each with a different calling. No single teaching has it all. It is a wisdom spread so wide that no single barrel of neurons is vast enough to contain it all.

Imagine you are shown that the tune a dung beetle plays is a thousand and one times more symphonic than our tidy little artworks. Indeed, what consequences, Theo, when you realize that whatever you meet, creeping, flying, greening, it knows some trick of Life much, much better than all mankind together does.

After the many centuries of man's domestication, a child may be born frail. But as with the grapevine before its grafting, it does not start out entirely domesticated. And here is the hope that puts the doomsayer to shame. The laborious taming process starts anew with every new generation under a thousand different masks. Many details, most of them barely noticeable: from the first minute under the blinding floodlight over the operating table when a sanitized rubber glove of a stranger touches the new baby, instead of a warm, sweaty mama hand. The separate beds, the painted and lifeless surfaces, the symmetry everywhere, a spotless landscape of cement and stainless steel, later the subtle proverbs and slogans, the Disneylands that distort the soul of animals and make them behave humanely, the taught aversion to daddy longlegs and to scavengers, to all that's wild, and to "blind" instinct. The notions of pests, sin, perversions, parasites, chaos, bestiality, brute nature, pathogens, are tattooed into that tender lover. Death, that dear and wise allotter of ample elbow room, is condemned for life to wear a sad mask and black dress. The arrogance of man-gods with our memes (our deep cultural engravings, tattooed on our minds), that we should be the stewards of the Earth, is driven home. The words of natural demands are given a bad taste to defame what they stand for. The curse of nakedness.

Each must think out for himself the details of this systematic isolation by way of the learned bio-phobias that our culture of make-believe teaches us. That culture labored hard to empty me of my mental wildlife, just as it has emptied the amazing epic of the maize plant into just bushels and bushels and more bushels of corn.

And so, my wild thoughts and guides have become shy and suspicious creatures that visit me only in the twilight between my sleep and my waking up, when my mind has not yet been combed by a strict credo. These inner guides see Life painted as one single canvas covering the Earth. They want to free me of the myths of supremacy that keep me in quarantine.

A woman or a man who could become high on serenity must have welcomed these defamed guides back. They must have radically disassembled the notions that soiled our trust in Life at large, washed these path-finders and distilled them in their poetic minds to a new radiance.

When I indulge my cultured preoccupation with the collective psyche of only mankind, it hinders me from lightening up the larger soul of Life. Kneading mankind's tiny sentence in the long storybook of Life, squeezing it up, down, left and right, I tried in vain to isolate our tiny part of the whole, and make it look and behave harmoniously and beautifully by itself. It is from this profound nonsense chasing my tail that I am healing me now.

There was a celebrated sculptor who was not contented with what he saw on the tip of the iceberg. Ignoring the vast yet obscure underneath, he started to very seriously chip-chop the visible part, trying to make it look harmonious by itself. And, flippety-flop, the whole marvelous thing lost balance, and in one cataclysmic spectacle, it turned upside down.

It seems to me that some very successful founders of religion were deprived, when young, of their connectedness and familiarity with all things wildly alive. Hence their teachings' preoccupation with cleansing, sorrows, and sin. Hence their PR campaigns addressing only man—not elephants, not wetland flowers, not owls. They cannot see that qualities they exclusively attribute to us, the other folks of Life's association most obviously do share with us, like: speech, soul, joy, intelligence, memory, social skill, learning capacity, mathematical talent, compassion, mastery of architecture and agriculture, to love, dance, weep and sing, fantastic courtship rites, fidelity, to mislead and to lie, to hypnotize, to keep slaves, to gossip, to play, to get bored and mischievous, to pay attention and get conscious of danger and communicate it to a partner, to build roads and air-conditioned homes and many other technologies, to move objects with their bare brainpower, to go to war, to keep pets, to show off and bolster reputation, to get so drunk from love or from their own mountain ash berry brew that the starlings fall tipsily, happy down from the berry tree, the use of lipsticks, the art of reconciliation, body paints, perfumes, to goof, scheme, brag and invent, the most extravagant sexual foreplay, the shedding of tears.

Plants produce herbicides as we do. Ants invented antibiotics to protect their fungus gardens. We do the miracle of creating, and write metaphors so our confidence may soar. Bees perform the miracle of the philosopher's stone, cooking magic food that gives ten extra life spans to those larvae chosen to be fed this brew and to become queens. In some circumstances, animals and plants use all our "crimes," they even share genocide with us—and, incredibly, they have learned to thrive on them. There are so many marvels the folks do on the other side of the fence, things that we have no idea how to do.

It seems to be this one cultural dead-end "gene" branding us as the exemption, this meme that education has been passing on from generation to generation, that holds us in a maddening disorientation, resulting in thousands of years of loneliness. And that loneliness will go on until that misspelled "gene" for our upbringing is isolated, made conscious and radically disarmed. Then that

Our children, when we encourage you to learn from all things again, what a marvelous classroom for metaphors is waiting for you. Organic thinking is waiting for you.

illusion will be drained of its enormous power supported by thousands of years of a macho-technology, of man-centered religions, the media and works of art that cannot see the land as our sisters and brothers. Do you see it? That misspelled gene made us an overly egotistic species, engrossed in an egotistic, lopsided science. Meanwhile, I get hints that Life has downgraded the worth of our species in compassion, and is now reluctant to give us more help on credit.

We are not alone. We are not so specially "good" or "bad." Freed from the spell of the myth of exemption, free to invent a new lifestyle. Go out and look.

> *Theo, work at being a tightrope walker. Work at not taking a side—not taking a side—not taking a side.*

5. The power of intent

The Irish Meadows homesteading along Shelikof Bay had a talk with me:

"We, the plants homesteading this juicy plot, we are more listeners and gossipers, healers and spellbinders than you think. When you look at one of us plants with an injurious eye or with a menacing thought, we suffer your curse the same way people do. We instantly start to withdraw and to slowly wilt. Just the sight of an herbicide makes us plants shudder, even faint. When you nibble too much with your pruning clippers on our branches, within seconds, on genetic order, our defense system churns out proteins that make us unappetizing, even poisonous. And we tell our neighbors to do the same. Old-fashioned, we still think you must be greedy caterpillars or deer. If you are gifted with a scientific mind, connect a galvanometer to that menaced 'Lady in Green' and find out.

"When you harbor negative feelings toward someone, don't take it lightly. You are into witchcraft as we are. Your energy field invokes the sun to turn black over her or him. You are that black sky. When you excommunicate a man from your love, you turn him into a ball of stingers from head to toe. Excommunicating is love that sucks. Each time you 'fuck-you' somebody, you cast an amateur curse, whether you know it or not. You send out a mean twister-wave nobody can surf.

"Ill-feelings can make a man poisonous. Ill feelings are enormously contagious. They can be aimed at many. They can sink a boat. They can sink a people. These toxic mental environments can cause a holocaust. A spell of a snake can paralyze a frog and turn him into a meal.

"You people are so much more potent than you think—for better or for worse. When you harbor benevolent feelings toward someone, don't take it lightly. Serious happenings start happening. You become an amateur hypnotist. You 'will' her well. The sea of fluids smooth out. Knots open up. She lets down her guards. Her face stops grimacing and turns into harmonious music. Your goodwill mesmerizes her into feeling spring. Her growth factors have a feast. Better health and vigor start taking hold of her. Her immune system puts on weight. She starts to tan. You are a good wave for her. Your enthusiasm, with its shining energy field, makes you an apprentice healer. You are the gardener with the green thumb. People and plants grow toward you. Wild woodpeckers and deer start to couple in your presence. This is nothing supernatural. Prayers for other people or for dogs or for geraniums emanate that beneficial will. So do benedictions. The psychokinetic winds of your thoughts are bringing warmth and spring. Think of the hypnotic power of simple petting. Science can tell you that your intentions can affect bacteria from far away, and yeast, plants, ants, chicks, mice, humans, cellular preparations, enzyme activity, and on and on.

"Prayers are spoken intents. Their words are not important. Their official addresses, whether a Holy Sun or a Holy Mary, are not important. The mailman of these gifts is not important. Thoughts are intents. In a split second they can change the body chemistry of somebody far away. They can bend a spoon. Genes obediently wake up or fall asleep when they hear your thoughts. A healer is an expert prayer. Neurochemicals listen in and follow up.

"And so, beyond all the wonderful chemistry it may ultimately be the love with which a treatment must be given that can give the ailing man's intuition that extraordinary power of self-healing. Theo, ask Paracelsus, alchemist and father of modern medicine, your compatriot, about these mysteries. It was his life's passion to explore the way of such mental climate makers.

"Needs *here* reinforce intents *there* in the ocean of the cosmic energy field. When the baby prays for milk here, a breast starts swelling there, and milk wants to flow toward that sweet little whiner. Such is the exceptional persuasive power of a spontaneous act. Once we stop our mind from gritting its teeth, and we open up to this godly Energy Field that is the worldwide databank, we can go fishing in it for memories and advice. Maybe it is through this energy field that Life mesmerizes all Her children. Some may call this universal memory Inner Voice, Love, The Mama, God, Father. Others may simply call it Grace—or whatever.

"Ah, if we could visualize the mental climate our thinking and our feelings continuously emanate: a gentle breeze in a sky, all spic-and-span jubilating songs of May—a menacing weather front rolling in, blackening the horizon! Gifted composers of 'holy books' can cast a benediction or a spell on their listeners that stays with them for life—for better or for worse.

"When you seed the air with your laughing exuberance, or you foul it with your cussing, don't take it lightly. You are a weather maker. Like fog moving in, your cussing bends in no time around every corner spreading through town. Sprouting seeds hurriedly curl up again into the husk in the hail of your scheming. Intimate flower thoughts, when you smile at them, stretch their necks to put their own smiles high up into the sky. Consider what the truly wonderful placebo effect of just wishing yourself well can do. Thoughts have such echoes.

"Mind the mental climate you continuously spread around you, wherever you go. Do people flock to your sunny beaches? Do they pack up and leave in prospect of a storm pelting them with complaints?

"There are people whose eyes become exceptionally strong when they focus their intent, for better or for worse. Remember, Theo, when the strong eyes of your friend, 'El Tigre' killed by accident your mama rabbit, just by looking at it. He loved so much to have her, yet you would not sell her to him. Eyes can make a plant faint in terror. They can do more magic things for plants than can pellets of nitrogen. Leave the notion of 'evil eye' to the unimaginative folks.

"Think of the healing power of a sea of pilgrims. The air is sizzling with goodwill; a hot tub filled with goodwill—one enormous concert hall—one great field of friendly mindsets, swaying and playing together in harmony! Disorder may be swayed into order again. What homecoming, what a mental massage for a crippled mind.

And these homesteaders of the Irish Meadows had pages and more pages of advice, a nourishing soup of advice, for Theo.

"Don't take your secret life lightly. We are all conductors of the orchestra, whether we remember it or not."

6. Joy laughs in a zillion different ways.

You and me, every little wriggling speck of love, are we not all ceaselessly attracted and seduced by Life to copulate with Her? The subtle orgasm of a soul laughing, the hearty embrace of the fox with the hare, a sturdy lie jubilating after withstanding a mighty attacker. Every creature is a different bundle of delights, bagged in some sort of membrane or skin. Every bag is custom filled with the tools for some specific chores. Everyone has his own custom-made sorrows and joys. To sing, to chisel, to bark, a sweet long-awaited farting, all these activities belong to those delights. Blessings to all the mamas who cook the so, so yummy blackberry jam. Blessings also too to the thicket of blackberry thorns that protect this delight. Blessings to the big-brother-lies that hide and protect a tiny seed not yet ready to sprout, or a tender baby truth not yet ready to defend itself. Glory to the zillion unappreciated little bubbles, eruptions, exhalations, burps, and the sweat of the Earth that continuously concoct our wonderful atmosphere, which gives breath to us all. A timid thank-you also to all those who hurt my feelings while pointing out the guests for whom guestrooms in my heart are still missing. Glory to the drought. Glory to the rain. Why doubt that all these exultations are not from the same tab, simply because some are not yet mentioned in our sacred books?

A woman or a man who could make peace with to-kill, to-lie, to-steal, to-rage, to-hurt when needed, so that these defamed qualities of Life become to them as *There is* sacred as singing or giving birth, they surely *something more* are closer to serenity than I. They could *than understanding* take nature as an advanced model for human *out there.* morals, and finally their moral laws and the natural laws would become synonyms for them. That this peace is possible is my dearest faith. This faith is the barn door I keep open to my wilder, deeper self, despite all the prudent saying: "Don't you do that, you are going to catch a cold!" So, when Grace is willing, I am ready to be let into the clearing to get a glimpse of that view so bright, the candles of my reasoning will go blind. There is something more than understanding out there.

My "Ugly Toads"

To help me along, I am out to patiently make peace also with my own "shortcomings": my untamable impatience, my tendency to brag and exaggerate, my awkwardness with very small children, my overtrained sense to see and exploit profitable opportunities, my battered old tendency to belittle others in order to please my own ghost of grandeur that's still kicking, my practical sense that's overdone, my sometimes overdone frugality, my shameless spontaneity that plays tricks on me, my tendency to scavenge and pick discarded items lying around, that for others may look close to stealing. My endless struggle to bring my passion for fishing in harmony with my Earth-First thinking, my red-green color blindness, my getting passionate and carried away when talking to you and thus becoming a bad listener, my spells of arrogance, my rather bum-like style of dressing, my migraines, and my horse-like laughter that tells Clara from two blocks away I am on my way home. My sly addiction to chocolate ice cream, my sneaky old wartime habit of licking my plate when nobody is around, my tendency to silently make nifty compliments to myself, my meek preoccupation with the impression I make on other people is also a horsefly still bothering me, my loud mouthing, especially when I feel exuberantly good, my feel-good shouts that don't ask per-mission, my overdone efficiency that often tramples on my and others' hearts, my "crime" of over-inclusiveness when I write and talk, which causes my children to poke fun of dad for his out-rageous stretching when he connects far-off likenesses, ah, and the thorn education lodged in my heart, always spurring me to compete. These are some of my special children, my ugly toads that, when cared about and loved, may share their secret with me about how they also make the Earth a more exciting place.

Wholeness surely is not made of just honey and milk. Thank God it happens that from my messy pile of grim thoughts with their loose, bleeding ends, I can sometimes cobble together a story that shoots one of my angers. Here starts my better world. When I have figured out what Life had up her sleeves when She blessed me with these unappreciated rascals, and I realize that they are also wind in my sails, I will invite you to celebrate with a boatload of honey beer.

Serenity

So, when you meet a serene person, don't take her lightly. You are meeting a woman or a man of extraordinary courage who has out-climbed, out-thought, and out-braved any ordinary Spiderman. They gave up comfy old habits of thought. They have disarmed, with their own bare intellect, mighty myths that kept them protectively confined in the compound made of convenient prejudices. With their passion for dangerously clear thinking and clear talking, they reached for viewpoints that are as iconoclastic as they are breathtaking. These delightful persons draw me to that wild Goodness so dazzlingly high, that the ghosts of my learning, the ghosts of my upbringing, the ghosts of my old mythology protest most viciously—ghosts that are out to drag me back into the safety behind the fence of our common sense. In the presence of such courage, a beaten bystander cannot help but to become that dead lamp that starts to flicker again into light.

I expect serenity-land to be a mindset wild with options to connect loose, bleeding ends and nothing gentle about the ride to get there. No sudden explosion of fireworks, but a bumpy, winding road to that upper room that at great risk is slowly, slowly cobblestoned with a new tolerance I pick up here and there. So, against all apparent commonsense evidence, I stubbornly refuse to outright undersign any deed as a crime. Thought-joist by thought-joist, I have started here to create my bridges. I create my metaphors. And is there a better purring wealth than a hatful of helpful likenesses?

Joy in Simplicity

Back to Theo's story, along with some personal details. I am fascinated by simplicity. My whole life has become a modest experiment in it. Look at the *Onyx*, my boat. She is a thirty-three-foot beauty of essentials, of color, of seaworthiness, with which I have been having a love story for forty-four years in Alaska.

I love to talk with people who cannot write and read, people who are not under the spell of the tame written word. And for forty-nine and a half years I have been getting the chance to do it. I love to talk with people who have no electricity and all that it brings. I got myself a taste of a no-electricity life. Clara and I, we lived with our family in a log cabin among hemlock and spruce for some years, with running water from the running creek. For about three years, I earned a living for all of us with a dugout and one paddle, night fishing the mangrove lagoons and the shallows of the tropical sea. I got good at dancing with mosquitoes doing so. Then I upgraded my fishing a little. I have had a car in my name for only three months of my life. And don't fear for a minute that I talk here of some whining sacrifice, of being married to only a bicycle. It's just that this is the best bargain from life I could figure out. A lifestyle that stimulates my own self-made opioids has been permanently on my shopping list. So, to break our stare, we have been trekking a good month each year in some far-off down-to-earth culture and land, for the last forty-seven years.

And now, how to get me on a high, so I can pass a friend with his boat all loaded down to the gunnels with fish, and my whole being falls in step with his smile, with absolutely no lump of envy in my feelings? I assure you, getting rid of the sneaky competitor in me will be a more amusing story than any comedy offered on TV.

Here is one more exotic item in Theo's bag of joys, if you will allow me a little bragging.

Of maybe a thousand shade trees I have been sneakily planting in the early mornings over the years, all over the small tropical fishing town to which we migrate each fall, about half are growing and do well. These shade-makers have started to do their good work.

And now, Clara, thank you for making fun of my crowing. I learn to be humble in your presence—and to better see the world and myself.

7. Song of the Earth

Here a very large symphony is played in evolutionary time. Species respond to species. High-pitched mountain ranges answer to the rumbling *pum-de-di-bums* of milled-out gorges. Storms shamelessly dance their rhapsodies with the sea in ecstasy. A people are uprooted by uncontrolled success, singing itself into a breathless high. That high tells the players of degeneration, "Grab your funeral drums. Play that march of victory lost in thin air down again to the sweet nourishing soil." Pathogens may be musicians, called to soothe the wildfire of a population that has spun out of control.

The banana trees shading my hammock are also expressive movement instruments. Their grand leaves flag and flutter their music to the afternoon breeze. Each day, they compose and play together with the winds new variations in the symphony. Green sounds of spring meadows respond to the sky playing its blues. A summer meadow in the noon-sun grabs all its instruments and in a swaying splendor of sounds, scents, shapes and colors, that whole troupe of musicians falls in step with the Song.

Centuries-long ebbs and tides played by the wobble of our planet's axis are deep, sounding musical instruments of the Earth. In their cadences they drive the Earth Music into hot, exuberant seasons, later downplaying these luminous celebrations into a thousand years of ice ages and pauses. All to a steady beat of night and day, where in a duo the sun and the moon are clapping, one with a golden shine, the other with a flag of silver.

In the glorious ascent of evolution, the good boys' well-behaved repetitions of the good and the proven sway us into periods of peaceful rest. And again we are driven out of that healing monotony by the rap of a full band of sinners, rebels, inventors, terrorists, mutations and clowns who excitedly trumpet their shocking new causes. The thief and the good-doer each play their note in the sky. An exuberant hand hurls lightning and spear. A seasoned hand heals and seeds again the wound. All this, while benefit and harm watch each other closely, so none oversteps its term and gives this glorious Song a limp. Anxiety that caught fire is muffled again in a blanket of routine. The rhythm of the ocean tides and the rhymes of Life's disintegrations and reconciliations add their own seasons to the entrancing Earth music. Peaceful and martial, each plays its lines of rhymes in Amazing Grace. In this orchestra, mankind may seem for a while to be the soloist, but so before were the blue algae as well.

In the tiny Bodélé depression of the Sahara in Chad, mountain ranges focus the winter winds. These winds scour the depression and lift from it about thirty-five thousand truckloads of diatomite sands each day. They air freight that fertilizer across the Atlantic, and the Amazon responds by adding its deep greens to the Song. Further north one glorious morning, the sun ignites a whole rapeseed field into a firework of yellows.

Jubilant Life itself, with its so amazing gift to memorize, to repeat, and to metamorphose the same theme with slightly different instruments yet again, entrances me with soothing predictability into binges of confidence.

And the Song of the Earth is considerate about my terror of change. Sparingly, it adds tentative mutations, syncopes, "missteps" and "sinners" while evermore developing its themes. It teases me along with plenty of rest stops, with comforting repetitions and credos, with long periods of stasis. Think of the spell of all harmonious manmade modest music—it is our super drug, enchanter, soothsayer and swayer that comes to fit any chord and size of intellect. Yes, our music makes me so darn complacent. It can lullaby my awareness. It brings back the heartbeat of the sweet held-in-arms experience. Crybabies start to dream and feel safe, when mama Beethoven sways them in her arms. Troop commanders know. They march-music us into their battle.

And the sphere-music also joins in. As all the souls' joys respond to their pains, they each pull their notes on our strings. Many different countries, many different ways our hearts sing their music. Hearts in high altitude have their music as well as hearts in solitude and in the desert dream up their solos. On the ocean shore they cook fish and fish music. Glory to the deep-cutting gorges, the borders, and the separations caused by different languages and by forbidding mountain ridges. Glory to all the kinds of membranes and skins that keep up the gorgeous diversity in egos and instruments. May these diverse musicians never mix to a one global Big Bang of a sullen gray.

The beauty of the Earth is a miracle. It reaches from beyond the South to beyond the North. I, one of the sober people, got used to handling just a trophy of that wild beauty. I wanted a manmade version of that "beast," killed, stuffed, vastly simplified and framed. But that Song of the Earth laughs at my mental sandcastles, laughs at precedents and norms. And where is the conclusion?

The sweetly intoxicating predictability composed in our manmade music is a cocoon made of sounds; vastly less demanding than the mighty Rhythm of the Earth. Few of us dare to keep our countless chords so fine-tuned and open that at times we just start dancing spontaneously to the Song of the Earth, all high and unconcerned. That's when in the middle of a great fishing day Theo might just anchor his boat in a lonely bay, go for a walk-about, pick ideas and mushrooms, and let his heart purr.

Yes, our homemade music can deliver a home sweet home for any size intellect. So, when old China wished an enemy crowd hard luck, it wished them to live to a demanding music; it wished them to live in an interesting time. Universal social skill though, the skill to not just play a quartet, but to play in tune with the whole rowdy family of species, seems the first requisite of a species to remain in Life's orchestra. Yet my little finger also keeps telling me that every cry, every crooked move, every anything is a reach toward happiness.

"Theo, march to that big band. Be entranced by the Song of the Earth!" That's what spontaneity is all about.

I am a slow listener still.

8. Too tired of not knowing, yet a seductive mirage kept him going.

It is from the gift to concoct his own illusions that a man may find his strength to keep on going when stuck in the dark of his ignorance. How many windows in our minds would be blank, were it not for the friendly or scary pictures we compose that fill in these puzzling blind spots our ignorance leaves along our roadside? How much more peacefully a man dies who is given comforting illusions (beliefs) that cheer up the void behind that gate into the unknown, calming his terror of stepping into that abyss.

Most fishermen now take the pill of an illusory long-range weather forecast before they head out, and they feel reassured. A brave fisher may say "no" to that new anxiety-killer-pill. And with all his own feelers out, he heads out bravely to the naked reality of the ocean, dancing in ecstasy with the winds that defy long-range forecasts.

Ah, the remedial placebo effect or the harming painebo effect of beliefs, pictures, stories, all composed by imaginative creators of religions, for better or for worse. Minds stressed out by too much awe and wonder may need such anxiety killers. Creators of myths and remedial fictions, they give us father figures. They give us addresses to hear our petitions, our thanks, and our confessions. The despairing and the orphans are given a feeling of having a mother. Some are deadly confused from not knowing, yet promises beautifully painted in a mirage give them solace and keep them going. Hundreds of helpful or punishing neurochemicals are triggered into play this way.

I see here mental "drugs" soothing us more gently than Prozac. I see placebos made of promising, fictitious answers for our tender minds shivering in the four winds of terribly few answers. And these mental wooly slippers keep our "feet" warm. Then, too, a mind can catch a cold when the "sweater" for that mind is so badly knitted that it leaves the owner's trust in Life full of holes.

Wildness with its awesome commandments may become too overpowering, mentally and physically, for those many of us who are untrained to live with anxiety. Our technical and our philosophical constructs can give us the needed greenhouses for our tender bodies and tender minds, just as some caddis-fly larvae in the lily pond construct portable cases made of sticks and mud to protect against a baffling water world of too many uncertainties and foes.

And so we became a species of mental nest builders. We took the idea of the twig builders a step further. We take bits of warm and comfy thoughts and weave with them weather-tight structures for our delicate intellects. In this business, few seem to be constructors. Many are renters with a deep urge for mental safety as natural as that of the puffins to burrow underground to nest.

And then, whose mind doesn't need a bench once in a while to rest on?

Are you ready for an adventure in perception? Bite off the biggest mouthful of naked reality without being choked by the anxiety of all its unknown. Take off with the smallest possible dose of beliefs. Stay open and vulnerable to the zillion and one questions pestering, teasing you to be taken on. And you must know your limits to avoid crash-landing in confusion. And beware! Out there philosophies wear out as fast as clothes. So many new challengers and new sights continuously nibble on these fabrics. Galileo tore a seam in his contemporaries' cozy mental overalls. That was his "crime."

The richer the planting, the richer the picking. May we become avid gardeners of our imagination and plant it with many pictures of daring experiences, with delightful thoughts that give us many kinds of erections. I give you access to my imagination. I give you the power to heal or to hurt me. A French love-seeking woman sings: "*ne parlez moi que d'amour*" (talk to me only of love). She pleads for her imagination to be fertilized. When her wish is fulfilled, her cheeks warm and soften, her smile, her buttocks do too. A wonderful chemistry in her responses makes her a radiant sun. We walk in the gardens of our imagination. Some walk in its hay meadows full of Summer Song. Others stamp, shivering, through deep snow.

Who is such a rough redneck, that he could dive into the mysteries of every day without the slightest illusory goal? Was it not the illusion of a fabulous wealth of spices that lured Columbus over the edge of the oceans, only to end up a guest in a fabulous tropical circus show never seen before? Was it not the illusion that we can improve the lot of mankind at the expense of all the "others" that coaxed us into becoming the highest paid martyrs for evolution, afflicted with an incurable creative fever?

Each needs his handrail of illusions or credos—and the more custom-made to fit his or her size of intellect, the better. No wonder the market of illusions for minds in the dark is crammed with sellers.

Remember, Theo, that her helpful illusions, her uncertainties and loose ends wrapped in some comforting conclusion, his models made of myths or of software or of mathematical constructs, these are the best sweaters and coats for their minds that they can at present intellectually afford.

I filter my personal assumptions through my daily experience. One day, one of them just wouldn't fit anymore. I need to molt out of it, like crabs do, to adjust their shells to their inner growth. For a keep-off sign in such extraordinary vulnerable, naked times, I may have to wrap myself in a blanket of arrogance. Perhaps to move beyond what we know, we must rely on imagination.

Each, with the finds of his own raggedy love, constructs in his imagination his own world. Chair by chair, garden bed by garden bed, enemy by enemy, friend by friend, his walls and the windows in his walls. Theo, construct an extra-extra-large home with a new balcony added each day. No need to compose an imagination spiked with fear, mistrust, horseflies, sins, barbed wires, snakebites and thought pictures that suck like shipwrecking in summer meadows. Compose an imagination that intoxicates you with the enormous goodwill and beauty of Life.

Ah, the art to expose our souls—and get a tan!

"Theo, how much exposure can you take?" Don't try to
wear a sweater into old age that's knitted for a child.

9. Fecundity of the mind

How can I love the wildness of Life, if I cannot jump the gar-
den fence around my domesticated mind and get a taste of the
wild thinking outside?

(Here my mind ran free and nibbled on all kinds of wild
thoughts—please allow me this treat.)

And what plate of yummy food did you serve your imagination today? Did you laugh off the terror of the strange and take your mind on a safari? Or did you bore your mind just to figure out the cheapest fare to not-much-where?

My mind is not only my property. It is also the property and keyboard of my environment.

What I hear and see and smell is full of hidden cues. My mental chemistry seems to use these hints to discreetly coordinate my response to Life's global construction site. These cues, which spring from the mostly unconscious dialogue I constantly keep up with my surroundings, seem to switch on and off in me guidelines, passions, suppressor genes and promoter proteins, according to the need of Life for builders and wreckers. That chorus of voices choreographs my dance with the Song of the Earth, a little like the way stem cells communicate to choreograph the construction site we ultimately call Theo.

Those who will shed light on this elusive internet among all species will give me a toolbox for tolerance. In this new light great violence in the movements of elements as well as great violence among human societies, the gentle settling of morning dew as well as a mama-hand caressing, can become part of the Earth's wondrous living progress. In this brighter light my pile of shocking things can shrink.

Our alphabetical language is a crude and clannish system of communication, a tiny communication system restricted to our species at best. With our overdone verbal skill, no wonder mankind is becoming a little deaf to the zillion discreet signals millions of other talkative species are sending to keep us all in tune. In our verbal hall of mirrors, the skunk cabbage and the knot weed do in vain all kinds of fancy show-off things to catch our nose, ears and eyes so to make their point: "We, too, we recite our complex poems for you!" Are we embarking on a journey into loneliness and into a success that is a fancy balloon with no string attached?

Did you ever walk in a cornfield ten feet high and try to orient yourself? I am wading now in our manmade information field, a huge monoculture of man-serving ideas. Its crop is standing so high that I need a stepladder or a pitcher of wine to get high enough to see the contours and the needs of the land beyond, and to find my way. Or think of the meager world of the written internet, a room of symbols, no plants, no animals, no elements, and no perfumes. In this monoculture of thoughts my social skill to communicate and interact with the other many species does not develop well. My mind becomes disoriented, when I am tightly surrounded and taken over by just man and manmade things and thoughts. I live for the precious moments of repose, when there is nothing that demands my action. Thank God for my thrifty lifestyle. It gives me time off to just curiously think and look around.

My deeper mind is born a lush Amazon with a mind-boggling wealth of capacities and designs. Millions of plug-ins are waiting for connectors. Millions of seed ideas in the making not yet ready to sprout. Billions of simultaneous happenings occurring in each soul. Yet only a completely uncommitted man, with no speck of scheming on his mirror, remains naked enough to absorb more than a spoonful of this ocean of informers. No wonder that a child while not yet tamed, trained and focused, is such a vulnerable, uninterrupted ecstasy. Ask an elephant trainer. Training is not about learning. It is mostly about forgetting. Ask a lush river trained to become all hydropower. It must forget most of its river and riverbank population, when it is forced to squeeze through a channel and is degraded to a wallet full of kilowatt-hours. To know how green and rich my mindscape has remained, I count the plants and the animals that today have shown up in my mind.

I also notice that in a crisis, like a worldwide flood of men, a continuous rush of adrenaline makes us so darn focused that we become semi-blind. The fancy periphery must be blacked out. Back to basics. Even greetings may get blacked out. The economy dictates that our immense heritage of capacities is a luxury that stands leisurely in the path of our escape route to our fallout shelters. So comes education with its bulldozers, fertilizers, irrigation ditches and plows, intoxicating ceremonies and diplomas. A professional mind is trained to be efficient, sterile, cleared of non-paying songbirds and meadow flowers; clean as an operating room with no creative sloppiness. Is that not how, on our exodus into our economy, a niche is secured? A hugely productive soya field further than you can see may grow on top of this well prepared, well composted soil, still full of weedy talents and seeds plowed under. There is continuous spraying, weeding and hacking needed, along with the orders, "Keep to your oil palms or your soya. Keep to your theme!" That spraying keeps that outrageous feast of possibilities, that "Burning Man" in each heart, curled up underground. This "bean field "is a very nice and very useful man who can settle nicely in our economy. No doubt, here is the key to our immense productivity.

When I go out of my way, when I go to rub against strange lands, strange people, strange ideas, I do it to nourish my hungry imagination. I fill my box of memories. The more pictures in my memory, the more lifelike my mental constructs. These mental Legos I collect are my lightweight wealth. They fit nicely in my pack. "To better listen to the news of the Earth in this work-drunken time, Theo, go build a platform high above common sense. In that unstressed environment, your view widens. In that high, clear altitude, the grouches, sucker ghosts and horseflies in your heart move out. You may become a little poetic again."

When I choose "solitude" I enter the "Great Pollen Path." Solitude comes from my step into a society greater than mankind. Here it is story time. And it is not just people who are the narrators.

Here a huge cauldron of every kind of pollen for my mind is served. Millions of ideas swarm around me. My mind gets fertilized not only by the "pollen" released by the mind of other men, but also by every critter in the world. Millions of new pictures in my memory become the yummy black soil, out of which a lush imagination can grow. I am getting a little de-educated. My mind learns to digest unprocessed information. In this fiery furnace, powerful metaphors for adult minds can form that bridge and connect me with other species and with how they solve the problems we all share. With such power-food an impotent mind gets an erection again. I throw my questions into that exuberant land, just like I throw a ball of clay. She fertilizes and kneads that ball into a nourishing answer and throws it back to me. Every act, every critter, is a sentence. They are news shouted into the cosmos. They want to become ingredients of my soul. My hacker-thinking has a feast. Here is my thank-you to the ocean. This scene of power and beauty massages my mind. In its presence, strong healthy seed thoughts in me start to put roots and feelers out.

10. Life is a trilliped.

There are many kinds of legs. Some legs are made for walking about among the deep-sea vents, some legs for getting a foothold on ice, legs for braving the scorching desert sun, to trip safely through the night, through a thicket of acacia thorns, legs with sex appeal balancing on high heels, legs to wriggle through tiny tubes and holes. A trillion different "legs" are stepping the trillion ways to quarry, to digest and re-digest the minerals of the Earth and to compose them into beautiful designs that laugh, sing and rhyme.

Life's countless researchers have to be properly locomoted, clothed and shoed. Life is a very big creature. Some of its physiology is its claws, its digesting microbes and brewers, its voice, its ferrymen, its poets, its dung, and its dung hole. Others are its celebrations, its soberness, its drunkenness, its perspiration, its September song, and its breaking wind. Endless artists file onto the stage for this roll call. All move about to fill a vital need. Ask a fancy rosebush what she needs for breakfast, ask a caribou, ask a wolf. Your backyard garden produces food for you. But there are gardens in the Cloud Forest that cook food for thousands of species every minute every day. Now that looks to me like generosity. And with the DNA's toolbox of just four letters (A, T, C and G) that can combine into sixty-four "words" (proteins) that can in turn combine into many more tendencies, and on and on, the Conductor cheers on his symphony, played by countless colonies of genes. Together they keep up with all of Life's different chores.

And try not to call some of her back-alley players by dirty names, like parasites, pathogens, executioners, sinners, liars, thieves, perverts, racists, composters, weeds and pests. These unimaginative words are for the blind. Give these discreet helpers beautiful names, like Zuleikah, Papagayo. Shout their glory. They deserve it all.

So it might happen that on a Sunday retreat even global blenders of mankind, and other celebrated breakers of borders and firebreaks, might wonder: why didn't Life invite the merry assortment of all the earthworm peoples to become one global culture, instead of encouraging them to celebrate racism and ultimately differentiate into 4,500 species and ways to tunnel into the Earth's soil, giving the soil its breath?

And don't think for a minute that for its higher complexity a critter is seated closer to the Creator. Each species is the least complex solution for a job that Life needs to have done. The worm has perfect complexity. To give that mud-muncher eyes, wouldn't that be a calamity worldwide? Who in clear sight of sweet summer fun and raspberries would feel gratitude at being swiftly allowed back underground to happily munch and toil the zillion tons of soil? The earthworms do.

In Life, there is no solitary individual. Hummingbirds socialize with flowers, with fleas, with streams of wind and on and on, sometimes even with other hummers too. Critters cook nettles, others digest granite, and some wash the river water. Others graciously cull a population about to explode. Falcons play with prairie mice, teaching them to prick their ears and peel their eyes. Some transport semen, others fly in pollen, some open wounds so viruses may feast and ferry in some of a neighboring species' precious genes. Still others make gifts of yummy dung. The clover family fixes nitrogen; worms munch out tunnels to give breath to sucker roots. Pathogens give us time off to reflect and dream. Plants hook up for energy with mama sun and nobody ever remembers ever receiving a utility bill. We socialize with landscapes, with celery, with the air that gives breath to all, with a setting sun, sometimes even with our neighbors. Ecology deals with the needed morals for this feast for all. Darwin, why didn't you make it simple, just declaring evolution one endless Olympic Games, competing in social skills?

In town, the air seems full with the smell of freshly sizzled bacon on mousetraps. And I wonder: is there anybody around me who truly wishes me well? "Yes, we do!" the chorus of the Earth shouts back to me. And even Ms. Mosquito and sneaky Mr. Banker who turned grand, legalized horseflies seem faraway voices in this shout, although I might not yet be allowed to know. To wish others well, nay, to wish the air we breathe well, the soil, the redwoods, the locusts and the mosquitoes, to wish the whole rowdy Earth without conditions well, is less an attribute of religion. It is the cardinal quality of every living thing. And is there a greater gift to Life than to break a moral code and to differentiate and create and furnish one more niche?

When my thinking comes to this crossroad, that hunch always sneaks up on me and pats me on the shoulder: "Remember Theo: the 'bacon sizzlers' leading you round and round by your nose are also wishing you well, yet how could they know?"

My legs walk me out of town. There I meet uncountable laboratories at work. There fifteen billion years of history is written down and spread out in front of me. What a canvas! What a classroom! That memory of memories begs me to translate its teaching stories and tune in. The cramp of my scheming loosens. As inspired scientists do, I open my arms wide. I ask this land: "Sway me in your arms, please, and tell me stories." Why sip wisdom secondhand from some patriarchs, cup by cup, when the whole ocean of wisdom out here shouts to me, "Dive in. Sacred books are for when you get stuck in town."

The longer I listen, the more excitingly beautiful I find Life's storybook. Still the impatient boy who long ago begged Mom at bedtime story time to keep on telling it all, I keep on wondering. Yet, She closed the book while in the bat cave so close to the treasure. "But, no, that's for tomorrow, my sweet little boy." That's how Life pulls me by my nose to beyond and beyond.

Inspired religions translate for us the Song
of the Earth in wonderful ways.

11. Seasons of good-heartedness

Tell me of the strong good-heartedness that leads me out of the blind alley that my culture of faintheartedness has cautiously herded me into. Tell me of the good-heartedness with enough frost that it can refresh me from the scorching friction in which our overpopulation and our over-economy are sizzling us.

Here is the "greenhouse goodness" my culture is teaching me: Skip fall and winter, go fast-forward from summer again to spring. Quickly turn all feelings that fade and take on the colors and aromas of fall into constructive, flowering feelings again. Haul sadness to the city dump. Give the tulips no rest in their bulbs. Whip them on to flower every month. Prohibit Life to retreat and rest underground, to take refuge in hatred, to rest in tubers, in egotism or hypothermia, under snow, in death. Prohibit the beaver to retreat in winter to dream in his den. Stop the sun from setting. Shoot the whistle winds. Springtime must be enforced at all times. Make the desert plants drop their thorns. Eradicate hunger. Allow no fitness tests and possible rejection for seed-lings and for our young. Death must be practical and reserved only for old age. Build huge fires under winter so it will abort its unsellable gifts of frost and winter crops that come from tilling the soil. Replace the "poverty" of a poetic lifestyle with a world-wide opulence that meets the dream living-standard of our nifty economists. Manipulate the plants and the animals; bend their genetics our way, so they may become good animals and good plants that set the table exclusively for man. Build an even big-ger plow. Turn the Earth into our farm. Let the sea, the forests, the skylarks, the grasslands, Nanuk, the great white bear, the "useless" butterflies, and all sundry vagabond souls pay the bill for the fallout. Drunk from the success of our cleverness, deliri-ous from a high fever of IQs, our inborn talent for moderation and success management gets shouted down.

I see a humane soft-heartedness at work so selectively, so thoughtlessly "good" that it gives us now a mankind so huge, prosperous and fat that to sustain it worldwide would require five additional planet Earths.

And now, when we are quiet, with all the entertainment centers turned off, we might hear the Earth crying in pain from all our good efforts to make the world a better place for man. The Earth is hurt by our "good work" that we often celebrate with a Nobel Prize. With a boyish excitement I am now on the lookout to see how Life finds us a way out of our enormous greenhouse that grows like smallpox all over its face.

No, kindness and meanness do not just fall from the sky. Like summer breeze or winter frost, these phenomena in our hearts are requirements dictated by the state of the world environment. Life does not perform according to my needs. Day after day I perform according to Life's needs. And is it not for this that Life is so soul-bogglingly beautiful? Love must hibernate or be given eyes according to what chore is needed to keep the Earth green.

I see our crowdedness now engenders a frugal goodness. Crowdedness guides us into a season of winter feelings, a season with many kinds of hibernation and abortion, a gradual loss of leaves, of warmth, of femininity, of neutering and vision, a lower sperm count, a worldwide action to use the condom of rationality, switching us to a deconstructive, smart shortsightedness and depression that sobers us up from our drunken consuming and feasting—a triumph of basics. A time when we start falling back on a very serious kind of Olympic Games—we compete to mislead each other and we train hard for it. A time when pulling brakes and dirty tricks and a kick-ass mentality becomes pleasure. With so many near copies of myself continuously crowding me, and the animals and plants becoming invisible and few, how can a mind avoid becoming shortsighted and information-poor?

In very chilling life situations, our souls seem quite able to enter hypothermia, resulting in a very slow soul beat and a trickle of lifeblood flowing only to the most basic love. Exuberant love may turn into autistic love. Silently the aromas and the colors of fall may spread in many souls.

Here a North Wind whispers to me, "Don't you sneer at these marvels of adaptation. They are also part of Life's health and goodness." Unimpressed by our whining faintheartedness, The Great Seasons quietly take their course.

Moaning, we clumsily start to adapt our thinking to this awesome mental climate change and weather front. We try to wean our conventional wisdom and compassion from being so darn homey. We start to redirect a few dimes of our love and money not to charities but toward those neighbors in Life that agonize beyond mankind's garden fence—toward the so beautiful weed-life that makes up ninety-nine percent of the wealth of the Earth—and of course toward our grandkids, waiting for and dreaming of a green Earth. We unearth in ourselves a lost robust goodness that encourages, like a bee, people to evict the drones (the males) in fall so to survive the barren winter. Ah, what a whale of goodness that for millions of years could keep all of Life's big and little folks humming, diversifying, evolving and trim.

I am challenged to bring to light again a goodness that my upbringing has systematically defamed. To feel comfy in these foreclosure times, I must now get out of my closet my mind of wintertime.

In life's community, in which we labored to become the filthy rich by turning the bears, the rivers, the fleet of geese and the forest into the miserably poor, a bird in me, much older than Theo, sings: "Steal from those filthy rich to make gifts and prayers for the poor. Stop recklessly jetting around. Give back to the Earth its breath! Join a new generation of nifty surfers whose boards are so slick, they barely leave a wake and are not yet appreciated by the givers of the Nobel Prize."

The Dear Wildlife in Us

The cure sure starts to look different from what I expected it to be. No, it is not the philosophers, not the police, not the preachers or politicians, not the technologists, not the ethics committees, nor my culture that concocts the cure. I note that it is the forgotten dear wildlife in us. It is our genetic police, under the command of our wild and not so wild environment, that takes over the concoction of our cure. Our class interests, sex interests, personal interests, humanistic interests, and bank interests are ignored. As normally nontoxic grasses and acacia trees are triggered to produce toxins when nibbled on too much, so our crisis-charged environment triggers latent options of our genes into play. They modulate our compassion, adjusting the proportion of freezing self-interest and warm fertile kindness in order to brake or accelerate our growth. The seasons of morals take their turns. We seem to do what our agronomists do when all their manmade pesticides fail. We turn to the wise genetic memory of our wild strains for help when our cultural remedies fail to bring us back into the Song.

This gets exciting and worth expanding. A volcano under pressure emits early a stream of seismic signals that tell the animals to forgo their routine and to hit the road. Our society under stress from its overproduction and overpopulation also engulfs our children in a cloud of such soul-altering signals: our absent-heartedness, our obsession to lie politely and our obsession with speed while things are running out, our obsession with the production of toxins, with hygiene and simplistic clarity, our preoccupation with the banal, our mean crowdedness and the readiness with which we sling the poisonous "fuck-you" around, the obsession with sports and celebrities, the whole menu of shallow food for our souls, the hoarse environment, the manmade chemicals that fool our hormones, the canned and the TV education with which we junk feed the minds of our kids, our love for them that's watered down to practicalities, our shaky sanity, our morals that become a carnival. There are many warning signals for our children.

The conversation of the Earth, with its zillion simultaneous pieces of information to each critter, is speaking to our children. And their genetic setting understands this non-alphabetic language. This crisis-signal charged environment awakens dormant genetic options for just such an emergency that in generous, spring times of hot "joie de vivre" are not called in to play. Our children are called to "sabotage" our runaway success and to starve and ruin it.

It is this poorly understood dialogue, above all, that I expect to silently bring about our healing.

You might lament, wondering what's the point of all this painful probing, squeezing, perverting of truths? As I see it, finding a cure is not important. The cure will be, welcomed or not. Life is wiser and stronger than you and me. "Theo, forget about inventing a cure. It is the diagnosis that is painful yet encouraging and light-giving. It's the diagnosis that is the vision quest, that becomes the abracadabra, that can turn a hell of a cure into one more exhilarating adventure in our journey to who-knows-where." It will be our most daring safari yet into Life's working. Every wood serenely flaming in its colors of fall sings to me, "We can undergo this cure with serenity!" A nightingale my culture has caged in my chest sings, "You are taken care of, Theo—you are taken care of, Theo." And that bird is madly flapping to get out and be heard.

And so, for instance, while most see a tyrannical madman as a simple piece of evil, cut loose from future and past, a few start to see in "mean" critters, fat or slim, whoever, whatever, messages from beyond and guides to the secret of Life.

The belief that a dandelion, or a porcupine, or the constellation Sagittarius, or you name it can ultimately be selfish has become for me an impossible belief. Expecting that a galaxy or a man can turn independently is to be expecting the most outrageous miracle to take place.

Are we not all waterwheels dipping differently shaped blades into the cosmic awareness stream, turning slow, and turning fast, each wheel doing its marvelous, unique thing?

I wrap a warmer winter coat around my shivering mind.
I rub my eyes and I look yet again. My confidence warms
and I come to think that I like it here, so much so that I
don't know anybody with whom I would trade my life.

12. A custom-made egoism for any size of job

The Lower Viewpoint

My mind has an adjustable focus. Here, at the public viewpoint I share with the crowd, I am nearly drowning in the commotion of little egotism, haggling all around. Here, natural selection commands the critters to protect and promote each its unique set of genes. That hungry self-promotion bites, gurgles, hisses, flashes and jubilates everywhere. Many kinds of peacock feathers and colorful lies! Here, within the walls of my thousand "I-hate-this-and-that" my personal, precise mind keeps its little self cozily locked in and keeps those thousand un-befriended memory bags of Life with teeth and claws at large locked out. Here colorblind people dig up and wreck beautiful flower gardens, looking desperately for pennies. In order to survive, little bandits leave great ships stranded, stealing their propellers for scrap metal. Here we do that old monkey business, showing off our trophies of wealth while pounding our chests. Here we indoctrinate and celebrate personal and collective egoism with our competitive sports. Hollowed one-generation people sell the health of thousands for a lay with an escort.

Others are more gifted. A lusty soul sees a nugget of happiness in every fellow creature surrounding her begging for a suitor—and she goes for it.

Far Above, in the Cascade of Love

Through the mist and roar of this commotion and well above in the cascade of love, I faintly make out the same commandment again but a little upgraded. Here I see the lucky child whose mom is gifted with a tremendously brave twosome egoism that protects the tender little lover with every tool, mean or charming, she can find in her heart. I have found myself a few times positioned between a mama grizzly and her cubs, and I got to feel what that brave mama egoism of teeth and claws could do if I wasn't able to smooth-talk her into comfort. And so I have a hunch that Clara would kill her "Abraham" before he could knife and sacrifice one of her sons, Ivan and Fabian, to some god to bolster his reputation as "the chosen one."

On this level also, the have-nots formed their worker unions to help each other consolidate their bargaining power. And here are those who have warmly shaken hands among themselves to globalize the economy and consolidate their power so to get at more raw work power. Here, that same commandment leads some highly social animals, like termites and bees, to sterility. They direct their sexual efforts into helping their extended kin to successfully transmit their genes. Call it charity, call it compassion, neighborly love, the dance of the beehive—whatever.

From this upper floor, for instance, puny egotism in sex looks like a dead-end street. It becomes quite obvious that with a little compassion and self-discipline, waves and more waves he can bring to her and himself, a firework of pleasures! This wonderful talent of self-control so to light up our partner, and to light her or him up again and again, is that not a precious part of our sex pleasures? To convert a quickie into a lasting orchestra; is that not one of our most down to earth creativities? On this upper floor of compassion, also, our heroic deeds are awarded their prizes and medals.

Even further up in that merry cascade of love I get hints of what must be the mother of all compassion. Here the direct evidence of my senses does not help me. Yet I can infer that the Song of the Earth discreetly persuades all selfish critters, even whole species, to make also sacrifices and to be servants to each other in order to protect and beautify the entire genome of Life. From this high, giddy viewpoint, raw, personal victory looks like a dead-end street surrounded by dark frustration and dark hearts scheming revenge. Seen from this top level, every critter seems to fall in step with all others and fully engaged in helping the others, mostly in a way beyond my old imagination. To keep the universal potlatch in plenty, some may be asked to reduce their virulence or armaments, others their seeds or litters. Some load vectors with a bag full of their own genetic memory as gifts for neighboring species. Again others help with interspecies etiquette and mutually useful table manners, like making arms agreements or producing yummy manure, or not pissing in the drinking water. All are also engaged to inspect and test the quality of others. Some digest rock and cook soup out of it for their neighbors. Individuals who break the great Law of Moderation by becoming personally too impenetrable or by becoming foragers too fit for the common good, are soon squeezed out of the Game for playing foul, or for leaving no lunch for their kids. Cannibals are asked not to go on a rampage, but to leave and care for the food for their children.

On this high level, compassion comes out as a rich sense of bargaining, so both sides come out winners. I make out an extra-extra-large selfishness that is outrageously compassionate. It's a huge onion of a layered selfishness that still adds and adds to its billion rings of growth. I call it the "good gardener" principle. It's Life, that glorious beast made of critters that is in love with itself.

From this scenic viewpoint, the noisy selfishness, that eye-for-eye combat, all these flimsy little ego-forms framed in names that first caught my eyes, start to evaporate. I make a headstand to break my old stare. I look and listen again. And lo, I see the whole world of actors happily clinging to the right of this huge selfishness, to its left, above, and deep below. Here behind my name, a thousand Theos are standing, Theos of which you and I might have met only one, or two, or ten.

Here the springtime of a woman being pregnant comes to my mind. Timeless, slowly, quietly transformed into a great generous passivity, she lets her flower within compose itself. No flirting for this special time, no games, a logic way beyond my logic takes over her love and blends her in. Her twosome becomes one. The first time Clara was pregnant, the male in me was all perplexed. I wondered, did I lose her love? I had to get used to the idea that we all discreetly make love to the whole world.

Now, for a Sunday treat, I sometimes look at a tragedy not through human eyes like those of a fisherman's. I look maybe through the eyes of a halibut or a tree. This change of identity sure can make fun of the complainer in me.

Life, what a bargain of a game. In this league of helpers, each critter, each species gets its free turn. And whatever the outcome of that turn, after they have passed on the ball, they come out of it proud contributors to Life's memory, and winners worth a Nobel Prize. Name anything you like to kick in the shin. A hunch pats me on the shoulder, "Life could point out to you that its contribution is worth far more than your contributions to the IRS."

Big, compassionate selfishness is a big, fat summer-gift.
Lean (mean) selfishness is a different, leaner winter-gift,
each an ideal tool for doing a job in Life's seasons.

Dear adventurer, I welcomed you aboard this book. I promised to aim at navigating the smoothest tags those waters allow. How do I do? This book is a process. I am an apprentice. Be patient with me, I am learning.

13. Let my encounters be my adventures.

In intellectual talk, well-dressed ladies and gents talk about the ocean experience. Others, not so conversant, go hide their clothes in the bushes, dive in, surf and swim.

"Stop that scheming for a safe future, Theo. Don't be nice. Don't go where it's safe. Be brave. Don't pose for a picture with a stuffed bear. Meet a real bear. Let your encounters tease you off-road or off-niceness right into the mysteries of her jungle. The meeting gets more fruitful the more she sees it not your way but from a different angle that is not accessible to you. Let her lend you her eyes."

My scheming funnels me into a long, narrow tunnel, a tiny bright target far ahead. In this tunnel there are many crybabies, fears, disappointments, blind spots, enormous limitations, mocking birds and run-in-the-walls. So much love-begging that I have to kick out of my way. Much energy is ground up with gritting teeth and pedaling stress to squeeze through this tunnel and bulldoze the path to my goal—while others merrily prefer the spring meadow of "take-any-turn-you-please." And while getting their scars of learning, those adventurous souls are having fun.

To be truthful is to make love. When Life turns us upside down, shakes out of our souls the old common sense and puny schemes, some cuss and moan. Others, we adventure through the thicket, using the light fixtures we have installed in our souls. To make of every encounter a work of art, is that not what our daily lovemaking is mostly about? Meetings of two naked minds have offspring.

In reconciliation, dare to hold each other by both hands and imagine you are on a safari. You cannot help it that shy truths of our shy inner jungle regions start to pop out of the brushes and walk right up to welcome you. When I am just nice to you, I meet you with a condom.

Overripe and at great risk, a man finally takes to his brave heart. With one daring swat he mows down his thicket of fears in which Mr. Prudence and Ms. Niceness have cautiously fenced him off. He mows down his polite ten-cent talk that was just a front for voices in him he did not yet dare to acknowledge in front of you. The lion in her rips through the limits of her expectations. With all her courage mobilized, she dares to see with stark naked eyes. She comes. She steps down to that naked simplicity and basement where her preoccupations and mine are quite the same. Every woman or man, whether in the limelight or in jail, has become for her a mountain to climb, another viewpoint of Life to be taken on, regardless of whatever challenges are offered on this climb. Here, finally, is conquest that draws no blood.

My culture cautiously disoriented many of my wilder talents, and, like a disoriented whale, they got beached. Meeting you, Clara, I met the incoming tide that surged under and over me. And floating once more, these talents of mine found a way to the ocean again. You let me discover that love is more, much more, than my childhood catechism talked about. You switched on a light in me so darn bright, I sometimes wished I had my sunglasses with me. In short, a more impolite, more deeply moving conversation from heart to heart started taking place. And now we both know a little better who we are. Are we not all born, each with her very own overly tender and overly tough spots that we want to respect when we love him or her? And so, we now know, for instance, that a "hedgehog" does not want to be petted just anyplace to feel loved.

Another, very different, encounter that also took me a long time to understand as more than a simple kill: it took me probably *twenty* deer to learn to talk from my heart with the deer before I take this generous animal down and home. It is said that only a hunter who can remain above the intoxicating adrenaline rush that comes during this tremendous encounter is a hunter worth more than his meat.

I look at the artwork of spontaneity with which the Earth is filled. And I say to myself, "Theo, let today be your day of surprise. Today let your encounters be free as the rainwater, to fit and use every contour of this day, free to choose among the ten thousand helpers that line your road to who-knows-where." That's how an adventurous mind learns to cross many streams. That's how contradictions unite which before have helplessly stared into each other's faces across these streams. That's how a man learns not to capitulate in a conversation, and to resist hiding behind being sarcastic or being simply nice.

When lazy, I bury myself in books. When adventurous, I ford a stream. In a person's or a tree's presence, bubbling with intimacies, I can learn truer things. Meeting with a pickpocket, visiting a lawyer, a fly drowning in my soup bowl; every encounter is a loud confrontation and a whispered invitation to my brave soul for a work of art. "Become creative. Get lost, Theo! Let Mother Grace bail you out of this creative mess." Ah! The adventure of plunging into a charged scene, with only the confidence in my inner voice as my lifeline, to surface again every which way, maybe the successful hunter, maybe the hunted.

> **When lazy, I bury myself in books. When adventurous, I ford a stream.**

"And do not doubt for a minute, Theo, that the hunted is not also an apprentice and winner. Away from books more real things start happening to you."

Listening and Seeking

Two blacksmiths bang and bend each his own glowing iron, each on his own anvil, each banging and bending his own argument. It's a banging competition. When in an argument I want to be the winner, there is not much profit for Theo the lover and seeker. I bet you also already found out that we are all each other's instruments, on which we play our daily music. And some of these instruments we make so awkwardly that they squeak terribly. Yes, other cultures teach a stronger taboo on raw confrontation than mine.

What a gift that we can hold down the impulse of our willpower. We can hold each other's hands when we dispute, with the promise that neither you nor I will try to win that debate and walk away with a trophy. I am a barrel full of undiscovered thoughts. Touch my skin, and these thoughts start to flow toward you. Don't talk to me about airplane tickets, schedules, prices. Talk to me about the lovebirds caged and flapping in your chest. We could learn from each other! We could bring to this feast of an encounter each of our very own ingredients. Together we could knead them into tasty raisin bread. We need not drown our listening in our own furious scheming and banging. Did you realize that listening is becoming an endangered act of love?

Did you realize that listening is becoming an endangered act of love?

Many of us have barely ever landed on this joyous world of compassionate talk. We have remained clams, just peeking out to get our bellies filled and to eject our sperms. Yet so infinitely much is calling to us, "Look at me, explore me, listen to me, tame me. Not by mutilation but with a *wow!* For eons we have been neighbors and each others' helpers. We might as well call each other by our first names." Savior, thief, ass, the bank of a river, whatever, they are all continents challenging us, "Land on me!" And each time I simply exclaim, "How ugly she is, or, what a pest, what an asshole!" In these moments, am I not also shouting, "My imagination is failing me"? I proclaim defeat. Ah, but to find her confusing—now here is a treasure cave stacked with teasing uncertainties, left open for me to explore. Or to find a night spent on an angry ocean not to be terribly terrible, but to be most challenging. And then it might happen. The bunker that was for so long my intellect's home gets wrecked into pieces, strewn all over the ground. "Take what you can salvage, Theo. Build with it your new hilltop home. Build high! Add those new window views that you have created in your mind." That's what confusion of your common sense can bring forth.

Reconciliation

I tried it out. Instead of retaliating with another offense when offended, I tried to instigate reconciliation and surpass the old bully in me with one more social skill. I realized that this is the "goofer's" and the "loser's" privilege, and *strength*. Reconciliation, not only with a woman or man, but also with an offensive ocean, is a potent power food. "Theo, get in the habit of making breakfast of it."

In a conversation, sometimes I dare to be the bow. Often, I am the arrow waiting for a brave bowman. Here I offer my thanks to those outdoor thinkers and speakers who shot Theo clear out of the window of his narrow old commonsense window-view. *Wow!* Things start to happen to him. And is not each of us pregnant with a wild world of capacities? We can be each other's midwife and deliver some of these special babies public school may mark for abortion. Now wouldn't that be a flower in your hair?

Give me wine—and all the hidden ghosts in me come out on the balcony. Social contracts are delicate curtains—veils and burkas that cannot withstand this open-sesame. Meet some of my beautiful inner jungle-land while taking me in your arms to protect me from harm. And so, we made a pact when we married. We promised to weave something wildly beautiful of Clara and Theo. We've now spent forty-nine years, not simply looking into the other's face. We explore our inner rainforests and, amazed, bring to light an Amazon so vibrant and rich, I never want to spend time in a tea garden again.

14. Basics for serenity

The question engraved over the gate to "Serenity Land" reads: "The story of Life you composed, is it roomy enough to accommodate all the beautiful follies of Life's reckless permissiveness?" And I, naively, lazily, expected to enter with my nursery rhymes.

Now, here I am, sweating, laughing, and adding an upstairs with a balcony to my downstairs-awareness. Upstairs, with its magnificent wide-angle view, I have less need for the dead-end notions needed by ground floor dwellers, such as pests, weeds, perversions, sins, and sundry apprentices of the devil or some evil, to keep their interpretation of Life's mystery-story going.

I have always hesitated with my praise for a thinker who professes that do-not-kill, do-not-lie, do-not-steal, have-no-anger, are divine laws. How to reach the upper room with such negative, dead-weight notions in my pack? In this world, so non-judging and full of beans, where Life continuously shuffles things around to evermore dress up its fest of organic fantasia, I reckon, for instance, the Creator is not fond of private possessions. Possessions are our slaves. I doubt it to be a divine law that we should be paid when others are taking from what we horde, or that the sun should send us a utility bill each month. Snooping around in the woods, the ocean and grasslands, I note that to "steal" is the common way of exchange. Things are borrowed, and later made a gift again to who-knows-whom. And this goes also for whatever I bag in the hide of Theo.

Do-Not-Kill

And this *do-not-kill*? Now here is a mighty vital raisin in Life's raisin bread, we put it in jail. This might not be so wise an ordinance as we wish, when I think of the Creator's fondness to let every one of his creatures migrate through this fruitful cycle of birth and death, with absolutely no private favors. Time and again, when so cooking, She adds in this way a new genetic ingredient to a dish—a new curl here, a new color or sidestep there. I watch a bald eagle swoop down on a sea otter pup. I see an eagle at peace with itself. I see the Sculptor with a feathered chisel at work.

When you marvel at a summer meadow playing full bloom, don't forget its helpers. It's due to the rich, yummy soil underneath. Destruction prepared this feast, so you may be the marveled spectator. In this wild generosity, killing may be one gesture of kindness. And look at the colors of decay in fall. Smell the rich aroma when Life brews the compost to nurse its future crop. Nobody has ever been exempted from contributing to this star number in the Great Show.

Take a caribou, take a wolf, take Theo, or a bacteria, take granite or limestone, take anything filthy rich or lousy poor—we all make food of others and we all become entirely food again for others in this mysterious dance of the giver and the gifted holding hands, choreographing ever more beautiful designs. These floods and ebbs are the heartbeat of the Earth.

And now, dear adventurer, imagine what would happen, should the mosquitoes only die of old age. Would not in a few years the Earth be pitch dark, with the sun completely blotted out by a worldwide cloud of buzzers a hundred feet thick? Today it's late May. The swallows returned. Each bird will kill up to 300 mosquitoes a day. Here is my thank-you to the Creator for the good help She sends.

And again, figure out for a minute how much killing is now needed so we can hold on to our dear, tremendous comfort. Why sneer at an animal or a man whom Life chooses to be that carving knife in Her creative hands—a plow, a hammer, a claw needed for Her emerging work of art? Should we question one of Her tools most worn down by Her imaginative hands?

Here, a story:

The caribou laments and cusses the wolf. The wolf: "Stop this moaning, stop seeing me as an offense. I gave you speed. I gave you wit and sharp sight. I keep your kind so few so that lichen and moss may always be plentiful for you. I am your helper in a thousand ways that I can only remember in my dreams. Stick with us and we may even make you fly!"

The caribou, a little ashamed, reflects while scratching the carpet of moss. The spirit of the caribou knows that this muncher has no better helper than the wolf. Each evening, while the animal beds down to ruminate on the lichen and the moss, that spirit whispers thanks to the Creator for providing such a perfectly benevolent foe.

Do-Not-Lie

And this *do-not-lie*? Any critter loves to take on the strongest truth it thinks it can handle without being sunk by it. Life sure seems to be more compassionate with critters badly in need for some survival strategy than our unimaginative moralists are. When a downpour is beyond what a man can take, Life provides him with an umbrella of polyester, or with a tough hide, or with a shelter of tightly woven lies to safely huddle under, out of the rain. There, that huddler may wait for some gentler truth to rise, a truth to take on that fits his size. Let he who has not received the gift of hibernating in forbidding times curl up undisturbed in a warm blanket of lies rather than sending him to sizzle in some hell. In a moment, when cornered by a monstrous truth full of teeth, is not the lizard encouraged to throw its wriggling tail at this menacing beast, misleading the foe, then run, hide and grow that tail again?

Any critter loves to take on the strongest truth it thinks it can handle without being sunk by it.

Whoever demands from you: "You shall not lie" wants to gut your verbal capacity of one of its oldest, most cherished and dangerous uses. He wants to disarm you. Defenseless, your truths, your most personal treasures, can easier become his property and his power over you. For self-protection, a lie might well outdo a gun. Here in the tropics I am living among people who respect an elegant lie more than karate for self-defense. I have learned to live among "armed" women and men.

Take a society, take an assembly of insects, take Life itself. Without a measure of lying, any of Her wonderfully unique designs would instantly go up in flame, or end up cooking in a stomach.

Here is one more good word for the defamed Goddess of lies we love to put in jail. She is every critter's gatekeeper. She promotes segregation, immunity, racism, firebreaks, and division. In short, she is the stout guardian of the glorious diversity among the peoples and the species. She keeps up the jubilant feast of the countless different perfumes and colors, of the thousand ways of cooking fish and making love. Could you spare a little thank-you for this raggedy beggar for love?

Yet when I love somebody and we share not only the pillow but also our hearts, I become a little you, and you become a little me. This is the magic that happens when a lie becomes an absurdity.

We can weave a more creative, more forgiving story for this survival strategy than the one our culture composes.

No, no social movement will do. No devoted crowd of followers, no collective egotism will do. It takes seven billion different, very, very quiet revolutions in as many hearts, each with its own name, and not a single drop of blood spilled, to start us on a trek to serenity.

Theo, make yourself a gift. Go to where there is no road. That land will rub you with an icy-hot soul lotion, a repellant against your mistrust and your pissed-off-ness, a merry gathering of storytellers ever-ready to tell you such brilliant stories, they turn your depressions into erections, they shine on your dormant seeds of ideas—and these little specks of intelligence start to neck for the sun!

Go for that safari beyond the puny personal "survival-of-the-fittest" into the mystery of that life-wide compassion. Switch from local to Life's Discovery Channel. Wild thinking, flowing through you, will feel good.

15. I am waist deep in blaming, and I am still shoveling to free myself.

There are acts so raw that my mind, with all its grinding, has not been able to digest them, Hence, my addiction to blaming. Like a hissing, sizzling turnip, angry at being stir-fried to bring out its flavor, I used to hiss and jump out of conversations that boiled my addiction to criticizing. Not anymore. I notice my deeper self has a craving for those conversations, and pays me well for such cookery when compassionately done. And, timidly, I may come back for more.

We are each a sailor's story: some a nice no-news story, some an odyssey, others a terribly sad sailor's story—a boat battered to splinters in a sea of mad winds and feelings—towering waves of strange knowledge, horrendous confusion, the rudder lost, the sails in shreds, no GPS, no sips of coffee, no sips of warm love, no compass. Yet still, again and again, somehow, every man, dandelion, and living fiber, are we not all headed for sunny beaches, tenderness and the Dreamland of Love?

I have devised here a quiz about how omnivorous Theo's love is. Which of these strange phenomena of Life can he digest, and so add another inch to his love? Which of these phenomena must he throw up and out of his heart into some jail or pit of evil?

1. A sailor paddles his splendid but broken rig with two-by-fours, pulling it desperately with bare hands through piles of kelp, living on droplets of stinky rainwater mopped up with rugs, and on crumbs of mildewed love.

2. This May, Theo tied his fishing vessel to his dingy when it drifted, dead in the water, into a pile of surging rocks. Furiously he paddled that big thing, inch by mile-long inch, toward the safe open sea— what perverted sailing, what a grotesque scene.

3. On the other side of the globe, a weather front blows the soul of a father to shreds—the batteries of his soul flooded, a dark, fright-drunken sailor in a damned, star-forsaken night. Blind with his blacked out soul, that battered man can make out and use but his own son for some sexual release. Do I have to throw him out?

4. And again, a mite falls into my coffee cup. Panicked, it uses its bare, delicate wings to paddle out of that hot brew to shore. Is this allowed?

What rawness! What tearful, terribly fertile scenes for inventiveness!

How did you test out, Theo?

These innumerable, far-off stories, continuously crisscrossing my way, are the clay out of which I squeeze, mold, and finger my world, my living Work of Art. Never mind my hands and my mind getting dirty.

A "bad man's" story has become part of an Everest of goodness to me, a huge, forbidding goodness I might only be able to climb with an oxygen mask. Halfway up, the evil man's story may open up and soften, and slowly, slowly turn into a sad story to me. Even further up, where a million trees melt together into a great Mama Wood, and the sunset and the sunrise become one, who knows how that story will look?

After so much common sense, I break into new scenic views. A "bad man's" story gives me deeper insights into the wonders of Life than the common tale of a "good guy." Yet vertigo is never far, and pulls me back to safe ground. Manmade goodness proved too shallow a pond for me to fish for deeper insights. Some climb Mt. Everest for a scenic view. Others climb the mount of a mole.

Tell any sailor's story right and whole to that weathered judge. When that judge is asked by the accused, before he sends the man to be shot, "Do you see me as guilty?" He replies, "No, son, but you are of a darn hard material, a rock in our communal bed. You can see yourself as a hero, if that helps, a hero who dies for the good of all of us, so we, the tender people, may sleep in softer dreams." And the judge, after his verdict, presses his coat into the hand of the accused, so he will not be cold, before he is shot.

In this overcrowded world, it is unbelievable what people are driven to invent in self-defense—what they devise, renounce, and leave behind, what degradation they accept to survive in this blistering competition. I see this extraordinary present environment triggering shame-suppressing proteins into action; allowing us to lie generously, with joy, and without blushing. In this Great Flood of men, people grab a chamber pot for a paddle, a barrel for a boat, a poodle or an internet site for a lover, a padded impenetrable lie to hide out, make do with only disposable relationships, throwing most of their vitality overboard so that they may hibernate in front of a TV set. Yet, we still have far to go to surpass the resourcefulness of the sea cucumber that ultimately eviscerates its whole inner anatomy to divert a foe and save its life. Later, it regrows that throwaway.

> *Nothing in either my religious or my public education has prepared me to live joyfully with these awesome treasures of life's playfulness. I am overtaken by a sense of awe.*

Nothing in either my religious or my public education has prepared me to live joyfully with these awesome treasures of life's playfulness. I am overtaken by a sense of awe. Whoever finds love beneath this mind-boggling playfulness will be my teacher. How to decipher a story that is three and a half billion years long? Serenity, the ultimate life-skill, is a steep climb.

Goodbye, Good and Evil

My imagination was so mired in the notion of fundamental evil that I barely could imagine a more compassionate way to deal with a difficult or a hurt man. I am now going to free myself of any concerns with the debate about being responsible and about free will. This practical illusion of good and evil has ultimately become a witch causing me much harm, much harshness and laziness of intellect. This nifty mental device has also given an elite the power to punish others with a meaner stick. Men, who want to see themselves as better, hold themselves above, love the idea of free will. Watch a hen. She loses no sweat fantasizing about guilt, responsibility or free will. She nestles a sickly chick with extra feathers, or pushes that misshapen chick out of the nest.

The notion of good and evil is always ready and tempting. This notion is a very handy prostitute for my mind, seducing me to be intellectually lazy and run to her for relief. She can instantly relieve me of so many painful enigmas with her clear classification for everything in hand. Here is cheap, easy, fake clarity for the crowd. Yet, like a whale sunken in the dark, breathless depth, if patient, I can sometimes breach. What a view! In this tremendous openness, I can see and compose out of my sack full of experiences a roomier, more enlightening story that can comfort my anxiety. Road signs out of my pissed-off-ness come in view. Here is the good work I am supposed to do. The other "good works" are mostly credit extensions. My criticism? An intellectual show-off.

I am an apprentice judge of sailors' stories, every minute, every day. I break limitations. I burst my padded cocoon. Broken open and confused, I bleed a new growth-ring to my soul, which is the only onion that never stops growing. I pile up my wealth. While so growing, ring by ring, I sometimes get a little high on the sips of serenity that start to seep in. That's when I forget all about blaming. Then my pissed-off-ness doesn't do so well and threatens to move out.

You want to know whether I am ready for graduation? That will be on the day I stop mean talking about others. Meanwhile, ask me how often I sing out of the blue when I am alone on the sea.

16. Thank you, Oceans and Forests, you are a hundred sisters and brothers to me.

At full moon, your mind might become lunatic. Likewise, fully in town, my mind might get townatic with many of my caged songbirds desperately flapping to nowhere, with many of my inner "beasts" going extinct for fault of habitat. Others are evicted into video games or parks. Others are jailed. Consider: when you enter your living room with the television on, you enter a high-tech factory. That factory produces your mind, a mind preferably addicted to what the corporate empire sells.

Away from town, where man's society is less in control, my mind gets its chance to play with that whole spectrum of memories. Memory bags crawling, flying, cooking fruits in the sun. My mind learns to ford many streams. That's how contradictions can unite after they have longingly stared into each other's faces across the stream. Here the diet of my mind may become such a potent brew that I become a little drunk and poetic from seeing so much. Not much stimulation here with what to buy and to consume. Yet with one breath in the woods I absorb hundreds of therapeutic aromas for my body and my mind. Here, sometimes, the company of Mrs. Nutkin and family becomes dearer to me than my kin. In this huge news arena, millions of species broadcast their news. Our own information network fits in as a modest one-species affair, competing with news from beetle-land, from turtle-land, from the stratosphere, from the ocean's biosphere, news from nifty spiders colonizing the riverbanks of the Amazon, bragging about their latest invention of a new, invisible filament. News from the mighty water hyacinth that landed on, and is now terribly successful in colonizing, the rivers and lakes of the Americas. News about starvation among a tribe of toucans after Nestlé's cash croppers invaded their homeland. News from an expedition of fire ants that successfully navigated the Caribbean Sea and are now slaying the native ants in their new world of North America, while spreading like hell. News from a rackety roadside plant that is violating the patent of the leguminous family, which claims exclusive rights to the use of nodules to fix nitrogen. News about a war the guardian spirits declared on the arrogance of mankind, and about their invasion of our dreams, raising hell. Intelligence about how a nocturnal moth invented the technology to outmaneuver the Doppler Effect used by bats. Rumors circulating in the microbe world, whispering about an obscure pathogen that cracked the code of mankind's immunity system and that there is now hope in Blue-Blossom-Land that overflowing mankind might get "help" so not to turn itself into a Great Flood. News released among the termite clans about a terrific enzyme that can digest cellulose in no time. Every critter is invited to be a broadcaster of news, and most of it can only be perceived by an attitude often discouraged by school.

Learning by way of professional teachers feeding verbalized knowledge to young people has not been very profitable for my soul. Sometimes it reminded me of feedlot animals being served the best of housing and food. And for what? For making the butcher smile. Professional education also follows a strict bible— the formula that makes our economy smile. The more departmentalized a curriculum becomes, the weaker education gets in holding together and passing on wisdom. Wise people die out. Smart cash-crop people abound. Yet I note, the "gifts" of excessive smartness ultimately bring results that are different from what we anticipate. Smartness lives high on unpaid, hidden debts. Ask the bankers, our new drug dealers, about the addiction to credit cards. As these cards, so the addiction of smartness, they are now the drugs of choice, outdoing coke.

Ah, but there are teachers of a more daring breed. They do not serve me steak. They fork my steak, flip it and sizzle it from a different side or point of view. Take the great, old Persian poets. They do not teach me. They bewilder me. They puzzle my common sense. They make me blink and look yet again. There is no way for two of us listeners to walk away together from such fertilization without a loaded interchange.

Would you ask a miner of diamonds for a wide worldview, or an expert in a niche for wisdom? These diggers are experts in information. For wisdom, I ask a vagabond. Would you try to fertilize a puritan with more diamonds or with yummy dung? Thousands of lost resources, thousands of forgotten opportunities come into play again with the treasures of impurities.

Vigorous ideas need to grow like weeds, slowly, slowly, with lots of ingredients that make little practical sense. If I force-feed and monoculture them strictly in one of the universities' domains, these framed super ideas on high heels might not pass the test of the outdoors. It is the pagan environment that has concocted much of the advice that makes my life more of a feast. It gave me back the magic spell of interspecial communication, which public school and the media had rather obscured. It is here, where the Book of Oracles and the I Ching went to school. There is no rush here, no wrongdoing, no guilt, no blaming. I fall in step with the quiet song of confidence the river sings, reaching the "long" way for the sea. Like the river, I fill up pits. Confronting a mountain I reverse, make many reversals, and, thundering, I fall over cliffs. I become stagnant, filling in sunken valleys and huge holes in flats. I rest in aquifers for years before I join the ocean crowd. Here, one lucky day, a man may even get the wonderful hunch that nothing, absolutely nothing bad can happen, without that the good Mother fulfills some promises on the shaded side of the moon, or in a species I don't even know. Safe from virtue and vice! With my confidence shouting, I open my arms wide: "Please give me your advice!"

While people in town look desperately for psychiatrists, flashlights, and sacred books, out here is all the free light and advice needed to find my Way through the obscurity of my nature and the mazes of fate.

May it never become the pride of our educational system to produce in our children a continuous trance of rationality by focusing their psyche on one single state of mind, and oblivion of all their other worlds.

Here a hint: Did you see the advertisement picturing neat and endless rows in a cornfield with which our agrochemical industry promotes their fertilizers and herbicides? Do we want a young man's mind under the plow of education getting readied for harvest to look the same? Are we going to stifle her merry weed-thoughts with bad grades? Are we going to spray a meandering soul with surges of adrenaline triggered from the stress of our exercises in willpower and dominance, stress from boredom and hours-long sitting still? Would such forced learning not smother the neurochemicals in our children that promote their love for creative daydreaming?

In a slow dance macabre, the "daisies and the gophers" may start to die in them. The earthworms, the thunderclouds, the gale birds, the soft blue moods of spring may start to die in their inner lands. A mercilessly rational, mercilessly "productive" cash crop mind might prevail. And is it not from such highly sanitized minds many of our brilliant technologists are bred? Rationality seems an organ in us, just as the udder is an organ of the cow. Both are essential body parts that we now breed into something rather dangerously intensive for society's own goal.

No wonder that sometimes our hearts keep on shouting "foul" and demand a taste of peyote or sparkling danger or champagne. These helpers can put our hyper-rationality to sleep. They deliver us from working in the stress of our souls torn apart. Such gifts from Life can relieve us from a tyrannical self-consciousness, from an endless cramp of scheming and tunneling in just the meager underworld of our personal memories. My unconscious is my roots of thinking. It demands its chance to connect with the Earth, which is my mind's most fertile compost pile and memory bank.

Did you ever wonder why the cormorants never build shrimp farms? Why the pigeons never invented cornfields? Why a whale does not wear a tie? Good question. Did you wonder why the poet doesn't just cultivate knowledge as does a scientist, but likes to hunt and gather it?

Out here on the ocean I am beyond prudence, politeness, and shame. In this grand immensity, wisdom can run free to do its very vast things like fertilizing my deeper mind. Out here, watching like a good mother over Darwin's neat theorem, the "Good Gardener Principle" comes in view. That principle protects every child of Life from excesses, leading them again and again back to The Way when too much exuberance carries these little bundles of joy away. The wealth of cues in the permissive environment of the wild coaxes my man-specific mind to switch career. My mind becomes less disciplined and more poetic. My mental system of participation gets its chance.

Oh, horror of horrors in the halls of Wall Street! Then on this analphabetic outdoor stage, endlessly different memories broadcast, not just in numbers but also in hieroglyphs, in petro-glyphs, in bioglyphs, in the dance of the heavenly bodies surround me. Memories in the shopping bag of my own brain and in *our* internet take up a modest corner. My mind is now an unleashed dog, yelping with joy. It dashes for the open land of spontaneous thinking. It sniffs out likenesses in these immense "classrooms" where highly structured education, with its pretended clarity, might discourage us to go to school. Yet these are the bones my larger mind enjoys. For that festive while, I am released of the locks forcing me into a niche of expertise. Adventures in percep-tion begin.

I can produce more than manure, more than children, more than a boatload of fish. To what would I amount, had I not pro-duced and shed some new blink of light?

Thank you, Oceans and Forests, you are a
hundred sisters and brothers to me.

17. Life, that glorious miracle of "injustice"

Jupiter complains to the Creator: "Why bless that minor Planet Earth with this miracle of Life, and not me?"

Look at that little tuft of moss, lying low. Where it camps, it's completely overshadowed by a giant redwood tree. Yet happily Lady Moss is filling her niche. Nobody ever heard her complain, "Why a whole acre for this greedy giant and only this sun-forsaken little crack for me?" And notice, she now seems ahead of these giants in the race to stay alive.

And why would Life give the salmon a bellyful of two thou-sand eggs while the stingray gets only five? What creative mischief has She up her sleeves? She crushes some salmon eggs between rocks for who-knows-the-reason. Many are served to mallards and gulls to be gobbled up. Others are delegated to set the table of a bunch of trout. She cradles a very view of the most promising eggs very, very carefully in Her palms so they may mature to retell the salmon story with a new twist all their own. And She does not necessarily just collapse gene systems. She may disengage them, and let them migrate in loose bundles to other species for better breeding grounds.

The lawyer in me complains, "Why all this injustice?" And the answer I get is that some works require a pauper. For other works, only dripping wealth will do. Every injustice cradles a seed of creativity. Creativity is injustice at its best. Creativity is taking two plus two, and coming up with five.

In Life's outdoor show, my learned sense of justice gets baffled to no end. The impatience of my logician plays such tricks on me.

Every injustice cradles a seed of creativity. Creativity is injustice at its best. Creativity is taking two plus two, and coming up with five.

In Life's wheeling and dealing over eons, what do a few generations' ups and downs matter, or a gift made to a species next door without a paycheck in the mail right away, a tiny exploratory sidestep, a step maybe onto a loose boulder and back again to the solid bank, when Life tries to cross a creek? Yet, at the slightest setback, my impatient intellect panics, cussing Life for breaking again what has been tentatively done, or for making me pay for another guest's bill.

Yet the curious lad in me has a fat smile. Each species runs up a debt. In that salmon story, that curious lad sees a hint in the way hungry Mrs. Salmon ultimately pays back the debts she accumulated with the many gifts she later so generously cooks in her belly and turns loose in that creek, inviting everybody for a banquet.

Every woman and man is a sentence in the revelation of how Life works. Theo, be brave. Open and seriously start to read that kinky her, him, or it. The title up front, the skimming through society's recommendations on the back of the storybook, a name-calling that stinks; these comments are for the dull. There is no lack of critics, persons so drunk with self-esteem that they burn to criticize the Creator's work. To go out of one's way and open one of Life's unappreciated storybooks, now this looks to me like first-class creativity. Here starts a man's story that counts. Who knows, whether an act produces smiles or tears may depend entirely on the different prescription glasses Life prescribes for each of her zillion wriggles of joy.

18. Comments on our western goodness that lives high on credit

Honorable moralists and historians continue to analyze Life's adventure with man using tools that do not give justice to human nature, nor justice to the mysterious aberrations, sins, and other mutations that bring forth the marvel of Life's evolution. So, on long terms, the result of the manmade moral laws we bend in our favor are slightly different from what we expected. Later, hidden debts are coming due.

The theory of relativity shows me that beyond Newton's law, a turning wheel is a tiny, tiny bit heavier than a wheel at rest. (Mass and speed = one). Yet on the cosmic scale of speed and mass, this interaction becomes big, big, and big. A new theory of morals, (human and nonhuman = one), shows me how these tiny, tiny unnoticeable side effects of my cultivated, man-centered acts, when accumulated over many generations and species, can become large and very large, discreetly changing

When I dare to look over the fence of our paradigms, I am dumbfounded to watch Life at large behave far more compassionately than we do, with our manmade compassion on a leash and our commandments.

the Earth, from the core to the stratosphere. Was it by ignoring these subtle interspecies reactions that the believers in our man-made, garden-variety goodness became so successful in ways fast and unhindered? The success of the green revolution the western religions started in our souls, when they manipulated our compassion so that our love serves only mankind, now starts to distort. For comparable reasons, the expected outcome of the Green Revolution that our agronomists started on our land has also started to distort.

We start to notice that the uncontrolled success of our "goodness on credit" has consequences. We begin to follow the mostly unnoticed and discreetly disturbing ripples our "virtuous" acts send out to our less glamorous friends: the woods, the oceans, the whole society of wilderness, and ultimately back to us. We start to weave these neglected connections together. And lo, we discover that the unappreciated wildness we heroically fight is engineered to work unexpectedly wisely, long-lastingly, and outrageously compassionately. My learned and imagined superiority has so skewed my view into a one-generation and one-species vision, that for a long time I could only see a terribly distorted beauty in Life at large.

The fathers of our western religions took on a love that lives far beyond our modest logic and brought it down into the circle of contemporary mankind. They teach an impatient, reasonable love that wants to see the smile it produces right now, and only on the face of a human.

I discover that it is the unnerving, cursed imperfections, the sins, irregularities, imbalances, the darn obsessions, the trespasses on the level of the individual and their barely noticeable inter-specific side effects, those are the things that make the family of Life work together so awesomely well. I discover that when seen, not from the individual's, not from our species' perspective, but from *Life's* point of view, these unnerving sidesteps (call them perversions, crimes, weeds, jumping genes, mutations, sins, impurities, parasites, sicknesses) are tools of life's magic goodness.

I discover that we cannot fathom the miracle of Life by taking the behavior of an individual, or a species, and holding a yardstick for goodness or for justice against it. I discover that a man is only a short sentence in the long, long story, and that this sentence, like the trigger of a gun, should not be judged by itself. I discover that the anatomy of an act is eternally bigger than a man, and nobody knows the deeper reason for his every movement. Every movement, whether in a heart or in a mountain range, seems an act of faith.

At first glance, the advantages of these new commandments for goodness are so obvious and so many. Here is a story: The minister of a humble country goes to a smart country. He signs an agreement. Happily he brings back a fat coffer of loans, help, and ideas on how to live on credit well. The feasting begins, the pesticides, the fertilizers, the dams, and the

Man is only a short sentence in the long, long story.

vaccines. Fewer are dying, less hunger, an oil palm plantation, a world bank project, maybe a McDonald's, the enormous power of strictly humane cooperation. Time for music, no weeds, no fevers of creativity and doubts, no wasting time in worshiping and lovemaking in a thousand different ways. Turn the Earth into OUR farm! The bubble of that human enterprise on credit engulfs the land. The crowd, now drunk with success, is clapping their hands and feet at their luck. Who remains sober enough to ask: is the payment of our loan from Life the birthday gift we present to our kids down the line?

Obediently, I assumed that the purpose of Life is to improve the lot of mankind. "Not so," said my brother the wind. "There are many qualities built into man that are not at all meant to help man. They are built into man to help Life." My genetic setting is older and wiser than Theo—even older than mankind. It loves Life first, mankind second, and Theo, my ego, third. Take our DNA. It contains instructions for a protein called reverse transcriptase. Science tells us that it does not help us, but serves

69

Life. Our DNA contains a foreclosure gene to keep our species ultimately lean. The poorly understood built-in genetic compassion sometimes takes from us to give to other species. And so, our deeper nature is the nightmare of most moralists.

My humanistic culture refined my perception like it refines sugar, and for similar reasons. Humanistic sacred books have invented a sack full of bad names for these mischievous loves of Life that don't deal us private favors. It takes a man who is much more than a man to love these vital components, these impurities of Life that we have demonized. And some of the "genes" (memes) of our civilizations are even younger, just giggling girls, still playing dolls in place of the real thing to come. Here, an interesting hint: our domestication, as well as the animal domestication for the last twenty thousand years, has left our brains, as well as theirs, smaller.

Every one of my words, my acts, my thoughts, provokes not only an echo from other people, but becomes a shout into the cosmos. Gazillions of echoes in as many forms respond back to me: sounds, perfumes, weather fronts, droughts, pests, ozone holes, oceanic dead zones, baskets heaped with summer's giveaways, thankful or revengeful. But they come unfailingly back to me, in God knows what language or form. Science tells me that changes in the social environment trigger hormones that promote adaptive changes in our mentalities. I am compelled to regard our morals (commandments), which I took for constant, as variable.

The dogmatic absolute of our commandments is challenged by the relative. Not only my neurochemicals react and adjust to the cosmic gossip. My whole psyche does, too. Take for illustration the shepherd's dilemma. He needs to impose a different, more Christian moral among his flock than for himself and his sheep dog. He must hold on to his wild ruses and saber's teeth to keep the docile sheep from being eaten by the wolf.

And there is good news. While moralists scratch for crumbs of justifications, I see tremendous assortments of mental tools for forgiveness hanging ripe in every tree and swimming in every tidal pool. When I explore with this new logic of relativity in mind, Life shocks me less and makes me purr more. My awe and my confidence in Life at large soar.

It will take a tremendous imagination to disassemble and re-engineer the western moral concepts to accommodate this new dimension. My mind is trained to be highly reasonable and shortcut to quickie conclusions. I am trained to find ways to make beautiful the life of our present generations, or of our species, and that's it.

As with Newton's law, our ten commandments are based on practical observations of how the human society works more efficiently over a generation or two. Its legislators also assume that we are better off, and more sacred, the more social we become among mankind. On this modest timescale, this model and its predictions have worked well. Tiny side effects of our practical behavior on the many hidden generations ahead, or on our fellow species, or on the atmosphere, or on the whole menagerie of Life, appeared negligible and so were not pondered. They were not included in the logic of that behavior model whose first laws were chiseled for eternity into some famous slab of desert rock.

Not considered in this tidy piece of legislation were its side effects on:

- the robustness of our bodies;

- the development of our wildly diverse talents;

- the way some of our vital genes are weeded out and others are highly bred;

- our most wonderful gift that a girl and a lad can independently self-procreate;

- our immune system and our self-maintenance;

- our sex appeal;

- our wonderful capacity to tolerate and to forgive;

- our need to keep our minds a big guesthouse with rooms for everything alive;

- how much knowledge remains off limit to us;

- side effects also on our neighbors: the nematodes, the algae, and the kangaroos;

- our neighbors, the winds, the rain, the climate, the stratosphere;

- the airstreams and the ocean-streams that give breath to us all;

- our gift to freely learn from the minerals, the animals, the plants, the heavenly bodies, from all critters that people our dreamtime and our memories and help us to think with the help of likenesses;

- our social skills when mingling and conversing with the motley crowd of all bundles of joy that sting, bake fruit in the sun, sing, and our gift to enjoy their goodwill and advice;

- our gift for critical thinking;

- our gift for ecstasy

And Ms. Cockatoo complains that our ten commandments contain no reminder, for us people to be courteous when we come to cockatoo-land and meet.

I have to stop. This roll call has no end. One thing becomes clear. When including these side effects in a model for our morals in evolutionary time, tremendous changes in predictions must occur. I think here of the dark side of the genius we cling to with our purely humane goodness. By high-breeding its virtues, we repress many messy, yet vital, functions of Life, or drive them into oblivion in the subconscious. Yet, I note the awesome life forces never tire in proving to me that they have their way of creating a new balance. They irk the good boy in me, when they make me realize that to create situations that give great fulfillment to the Medecins Sans Frontieres, the Creator does not enroll "saints." Thoughts greater than Theo that are kept in the eggshell of a one-generation mind start to squeak and to get rebellious, for in such a tight credo there is no room for these thoughts to spread their wings.

Watch how healthy egoism, driven into the underworld, surfaces after generations again, now masked in a grotesque consumerism. If I am not allowed to test myself and be a little egoistic with my neighbors, then watch out, trees, animals, the laughing waters, the kids five generations up the hill. In the western heaven, you might not have an advocate when your case is argued. We are still very healthy coyotes, yet professionals at wearing sheep's clothing.

Look at the animals, the plants, the great glaciers and coral reefs. Many are in terror of our applied sciences, which have become deadlier to them than all the scorpions' tails combined. Our technologists put condoms and chastity belts on the wildness of Life, on the rivers that love to produce and reproduce in their very own curls and curves, on the visible and invisible critters that also have nicely installed themselves at the banquet for all. We catch our wild thoughts in condoms and call ourselves polite. Few see a conversation as a chance to join an everyday safari, where each reveals her or his deeper, wilder delights.

My culture has left my psyche with a few very bright spots and with many wounds. I had to become my own wound-dresser. That culture tinkered with my soul as we tinker with the soul of the sheep and the wolf when domesticating these children of Life.

To make sense, people all over must now ferociously hang on the notion of evil. Have we become feeble Eskimos who have to hang onto our winter coats year-round? Our domesticated new intellect is not up to this tremendous goodness out there. To avoid getting completely lost in the mystery, our intellect puts up mental shelters. Few dare to step out of this mental sleeping bag into the wide-open weather fronts of God. I don't know anymore what to do with the notion of evil that continues to tempt me.

Yes, it gives me a fine excuse to keep my delicate intellect under protective house arrest.

When I look through any eye that is not a human eye, our manmade goodness becomes to all other critters a somewhat distorted benevolence. Our goodness may be their fear, their desperation, and their hell. It may be the goodness of the Holstein cow we made into a monstrous udder, gushing thirty thousand pounds of milk per year. It might be the goodness of our worthy Red Cross or of our clinical medicine that doubles our world population every two generations, naively crowding out the other tenants of this inspired Earth. Life is that great university where every one of its players does or does not graduate to the level of being allowed to reproduce according to what it learned. Is the medical industry becoming the honorable cheating enterprise, whispering the answers to the students when we fail the test of self-maintenance? No wonder in this tremendous flood of our technology's "good" works, the wild genetic wisdom of people starts to pray for a drought in that "good" work. It is man's table manners that beg now for an edict to be added to our ten simplistic commandments.

By their deeper nature, a man and woman are an infinitely fine-tuned mixture of hard and soft, of lies and truthfulness, of attracting-loving and of repelling-hating, of being aggressive-asserting and of being vulnerable and giving. A man and woman's life is a hunk of soil. Not only the beauty of their children or the beauty of their tribe will grow out of this soil. All the Earth's storytellers big, small, and very small depend on the awakening of this hunk of soil, so story time never becomes dull. And so, I take my conscious sense of goodness as a shy new organ peeking, a toy just to play with and slowly learn of Life's awesome generosity.

To make peace, any peace, nothing, absolutely noth-
ing visible may need changing on Earth. Peace is made up
of handshakes that take place entirely in my mind.

My faith: when I see how Theo fits into the ongoing story
of life, I will be healed. I will be all well and beautiful.

19. Should I become known? Or should I become a slick boat that leaves the least wake behind?

Many people are now bred for quiet obedience. They are delegated into a shy professional niche, deep down in society's bowels.
They become invisible. Nobody can hear their modest yet vital
shout: "I am here. I want to be heard, seen, loved." Doesn't such
a society also produce the loudest professional shouters? "I am
here. Look, look, look at me, applaud!" The brighter and louder
the celebrities, the paler and more unnoticed the multitude that
lives in the shade.

Celebrity Life

So, to elicit gossip, I would have to shine and clown heroically in
front of a crowd that labors, forgotten, in the dark. I would have
to become a dancing elephant of an egotist. I would pump my
relationships into fantastic soap bubbles, then pop these bubbles
again as fast as a circus clown pops balloons hidden under his
pants. A show of hilarious greed or wealth, or a sex life that's a
shamelessly open wound, might make them buy a ticket to my
striptease. The masses of the Bystander Club love to be tickled
by the bizarre acts of an exhibitionist. Celebrities are society's
highest paid clowns. But why ask Theo to do stressful faces to
entertain?

To become famous, I have to perform as a slightly extended egotist, by which I mean a humanist. In this collective egotism, my dear next-door neighbor and my dear next-door generation do not only gossip about me. They applaud with medals the private favors that I shower on them. Yet the huge multitude of the generations and the species across the fence or beyond the hill may shake fists and call my favoritism a cheat for leaving them neglected out in the cold, or for having to pay my debts. They love a general practitioner, not a good-doer humanist.

"Good" reputation is a noisy, demanding bird in a cumbersome birdcage tied to my backpack, when, in my quest for learning, I try to weasel through the thicket of life. Like being crowned a master, a guru, a teacher, a "good" reputation can be a hindrance for learning. It slows a traveler down. To stand in the limelight or to receive medals of honor, Mr. Goodwill must look over his shoulders, instead of ahead. And there is danger; do-gooders seem often to be punished with fame.

Ah, the temptation to become the *best* at anything. How can such title winners avoid the economy's recruiters, who are always out hunting for such trophies for humans' use? Think of the high yield rubber tree. Society finds that tree, makes incisions in it, and saps its blood.

Maybe my stubborn, inborn stage fright comes from a wise, old feeling of feeling ashamed to stand out. Maybe it is because of this that in my life I have only once or twice spoken in front of more than a dozen people.

To Remain Unknown

To dare to remain unknown and live by my own dear self-esteem; here luxuries are offered that I like. A general practitioner, I hold on to my sack full of options, to all my allowance of leisure time, to a world that opens to a huge arena crowded with people and critters of every kind, all together discreetly, amicably exploring with me the Way. I shake fins, hands, branches, paws. So many kinds of neighbors! My admiration and my entertainments settle on the saint and on the pesterer, on the cheater and on the cheated, on the redwood and the logger alike, as does the dew, the rain, the sun. To be hypnotized by nobody, to be angry with nobody, to belittle nobody—now is that not a sweet deal? Greetings to any eager guest! Anybody is invited to paint their joys and their sorrows on the canvas of Theo's mind. Barely noticed, I blend in as the sun yellows get harmoniously absorbed in a Van Gogh. Here is talkative solitude I like. Heroes, celebrities, and other out-standers are stress-spots in the vast canvas of Life.

Nothing "heroic"! I do not wish to be corralled in the niche of some cause; *no "good" deeds!*

Enough of the self-proclaimed lords of Life, lording it over the Earth with their private favors. Let me scatter my affections and my martial arts evenly, beautifully, through the whole assembly of the generations, the species, the elements. I do my share of providing, of killing and of giving birth. I reason with the Earth. Sweet murmurs for playing fair from every critter, gentle or mean, intoxicate me. I resound cheerfully to these cheers. Here, very large harmonies are played. Some are hundreds of generations long, harmonies that are not as obvious to a domesticated mind as are the short local *pum-pa-di-pums* our scientists, moralists, musicians, economists and the sundry Theos may compose, according to the commandments of what we know. I am safe from the blinding spotlight that newscasters may focus on an outstanding man. I am safe from Theo the show-off. Fame makes a man so darn self-conscious. It sucks spontaneity.

> *To be hypnotized by nobody, to be angry with nobody, to belittle nobody—now is that not a sweet deal?*

And while no particular crowd of darlings monopolizes my mental scene, my soul yells from joy to be a guesthouse for all. I am free to improvise in this hugely permissive openness that may cook a dish of serenity for those merry draft dodgers who did not fossilize into a golden statue of fame.

Theo, do what the Storyteller from the depth of your thousand and one layers of memories tells you is the right thing to do. **The results are not important. They are mysterious. The bystanders** *are not so important.* Through thick and thin, this one mantra has become my most helpful companion. It's a candlelight in the dark that never goes out, whatever the wind. It helps me to brace the political storms without falling to one side. We are all magic flutes. "Theo, keep those holes open. Stand in the wind. The whole band of Life will play good music with your help. Slowly you will get the rhythm. Here is the reward. May your life be a streetlight."

> *The results are not important. They are mysterious. The bystanders are not so important.*

Be frugal with the back rubs, compliments, honors and gun salutes. With just two shots of this brew I would get drunk. When my trickster, that rascal guardian spirit in me, sends from deep down in my toes a "Theo—well done!" that should be compliment enough.

20. Life smiles permissively at our stern, manmade commandments.

Show me one critter, one people, one anything alive that does not successfully break any of our commandments in some circumstances, and I will vote for you.

With a big shout, our universe bursts forth from the belly of the multiverse to stand on its own. The fireworks of egos are being born. Whole galaxies break loose, some very large, others very small, some fast, others slower than an army of snails. Atoms, cyclones, microbes, Milky Ways. In that enormous stillness of uniformity, all hell breaks loose. Life, that miracle of egotism, is here. You, me, it—we are a violation of peace.

On the baby planet Earth the lava beds are still at peace, the mud flats smooth. Look, but something starts to wriggle that should not wriggle, another to breathe, yet another to fart.

A handful of dust starts to blink and to look around. In the sea of uniformity, islands of confusion begin to behave in baffling curls. Promising little centers of greed start to Sufi dance around themselves. Ecstatically they shout, "I, I, I." Little crystals, little egos, come alive. Here, a fire wheel takes off; there the idea of a sunflower tries its first turn. The living Earth is here! Zillions of arguments and genetic conflicts—a firework of arguments—and as many reconciliations! And think of all the new designs this bickering brings forth. Ever more exotic flowers of greed keep the miracle up. And it's the marvelous strangeness effect that keeps the clover and the grass, the Eskimos and the Chinese, the wasps and the bees, from falling again into each other's arms.

Each little bundle of joy shouts, "I am going to be heard, seen, felt. I claim a home. I bite and fart. I am alive and kicking. I cast a shadow. I am going to push others aside. I play all kinds of violent tunes to get my belly filled. And yes, I also cook lots of food for that banquet for all. I help to fill the universe with joy."

First, I am a baby squalling for milk, simply loving my baby self. Then I start to love my toys, my garden plants, and my next-door neighbor. Then I realize that my soul pays me well for adding to my love-garden those beyond my neighborhood and those beyond the generations I can see. "Theo, keep that roll call going. Theo, keep that onion of love, ring by ring, growing." You may argue with Theo that he does not always live up to the ideology he professes. I hope I prove your argument right, a hundred times right! A growing Theo needs ever-wider elbow room.

Thank God, we soon encounter and can love more exciting things than just our neighbors. Windsong told me that if you do not sometimes break out of man's commandments, you may be the darling of man but you are not a first-class child of Life. Did Windsong mean I am to walk the tightrope between benefit and harm, between yin and yang?

Maybe Rasputin had a glimpse of a healing-way the Puritans had never seen. Sins, crimes, misdemeanors, demonic and heroic works, all transgressions and other "miracles" seem mostly to deliver the new building blocks for Life's new adventures. Life ultimately fingers together new artworks of these aberrations that stand up, bend, walk, turn around—that ultimately sail their hats up into the air in thanksgiving joy. Is it not for these darn transgressions that Life became so darn versatile in its love-making? Without such violations of peace the Earth remains a soup of mud. And thank God, Life is still looking for more trouble.

No implant in my mind has produced more garbage and traffic jams than my regrets and my pangs of blaming others and myself. These add-ons, nifty "courtesies" of the tamers, proved to be unprofitable ballast and anchors for my inquisitive mind to drag along. I look at the hilarious missteps Life makes—everywhere—and I look at the results—more marvelous than the work of a million saints! And my self-hate evaporates.

There are also innumerable lies that are badly placed, break-ins beside an open door, an arm forced into being where there should be a leg. These are acts that seem totally misplaced, and therefore we call them crimes and sins. But who knows? Windsong told me that the Creator uses such pains and goofs, together with standard Legos, to build an upstairs in my soul. Some of my helpful posts and beams of thoughts are formed with the help of my migraines.

More opportunities, more challenges to live to the hilt, offer themselves to me in town than when I am alone at sea. Yet in the city these invitations are more easily avoided. In the city, politeness, which means avoidance, is ever ready to put my vitality in a box. On the sea, there are no such agreements. The wind does not lie down when I am petting him.

As you see, these mind-altering scenes that my mind continuously inhales in the wild open sea set my mind dangerously free from humanism's leash.

21. May a religion's story enchant us better than Prozac.

Why is it that some religions have an endless grudge with Life on this enchanted Earth?

Like: Life on the Earth is the pits from which we are to liberate ourselves, never to return. Or, we are supposed to be born with a fifty-pound stone of original guilt tied to our backs. Or, to graduate to some better yonder life, we are to cut our feelings and our natural acts from our living flesh with the knife of self-denial. Or, here is misery and suffering; the good life is not from this world.

Tell me how to expect help from such bashers of the Creator? Help that will keep Life on Earth lush, beautiful, and diverse?

The great fleet of cumuli meandering the summer sky, the wader-birds, the Earth's waterworks, every critter with no hat or shoes, they plead, tickle, stand on their heads to catch the eyes of the present leaders of such world religions. They call them to a change of heart, to stop advertising the living Earth as a morbid, lowly place good only for escaping.

This world right here is the best world for me. The better world? It's even more of it. Don't moan for a better world. If you are too feeble to swallow what you bite off, moan for a meeker world, a spaded world. Moan for globalization, that emergency autonomy of our so luxurious, wildly profuse, and lusty diversity, for an emergency massacre of costly cultures. In this exodus, people stand now in line to pawn their dearest peacock feathers for a bag of safety and a bowl of cheap global soup. To wish for a "better" ocean, an ocean with no whistle winds and no cresting seas? Never, never, never! Don't rob me of my source for bragging. Don't rob me of my dangers and risks, the healthiest drugs I know. I have a hunch that the prophets of a globalized economy were sad, fearful, and frail girls and boys who had little fun when young.

*The longer I get to listen and observe Creativity at work, the
more inspired Life itself gloriously shouts to me, "Your goofs,
stabs, and missteps are all accepted, no strings attached."*

*Even better, I hear, "Look and learn from me. Marvel at what mar-
vels Life can do with all what you condemn. Empty your backpack
of the rocks of blame and guilt that weigh you down—and fly!"*

22. To compete in truthfulness is the first discipline in Life's Olympic Games.

The "crime" of wildness is maximum truthfulness. The "virtue" of being cultured is self-denial and cover-ups. The one gives Life the rugged general practitioner—the other the vulnerable, fine specialist. This seems so for plants, animals, and people.

It takes physical strength, mental strength, and a large muscular vision to be truthful and to stand one's ground, more so than to retreat in a lie. In that game, the last player to stand her ground is the survivor. When I am truthful, I shoulder that extra bundle of life that the liar does not.

Each player has to watch his load and his backbone. Each has to know his personal inventory so to choose well when to fight and when to hibernate in some lie.

Barely noticeably, do I not ask myself a hundred times each day: can I handle this with truthfulness or not? To be truthful is dangerous, to be nice is safe. To live a poetic lifestyle is dangerous. To take refuge in the safe gardens of citing poetry is not.

Sometimes cowardice is needed to survive. Other times courage is required. Sometimes it's hibernation. Other times confrontation is the pill. The beaver is a wise "coward." He knows when it is time to be a coward and to curl up in his winter den. In spring the tree opens in leaves, flowers, and fruits. When it snows, the tree takes refuge in its bark.

To be truthful makes me a bigger target. To weigh whether to go for truthfulness or not is one of the oldest biological games. Can I confront? Do I have to hide?

And each tiptoes along his very own tightrope between being truthful and being polite, each respecting the limitations with which she was born.

How big a chunk of life can I bite off? How much vulnerability can I take without being choked by what

To be truthful is dangerous, to be nice is safe. To live a poetic lifestyle is dangerous. To take refuge in the safe gardens of citing poetry is not.

I take on? Some can handle an extra serving of truthfulness, others cannot. On the ocean of challenges, truthfulness can truly overload a man—and he sinks. Look at a drunk. With his filters burnt, he is drunk and shaky with too much truth. That is the crime of wine. Truthfulness let loose on others can be a roaring fire. Theo, use it with compassion. Confine it to a stove. Slowly released, truthfulness will warm you and the bystanders too. If you ask truthfulness of her that she cannot afford, you are not her friend. No organism is known that can fully skin itself and survive in such nakedness. And never underestimate what marvels a compassionate lie administrated as a placebo can do.

You want to peek into my naked innermost? No polite haggling in a comfy conference room will do. Go out with me in a storm that pelts our makeup away.

When truthfulness has a feast with me, I am a wild man. In such strong times, my talk wants to be raw well water—all transparent, no sweetener added, a mirror with no ripples. Any rhyme, perfume, politeness, conclusion added would lessen its transparency. Drunk with joy to be alive, I shake off hibernation, niceness, sunglasses, and all the fashion garments of my mind. I join the exuberant song of spring. In this inspired state, bursting with truth in heat, serious things start happening to you and me.

So. Nobody lies for pleasure. Those who have to lie surely are more urgently in need of some alms than those who can afford the truth. And yes, there are truths that only in our most loving intimacies do not stink like dirty socks. In passion, a woman or man can be helplessly overwhelmed with honesty. Therefore, in all but such intimacies, honesty must have its taboos.

You ask for a truthful person who has no temper? You might as well ask for a rich pregnant sky with no downpour after an over-heated day. Yet doesn't shameless truthfulness, when served compassionately with humor, have the heartiest laugh? It's a loaded camel that bucks, kicks and tosses off its cargo and starts to sprint, yelp in joy, and dance.

Evasive niceness has its consequences later on. All these little brush fires swiftly extinguished with cool politeness leave much unspent tinder to accumulate in our hearts, waiting to later ignite into the hottest, most destructive confrontations and cruelties. Anybody who can become angry, yet has to press that anger down under again and again, knows why and how atrocities happen. Just as the Earth's many little burps and farts held back too long build up to a tsunami, a million little frustrations without a release can ultimately move mountains, or produce a massacre or a genocide. Our history is full of these painful learning experiences.

I note that we now breed polite people, untrained in truth-fulness, who cannot take the stress of standing firm in the four winds—people who can only survive with the massive shield of beautifully ornate lies an authoritarian government puts around and before them. May the courage be with me to be truthful to my very limits. May I be given the wisdom to embrace a lie, if lying must be, and to pull down the sails when my rigging is not up to the challenge of a mad sea?

The Earth sounds and resounds with the beautiful song of its hide and seek. "Theo, sing loud—from the top of the mast!"

Thank you, Clara, for never misleading me with flatteries. In my ocean nights, there always cruises above me a bright path-finding star. This phenomenon in my sky, that's you.

84

23. As for you, so for a piece of land, it's the absolute necessity that you are as you are.

In a hush of "my-soul-is-having-fun," I can shut my eyes to that person I know as your name. Instead I can see you as the age-old, unique piece of land you really are.

Think of a Sonora desert, that grows its absolute best with what is at hand: cacti that ferociously defend their precious bellyful of water with a full-size coat of thorns and lies. Lovely, luxurious lushness is low on their shopping list. Who needs loud eye-catching makeup when you are mostly alone on the village square? Here, a bouquet of the best kinds of prickly solitude is produced: songs of waving dunes of sand, or any specialty this good mother of scarcity has the means to invent.

Think of a Nordic range of frosty peaks with just sprinkles of green. Think of a few acres of a raw bulldozer mess, chewed into marvelous jungle green as far as you can see, or a gaping hole of pregnant nothing, which a natural disaster has recently plowed and readied for a new who-knows-what. Name any brand of land, meager or fat, and I think I can show you a man whose inner landscape equals that piece of land.

Each named and unnamed land is madly busy out there trying to grow its absolute best with what Life has put into its gift box. Some human emotions will grow in it, others will not. Some qualities it can afford. For others there is no cash in hand. I see a law at work as basic as gravity. No seed can resist a waterhole.

When I can shut my eyes to that *you* with your name branded on it, which is really a gross underestimation of you, I go on vacation. This is the moment to give up judgment, and to fire any mean ghost of some judgment day. These precious moments need conditions to grow that are as rare as those in which diamonds can form. Yet these morsels of serenity are the invisible game I am out to hunt. No grim "god" squats in some roadblock, interrogating, on my way to the serenity fest.

Theo, when you complain about the meager crop of love some men may grow, think of Mars. And then even the most awkward wriggle of life on Earth seems to do well.

There are many exotic flowers that can never grow on Christian soil. There is missionized soil that can give birth to communal flowers absolutely no individual hunk of soil by itself can bring forth.

Whether he is a man of a bitter brew and he protects his precious little desert tuft of truth with thorns and lies, whether he is a soil so filthy rich that he can generously leak and tell me all, and then simply get more, he does his absolute best. Even a critter we put in jail or we round up with Monsanto's weed Roundup is a million times more valuable than the best of Jupiter's live crop.

There are far too many tools in Life's toolbox to all figure out their uses. She is an indescribable tool. He is a medicine not yet revealed. Every quality of Life is a message, a revelation. My hunch: if all our naive manmade you-shoulds and you-should-nots were fulfilled, then in the departments of the great shopping mall of our hearts, one by one, the lights would go out.

In my sweet moments of "no-judgment-and-no-Judgment-Day," my deeper mind elevates even the most shocking happening to a blessed natural "disaster"—a mysterious act of God. I might want to get out of its reach, or under an umbrella. Yet evil it is not. That disaster firmly remains a proud associate of the beauty of Life.

Did you note? I am helping Theo on to also be kinder to himself. Although, I guess, it must at times be a harder chore to love this rascal than to unload a truck of coal.

24. A language more refined than words

Beyond the confused, verbal outbursts of our moralists, is it not our genetics that quietly talk to us and prescribe our needed behaviors and our cures?

Take a handful of our environment—millions of messages: seismic, magnetic, visual, audible, molecular, subatomic, the whole spectrum of waves, perfumes, signs and dreams. Every wink of an eye is a message. The slightest tremor of fear, the steps of the dancing molecules and the unique design of their magnetic field, each charged particle racing across the universe, each one broadcasts. They are part of the universal language.

Every critter of the Earth receives, processes, and answers that mass of uncountable messages. My body is one of these million-stringed instruments. Our entire literature is a raindrop that makes its ripples on this sea. And who whispers to the tulip, "Spring is here"? Our environment is a million times more gossipy than all our nice ladies are when they meet for tea. If Life had a communication system as crude as our verbal capacity, it would instantly collapse into mud.

With our love affair with the written language we made, like no other species, our communication turns into a simplistic one-species affair. When I read, I enter into a hall of mirrors. Visiting no man's lands helps me to break out of that spell. I tune in to the Earth's wordless subtleties again.

A species seems to survive for long because again and again it manages to balance what it does for its own benefit with what it listens to and does for the needs of other tenants in life's apartment house. In the lobby of this grand place, every guest of the Earth is welcomed with an approximate set of rules. Modest extravaganzas are encouraged so nobody has to yawn, "Do we have to do this again?" Daring to tentatively sidestep life's simple ordinance of moderation, our science and its technology has listened lately a little too much to our books and fattened mankind. In fact, we have truly become the species of exaggerators.

Literacy focuses a mind enormously. It makes our mind so darn man-specific. Literacy is that telescope that focuses my mind on that one star number, the needs of mankind, bringing out an awesome wealth of helpful details, of practical advice and power. Literacy helps me little to become a good apprentice in the universal language of Life. It stuffs the mind mostly with raw mental calories. It is often a temptation for our ecstatic minds to become lazy and obese. Now, how do I write so as to tease the reader to leave the reading of bear stories, and venture out to meet the real bear?

Mankind looks a little pale, overweight, and diluted from too many private favors and cures we have showered on ourselves. Tenants of other niches are up in arms for being ignored and squeezed. They talk and act back to us in a language that my genetics understands. My genetic setting seems to have a telephone line to every critter in the world. And is not each mind a cell of the Universal Mind? No, I do not expect it to be one more sacred book or technological fix, an even better exaggeration of our benefits, a super cereal or a super iPod, a mightier plow, a breakthrough of our clinical medicine, a cleaner energy resource, one more credit extension, that will make us again slim, wise and fewer.

Let me expand. A volcano under pressure starts to emit a discreet stream of seismic gurgles and tremors—many kinds of signals, in a language well beyond our intellect. Early, the animals are told to forgo their sweet routine and hit the road. In rock crevasses, hibernating snakes wake up and wriggle to safer grounds, burrowing rodents hear the message, dogs get antsy, bark, get outside. Visual, chemical, sound signals, even vibrations can talk amphibians into drastically changing their morphogenesis, changing from standard editions to huge exaggerated predators when stressed.

Plants, also, are not primitive communicators. Plants continuously emanate a discreet cloud of thousands of different molecules. They are adaptive molecules of evolution. A plant speaks thousands of different sentences at any time. Sentences like, "I have an invasion of caterpillars, can the wasps please home in on me and have a feast, and relieve me of that itch?" And the fleet of wasps is hearing it too. They follow up. Other plants listen in and, on genetic order, their cells quickly start to churn out chemicals that make them also unappetizing or indigestible for these caterpillars, before the gobblers invade them too.

A troop of deer recklessly chews a sage bush to pieces. Within seconds, that bush churns out methyl jasminate (used in Chanel No. 5, by the way). The volatile chemical stimulates the production of toxic defense compounds. Other plant species listen in on the alarm signal and crank up their own chemical defenses. Warnings and medicines go back and forth. Take terpene aerosol. It's the SOS produced by plants in response to invasive damage. When the salmon berries need transportation, they put the ripest berries with all their sexy colors and perfumes out, shouting to anybody with wings, "Eat me! We need a ride to a new home." And listen to a summer meadow—two thousand species of grasshoppers—each species broadcasting with its very own love songs. Listen to a man's clothing. It is also talking. Yet who finds time to translate all these intimate, hidden meanings?

When the time is ripe in a Monarch butterfly, an urge wells up in her. She starts to dream of Michoacán and flies, flies over thorn bushes, over oceans, over dunes, "fly, fly, to your best wintering grounds." Demonic knowledge, cooked and recooked for a million years, is piloting her. In the pitch dark, invisible forms show up in her. Voiceless voices are talking to her. All this high-level communication goes on while many among us cannot even speak anymore in more than a thousand words. Our words have become simple echoes of the media. Other, more experienced social animals must have more refined languages than us. Otherwise how could they be so successfully social?

Our society, under stress from its overproduction and overpopulation, engulfs our children also in a cloud of extraordinary signals. Thousands of crisis and stress related molecules are emitted as well as cues from our confused stares, from our too many lies, and our obsession with speed, and all the while resources and elbow room are running out. They get cues from our harshness when we converse, from our love-affair with junk-food, from a mistreated environment that has tears in its eyes, from the air poisoned with the curses of our "fuck-yous" from the canned and screened education and advertisements with which we junk-feed their minds, from our love for them that got a little watered down. They get cues from the many minds that are pale and skinny from the absence of wild, nourishing sights and organic thoughts. Every single thought, science told me today, can trigger genes to spring into action.

Our environment and our parental behavior speak to our children, and their genetic setting understands those analphabetic crisis alerts. Our weeping and our cussing are languages so forceful; they make our verbal outpourings seem like lame blah-blah-blahs. Consider your body—countless millions of cells, each cell undergoing some hundred thousand chemical reactions every second. Each cell is involved in the dialogue with the environment and knows the sentences to produce an alphabet of three hundred thousand different proteins, from which it composes the harmonizing answers. One cell's metabolism dwarfs the chemistry of all the world's labs and chemical plants combined.

Throughout Life, for example, environmental stress talks us into promoting maleness. When resources are getting scarce, some of man's male talents are force-fed. Testosterone replacement therapies become headlines. Motherly talents are starved. Male qualities in a woman are ordered to become dominant.

Genes have recipes for proteins, neurochemicals and dreams at hand to bring a lost son back home. There is cannibalism when needed, mothballing in egotism, retreats into mental hypothermia, confusion of the sense of direction, proteins that can send our exaggerated activity on a vacation to a depression, or to games of self-satisfaction. They can reorient our zest into a poetic vision, a devotion to endangered elephants, or an "Earth First!" mission. When needed, sex may be talked into resting for a while, or told to cool its fire on the internet or in a virgin sisterhood, or a playboy-hood.

A non-economy may be triggered that, in order to drain our overaggression, makes us bag the desert's sand and dump it on our neighbor's land, or exhaust ourselves fighting over money to no end. Name here any phobia, obsession, aversion, or devotion that puts the brakes on our runaway successes. Then, too, a species may run a high fever, may lie low in depression, may starve, may faint, may get the runs—as part of its healing process. Millions of demand lists and supplies go back and forth.

No, a gene set does not function as an individual. It functions as a mirror for its environment. It communicates with the environment, including the individual in which it resides. That's how very natural our social instinct is. That's how we are all connected with Life's internet.

Now, take a handful of this universe. You hold countless messages in your hand. Poke a wire in this handful. You can extract the sum total of the internet from it. You can extract from its spectrum of waves, from the huge radio waves to the tiny gamma rays, a zillion messages at one time—all the time.

And how many different levels of languages! Cells chatter among cells. Individuals in a species talk among themselves. Species gossip with species, genes with genes. Growth factors of my body call in their shopping lists. Stars have much more to say to each other than just "good morning." Sunflowers beam their invitations to all the little flyers to deliver pollen. Microbes are also much more talkative in their microbial language, and cleverer than we guessed. Think of the slime mold. When meeting en masse, these little microbe slimers switch on quorum sensing—chemical messages of awesome complexity—to coordinate teamwork for doing fantastic things no single microbe can do. What enormous vocabularies! Our dreams have their own history and memory, and are also very talkative with us.

On my boat, how many thousand times my eyes have reached for the ocean sky, reading its clouds, their movements, their forms and their colors, the hue of the horizon, guessing what the mother of the weathers has in mind for me—listening, smelling what the sky has to say. That sky of Southeast Alaska is more talkative than a schoolyard alive with twenty jabbering girls in recess.

This is the nourishing soup of information I swim in, get nourished by, and by which my ego ultimately gets overridden when lost, only to be let back home and into the center stage again. I am breathing a very nourishing atmosphere of languages. Science tells me that out of the two hundred billion bits of information Theo processes, only two thousand make it into his consciousness. With this in mind, my pride at being a conscious being becomes a little lame.

Now watch a young raven. She will not miss inspecting anything new. Why then do we put our children's wildly exuberant curiosity on a leash, on a diet of only words? Luckily for me and to the desperation of my educators, I could not be made to read a book until I was fourteen.

Lucky me, for having been loved by Mocho, my dearest friend in the tropics for forty-three years—a supreme man and fisher, whom I have never seen afraid, who could not write nor read, with a heart as large as a football field.

Sun, sun, go away. I want now to hear what all the forms beyond the forms of visible light have to say. Google, Google, give me a break, I do not want to turn into an incestuous mind that strictly sleeps within our little family of the written word.

In the vast spectrum of information, visible light is only a narrow slit of brightness. A man to whom as a child nobody had sung to soothe him into comfort and confidence and sweet dreams—who will sing to him now? Who will melt away the ice that immobilizes his soul? What no words can do, the touching and the talking of her hands, while she sings and restores his battered love, are healing a frostbitten man. Sometimes I just listen to the melody of your talk and I learn more about your needs than by listening to your words. Yes, raw language as raw carrots are darned health-giving. Yet the crowd likes language processed into smoothies.

In our environment so flooded with puny bagatelles, I had to become an excellent surveyor, a night glider and passionate observer, and above all a bad alphabetic listener. I am walking chest deep in puny verbalized details, most of them utterly overly fancy dressed for their worth.

It is from that awesomely complex dialogue we unknowingly entertain with all these "guardian spirits" before all, that I expect our deeper nature to concoct our unappreciated cure again and again, so the plants and the animals may be plentiful and our population in tune.

Here a personal anecdote of an unaccustomed communication: Last Tuesday night on my boat at anchor in Gilmore Bay, Alaska, I had a terribly vivid dream. I was told that somebody in the tropics, someone very close to me, had died. I never had such a compelling dream that shook me all awake, sweating and breathing heavily. Maybe my brother? Maybe Lupe or Mocho? But it was only a dream! Yet what if I come home and I am told it was real? And so it happened, I found, when back in port. Without warning, Lupe left us at that time of my dreaming.

May I never be so blinded by bad faith that I can-
not hear the Song of the Earth.

25. Are the general practitioners becoming an endangered species?

Each time I buy, do I not cheat a capacity of mine out of its joy to live? Use it or lose it—child after child in my family of talents starts to get pale and left behind this way. I am a fish, born to swim free and take on the ocean. With all the goodies winking "buy me, buy me," how could that simple fish resist a job in a fish farm, and not go for those winks? There, no sweat, he can buy his food, his safety, his health, his erection, cheap imitations that seem to fulfill his dreams, bargains in luxuries never before seen. All this that fish could buy, in exchange for the quality meat he produces.

My pillow wants to know, "Theo, God just loves to make love with you: how much of your lovemaking are you going to farm out, so you can sleep lazily just with some dear, little routine? Be brave, wean yourself from your addiction to just live practically. Listen, every bird sings his inborn joy of being able to fly on his own." We, too, we spontaneously pledged as children allegiance to an unencumbered self-made life, as ecstatic queens and kings of our pains and joys. Yet to the birds' great surprise, we soon started to progress step by glorious step, into the contrary of that spontaneous life with its sack full of leisure time. With a pride so strange to my heart, we now buy and buy and pile up our dependencies that we soon empty our sack full of leisure and refill it with a chore list. This is what the battle among the business corporations can do to us when they compete to rewire our minds so we become their customer underlings.

Name any capacity of my body and mind. It can be bought with the paycheck I get for forcing the loudest, most outstanding faculty of mine into "prostitution"—an expert walking the economy's merry Broadway. Who can still sing by himself, out of the blue, now that the iPod is here? Enchanters kindle spendy phobias in me. Did they plant in your mind lately poison ivies of fear, so they could sell you an anti-fear pill?

Spare me the expert's syndrome. This force-fed narrow focus to excel in one detail comes at the expense of my bigger picture. I will fail my calling if I become a prizewinner. This modern condition brings to mind a gentle form of autism, with the few splinter-skills that affliction can prodigiously develop. One is the result of dubious memes, the other the result of dubious genes. Spare me that economy that becomes the magnificent super-whore who shamelessly, expertly sneaks her hand right into my pants till all my chemistry says "yes!" She sure can permanently erect our penises, and our guns. Eye-catching overconsumption has become the peacock plumage for those with nothing better to show. There are forty-five thousand items in a supermarket from which to choose.

Think now of a mind born free to roam the exciting take-any-turn-you-please trail, a mind with a gusto for pleasures that are not purchased, but paid for with healthy hardships and growing pains. What a dramatic happening when this curiously meandering mind is lassoed, corralled, branded and baited with fame in order to become an expert of things, a mind confined to safely mine some very specific knowledge, highly profitable on the mental commodity exchange.

Did you notice that an expert is more preoccupied with speed and lavish consumption than a general practitioner? Time becomes rationed. With just a few very specific peepholes in his mine-tunnel, that miner's mind feels at home only in very specific far-apart places and friends. It's a mind mostly on the run.

The more highly cultivated I become, the more options and players in my soul have to be laid off. Read up on the outside help New Leaf potatoes need to stay alive. They are big consumers. Without agro-businesses' weapons of mass destruction and food-additives, that super potato does not do well. Life's general practitioners can afford to be slowpokes. They run into an associate and a meal waiting in every ditch, sidewalk, and niche while meandering along the way. These draft-dodgers remain in the arts of social skills.

This beautiful Earth, so alive and sexy, has certainly not been made by a search for comfort.

This beautiful Earth, so alive and sexy, has certainly not been made by a search for comfort. Yesterday a flock of Canadian honkers on their flight South were teasing me: "You want to learn about light-winged living? Don't look at your Airbus and your pile of luggage. Look at us. Note our baggage!"

Theo, have yourself tied to the mast, as Odysseus did, when your ship passes close by mighty Television Land with its enchanting siren songs. Prepare your wits. The sexiest warrior thoughts grapple aboard and battle with your own little troop of thoughts. No army of pulpits, no other missionary organization, beats the power of this mental colonization tool.

A country with a vast budget tempts its women and men to avoid maturity. With hundreds of agencies taking over hundreds of my responsibilities, how to avoid remaining a puppy for life? It offers an Eden I do not like.

Practicality can cause an affliction in the class of vitamin-deficiency. In this badly nourished environment in which only this most simplistic dimension of our awareness is fed, a mind so deficient in "lightamines" can become numb to all responsibilities but those for present mankind.

Each man is now challenged to create with his own bleeding mind, word by word, sentence by sentence, his very own conscious immunity against the nifty little logic of practicality charming him. And how untrained we are in this task. Each is also challenged to create his own vaccine against the low self-assurance, beamed by the media into each of us, which continuously forces us to prove ourselves with a ridiculous trophy show of wealth. Damned macho show. Yes, practicality is a salesman who has all the easy arguments on his side. And did you notice: the more we become experts, the more we become consumers. Did you notice, an expert, neglector of a thousand of his talents and points of view, becomes a more irritable, less tolerant man than a general practitioner? An umbrella, please, against that downpour of slogans of the international corporate democracy. Through its crooked contact lenses the customers are

Each man is now challenged to create with his own bleeding mind, word by word, sentence by sentence, his very own conscious immunity against the nifty little logic of practicality charming him. And how untrained we are in this task.

the enemies, along with the wilderness and its resources to be exploited by the few competing fellow-corporations, who are discreetly friends with one another.

I think here of mentology versus technology—about sculpting light with my mind. I love to reinvent my life with a mental technology. My bridge-supports can be made of thoughts. I create my comfort by visualizing encouraging strings of pictures that include, for example, what wonders birth pains can bring forth. I can abolish fears by adding new balconies to my mind, so that fearful views can reunite with the flock of ideas that know how to re-engineer an enemy into an opponent, turning him, for instance, into a sharpening stone for my mind.

A Grand Prix, please, for those rare inventions that I do not have to pay for with my self-reliance. I can grow wings for my mind on my own. A gift of a metaphor that mows down a thicket of my fears, a stepladder to a lost reality, a shaft to my buried capacities, a stimulant that teases awake a dormant talent or a Sleeping Beauty buried in my sediments, a new enlightened story that turns an old pain-mythology into Prozac. To calm my terror of change, I can think of our great Common Wealth, which resides in the many strategies human races and societies have invented to survive and to govern themselves. Has this magnificent quilt of backup systems become a luxury we can no longer afford? I can bring to mind the great ant civilizations that didn't go for globalization. They are brave. They didn't massacre their many cultures. They evolved into 20,000 species so they keep up for instance 20,000 ways to govern themselves—20,000 backup systems! And they do well—with such a diversity there is no ant sweat lost worrying about climate changes.

Life laughs at simplicity. It loves to complicate, squeeze in another curl here, another predator there. From a flat face it squeezes out a nose. From a desert people it flowers a new kind of prickly desert religion. The Creator's sword swats and severs— and, lo, another niche! Soon another species exults, "hello!" Life's motto? The smaller the crowds, the fewer the fools.

Now listen to a wetland littered with critters, all happily waking up in the morning—incredible bags of delight, all shouting, "See! See! Listen to me!" Each of these many different free-wheelers worked out its own strategy to beat the idea of monoculture. This is creativity. Think of a critter we label as a pest. That's just a story badly told. Be an artist. Sculpt a brighter story for this unappreciated child of God. This is creativity. Look at the explosion of beauty from pole to pole that diversity in its stubborn responses has brought forth. Is it not in these cussed, symmetry-breaking, common-sense-breaking, practicality and mindset-breaking spells that our energy diverges into differentiated mindsets, sporting new blues and pinks? Did you ever wonder why the birds do not twitter for shopping malls, but happily inaugurate each day chirping their joy?

In order to remember my native gift of fending for myself, I asked Ivan, our oldest son, to beach me on Kruzof, an unpopulated island off Southeast Alaska in October (a wet and stormy month of short days), to be picked up after eight days. My baggage: my rifle, my clothes, my education, a sleeping bag, and a box of matches. Such shifts of independence can wean me a little of my addiction to simply lean against my fellow men, to shamelessly consume, to hang on their man-only, all-permeating intercom when I face a challenge.

Ah, the adventure of not being a customer. Beating the bushes, I ran into a mining port in me I had given up for lost.

26. Remember, Theo, when you lament your loss of freedom, your lament is also an ode to freedom, the freedom of another man, or another wind, to keep you lying low.

The pursuit of "freedom" is a ball game. Continuously, "freedom" has to change hands. In this game we play simultaneously at different levels in the hierarchies of freedoms. In fact, it is the game we all play to step up or down in the Hierarchy of Dependences.

Sometimes we play man-against-man. More often we now play this "tug of war" individual-against-society, and the individual is losing ground. Right now, a billion people eagerly await their daily serving of information (news), the command rooms of the media administers, every ingredient of it calibrated by experts to enhance your mood and make it favorable to the elite's cause. And many just love to be leashed to their beloved leaders. Few are alert amateur listeners, still in the spell of their own strong inner voices, able to grab the media's ball and answer back.

Sometimes a formidable man may wrestle himself free from his culture's nose ring and bridle so that he may amicably play solo against all of life's players. A woman or man who is obedient to his or her own inner voice is a slave I respect. She remained one of God's personal leash dogs.

And tell me: how freedom could ever be given; how a passion could be given? Here is a gift no man can possibly give. I never fight for freedom, neither for myself nor for others. My fight *is* my freedom. His fight *is* his freedom.

Ninety-nine percent of what you frame in my name is fortunately beyond Theo. With all my gritting of teeth, I still have absolutely no free access to that magic storehouse you might mistakenly call Theo. I shout at it, "Left!" And completely unconcerned it may trod to the right. I shout at it, "Feel good!" And it sobs and sobs. I plead with it to fast, fast heal my wound— and it keeps to its own schedule. I order it to listen to my smart ideas. It keeps tuned in to the voice of the Earth.

A man gets older and his penis will not stand up to his command. Ask him about his free will, about willing that penis up. It's his fantastic tool that decides when it's time for sunrise. A woman gets ripe and ready to close shop. Ask her about her free will, and her willing herself to stay on.

I am, mind, body and all, a waterwheel dipped into the Great Stream. One other wheel, just yards away, turns opposite to mine. That stream is full of back eddies. In fact, it is the only stream with no single direction and way. Left, right, up, in reverse and down, that's how Life gets all her chores done and without risk of overflowing. And don't forget how that stream always gets to the mountaintop again.

Ah, to be a little free, to make do with little help or commands from others. Even better, to scavenge the courage to live with a morsel of spontaneity and be the Creator's personal clown, available to sometimes march solo to the Song of the Earth, banging one of God's drums just by myself, able to work little and do much just by being a flag all unfolded fluttering in God's winds, available to be entirely a fiddle with a thousand strings on which Life's zillion fingers fiddle her gypsy tune.

Wouldn't independence break any kind of law, from the law of gravity to all the way up and down? How could there be anything but grace? Independence and free will would truly be a miracle. One has to retire this humbug talk of man's free will and that we can defy Grace. Independence and free will are deadly fantasies. The Earth is far too risky a place not to hold hands. No, these twin notions cannot choke off the ground water that wants to seep toward the thirsty corn. They cannot cut off the love that wants to flow toward a woman's and a man's heart. But these phantoms sure can tie a heavy guilt burden onto our backs and suck our sap.

The pretense of free will delivered the uninspired "cure" of punishing sad, little Theo when he wetted his bed, instead of Mom taking him into her arms. This notion is a black cloud that for too long obscured my road signs to forgiveness. And do we not all still at times wet the pants of our souls? The notion of free will is a punishing phantom idea planted in our hearts by clever commanders who want to dominate others, a justification for them to punish the rebels with a double whip, one whip for defying these commanders, the other for supposedly defying God.

May I never become a campfire left behind to burn itself down as I "celebrate" my free will and Independence Day.

27. The Earth is lush with the beautiful flowers of apparent injustice.

"To get comfy with Life's extra-large justice, Theo, don't talk with a referee in a football game. Add another balcony to your mind's jury box."

My sense of justice is a mighty flexible shopping bag. Heaps of generations, heaps of species can or cannot be befriended and stuffed into this bag, according to what I become aware of and can lovingly cradle in my arms. "Theo, for goodness' sake, add more seats to your jury box. Rediscover your wild, multigeneration, multispecies sense of justice, and fewer injustices will annoy you. Look at the cactus. With a bag of sand and just one spoonful of the enormous resources we have here in Blue Blossom Land, this expert in frugality has also found a way to enjoy herself."

Meanwhile, as the believers in obvious justice and the enforcers of it, we act out our justice's beauty-in-the-box with rituals like classical music, or two steps to the left, two steps to the right and one turn, or with meticulously sharing a pie. Here the millions of

Life's other dancers in her Great Dance have to freeze and play dead, so our befriended handful of actors may play for a moment our nice little harmonies-in-the-box without being disturbed. Yet when we grow up, it might happen that we want to throw away some of our most simplistic toys of justice—*too tight, done with it!*

Each critter is allotted a different blindfold according to his job—the leader and the led, a sucker of a man and the sucked. Some get bifocals, other mono or multifocals. The worm gets none. And wouldn't the prairie mice be totally lost without the rattler in their land? How would these voracious little mice, with three litters a year, pay their debts without the help of this dear, slick brother in disguise?

Everyone is called out to accomplish a different chore. Each chore needs a different kind of shortsightedness. Take the Marine's expert killer caressing his AK-47. Ah, if he could see all the consequences, the children of the man in his crosshair, that "bad man's" little girl with her pussycat, the empty soup kettle, and the woman mending that "bad man's" socks. No way. He needs to see behind his crosshair the bad man, the medals, the honors, the buddies slapping his back for being the best of the triggers—and nothing more. That must be his frame of justice. There are some among us who truly would die if they could not kill. There are others who would truly die if they killed.

Some wish themselves this luck: may the eyeglasses Life made by hand for my special niche never fog up, so I may never fail to see my little niche as my kingdom and remain its defender. Others are more adventurous. They hold tight onto their blessed unrest and the growing pains in their sense of justice. For them, an apparent injustice may become one of the not yet interpreted, glorious sounds, or one of the many glorious pauses the Conductor calls each of us to sing in the Song of the Earth. Glory to the healer, glory to the inflictor of wounds. Glory to the rattlers, glory to the voracious mice.

Glory to the stingray that nearly killed one of Theo's legs and taught him to peel his eyes.

As we lovingly mislead our children with scaled down stories when truth is too awesome, so do the simplistic myths of some religions cautiously mislead. They simply add up the momentary gains and losses a person accumulates, allotting him a job to frolic in a heaven or to roast in some hell. It is this simplistic, childish judging of him or her personally that misled me. It fogged up the wild, multigenerational love affairs I have with Life. It turned me into a grim, losing fighter for an impatient justice that, to fulfill it, wouldn't even allow me seven lifetimes. A million storytellers also soon surrounded me, making fun of a grim man. Old cocoons are cracking, now that I am after a sense of justice for grownups.

You, I, she, the grasses and the pepper trees, a prophet or a man of a bitter brew, all you can see and not see, we are all billionaires in IQs. We may all be blessed ingredients, perhaps to be used for do-gooders or seers, others to be fermenters or to be fermented to yummy compost out of which, later, sweetly intoxicating poets may grow. Some need to grow their peacock feathers a hundred feet tall or a billion dollars wide, to feel cock. They don't mind becoming heavy, flightless birds while becoming experts in this show-off business. Each has to play the instrument he is given. And I bet some four-stringed souls at the beach beer-party right now down on the bay have as much fun as I do, playing my ten-stringed instrument while scribbling this down.

To write this and be cocky about it? Ridiculous. It's just another job in the Creator's enterprise, paid with the same cash as digging manioc or husking nuts. And so the zillion earthworms still happily tunnel their million miles of tunnels a day to till and give breath to the soil. What if the worms demanded justice, to be given eyes, to see the raspberries? Who would then give breath to the sucker roots and recycle the dung? So the Divine Gardener decrees, "No eyes for the worms!"

Holding on as an adult to a childish idea of justice had condemned me to hold, day and night, some grudge with Life. This misfortune was the hindrance to getting Theo a little high on a sniff of serenity.

After that long hibernation, my inborn sense of justice, such as it is in Life, not such as man's own reasons would have it be, is now stirring again in me. I look. I rub my eyes and look yet again. Every critter around me seems to know that to make Life's creation a more just place has little to do with redistributing personal rights. This cure of my myopic sense of justice slowly takes place when I invite more and more generations and species to become partners of my mind. A telescope, please, for my shortsighted eyes that keep seeing much injustice in The Great Show and, frustrated, make me yell "foul."

Theo, climb Mt. Everclear to push the limits of your view.

28. Take hatred, Theo. Sit down with this unwanted child, and hear it out.

Hold on to your faith in the goodness of Life and surf these rebellious thoughts with me.

Hatred, that unwanted child, laments: why this anger with me? I have results as blessed as those of tender love. I am maker of isolation, quarantines, and firebreaks. I am guardian of diversity. I can build up mountain-moving intensity among pale, shallow niceness never seen.

I hate tuberculosis for you, and give this sucker microbe hell. When you cannot digest food, you throw it up. When you are pelted with behaviors, thoughts, deeds, or beliefs too far off, or you are confronted with happenings in Life that are totally indigestible to your mental chemistry, I am your "faculty" to throw them up and out of your life. Do you understand why a fish must hate land? Prone lately to altitude-sickness, do you understand, Theo, why you must now hate high altitudes? I am one of the mind's most effective repellants. I am a basic cure for mental indigestion.

I am the mother of the little fighters in your immunity system. I am a biological necessity.

I am speaker for unspeakable truths. For a man with little imagination I am one of his tools for self-defense. I am opportunity for clean, new starts. I am guardian of secrets. In my high voltage, people may remove their mask. I am fence pole and Chinese Wall. I am preventer of leaks so the fireweed's purple and the marigold's gold will not interbreed and turn grey. Among the idolaters of one global economy, I am the seed-man of misunderstandings and of different languages, so each society lives in its very own color of lifestyle and builds its own tower into the sky. Think of what happens if the uranium atoms stop "hating" each other and stop keeping their distance. I am also a protector from another such meltdown. I dismantle your global information bomb that, to the ultimate terror of all other critters on Earth, could now inbreed worldwide man's virulence and, in a luminous flush of power, could drive to extinction many of the animals and plants.

Governments abuse me to demonize their enemy and put extra hate-fire in the firepower of their soldiers. The English and early American settlers abused me as the terrible, intoxicating mantra, "a dead Indian is a good Indian." Stoned on this deadly mantra and freed from any compassionate restraint, the blue coats overwhelmed the Natives of America. They used me instead of a thousand more guns.

The Creator cradles me dearly for being one of his jack-hammers. I do for Him what sweet lovers cannot do. I break up unbreakable rocks—and the hungry, tender roots pay me well for doing so. I am the unbridgeable divide between the different colors of religions, or the different colors of flowers, or the different species of swallows. I am the mighty impassable river that can split one species into two. I am the chemistry that produces the tough sinew of your mental skin. I am the hissing steam when the glowing iron meets the water to be hardened. And listen to what the meandering creek tells the oil well, "I must hate you—it's my nature. We are not allowed to socialize and hold hands for now."

Yes, I am a dark continent not yet explored. Life is esoteric, and I am one of its tools to keep it so. I go to far greater pain than the "saints" to add new designs and colors to the coat of God. I am the energy that split the primal union, and flung its pieces in the Big Bang as galaxies, stars, meteors into a cosmos soon to become so rich in loose fragments and options that Life could use to compose.

Biologists are friendlier toward me. They call me the wise *strangeness effect*. Become Captain Courageous. Become creative. Make your mind more omnivorous. And you will have less need for my rather rough and old-fashioned barfing treatment when mentally or physically you must refuse some of Life's servings. From now on, please call me by my biological, more forgiving name. Do I not merit a little thank-you for my gifts? If evolution had not valued my creative mischief, it would have closed my department by now.

29. And now, what will Theo do with the heap of people, acts and things he has learned to demonize?

Here Theo, I filed a key out of your prison. Go free to socialize with Life's zillion lifted skirts of try-me-outs!

I wish I could deal with people I am supposed to hate as I can deal with the rain and hail. Then I could confront them as natural phenomena that are not demonized, maybe simply using a repellant, just as a man prone to devastating confusion protects his simple niche of believes with a vest armored with hate, a woman fights a downpour with an umbrella, an immune system springs into action, a mama-cat not ready to mate growls.

For my deeper, blessed Soul of the Earth, there is no moral problem. No need to translate rain into evil. My aversion is a simple defense against a soaking that may drench me to the skin of my body or my mind, if I do not keep my distance. From under my umbrella, I can honor that soaking downpour. I can make of my supposed "devil" a synonym of the very natural "strangeness effect" and erase its evil.

From behind my pile of things and the people I learned to give hell, my brave heart also hears a shy invitation from such fearsome treasures of Life: "Approach me. I am a new America begging to be explored."

Remember, Theo, when you condemn or give hell: Life has etched every one of its tricks for a reason. Just asking and answering one question about the man in the crosshair of your hate, of your aggression, or of your AK-47, makes that man much more difficult to hate. Just to know that he loves cashews, but not pumpkin seeds, turns that target from a faceless nuisance into a man with one of his pockets full of joys.

Here, the thunderstorms in Clara's temper want to be mentioned. No ego-anger. Her angers have tears in their eyes—breakthroughs of her wildly beautiful soul, on which I naively trampled minutes ago. Her downpour starts serious talk, yielding treasures of learning. To be with her then, I start out on a safari. And our potatoes, so fertilized, start to grow big. Out of an erupting temper, hocus-pocus, Life pulls out of that magic hat reconciliation. And, no, I am not back to where I was before. In Clara's beautiful jungle land, I am ten discoveries ahead. I am a wealthier man. That's what, soon after, the bittersweet tears in her eyes are telling me.

Hate and love, repulsion and attraction, anger and reconciliation, I watch Life combining these forces, stirring and cooking them till the flavor is just right. "And here are your newly cooked delights!" Out of the thorny bushes, the so yummy blackberry jam comes to light. A homemade reconciliation with tears in its eyes beats a visit to a shrink any time.

When I dare to make this mental space jump from dutifully hating to simply and cautiously marveling at this biological phenomenon, from under cover that frozen corner in my mind may burst into a spring I have never felt before. My mind becomes a more omnivorous mind. How do I know? For this is what I have done.

After we have been demonizing this biological keep-off sign for so long, hate pleads for a new name.

30. The helpful abnormalities and defects

Impurities and imperfections have a catalytic effect on my mind. They infect it with endless new options. Ask a metallurgist how traces of impurities added to a metal can give it new and revolutionary properties.

A cell goofs, it steps in a sewer hole, it mutates, it "sins." It does not need to blush. Its "sins" and mutations are not wasted acts. It does not try to eliminate and forget these experiences as something rotten. It remembers them in order to fish later in these "failed" experiences for new options. How farsighted of our genetic memory to remember and store, with the help of "chaperone" proteins like HSP 90, the blueprints of its perversions, mutations and sundry missteps. It creates pay dirt that it plays out when needed in a crisis, sifting for nuggets, beneficial mutations, new solutions. Life is more perfect with these rascally acts. These precious memories of our failures put adaptation on the fast track. There's no need for these little rascals to degrade themselves with an apology.

We, too, memorize the formulas of our sometimes strangely creative misbehavior. In sweet times, our transgressions are papered over by the memes of culture. When basking happily in our good luck, we tend to do what is proven, over and over. As soon as things get tough for either mankind or for the pathogens, both mobilize their repair machines. Both increase their mutation rates. Both open wide their capacities to sin, to pervert, to stumble into the dark storeroom of the unproven, exploring the forbidden and whatever we exiled behind fences and morals. Stray people and stray dogs are out *en masse* to explore beyond our sweet routine. New varieties of options have to be churned out, which may save us.

For instance, in a population explosion, these recipes for wrongdoings we have stashed away can unfold curative "epidemics" of prodigious nearsightedness. Call it egotism, call it smartness, call it a passion for reckless, daring inventions of I-give-a-damn. Is egotism not the mother of the inventors, the daredevils, mutants, the ever busies, the explorers, the non-mothers? In this mobilization, pure souls, as white and nourishing as white bread, as well as the old noble savage or the old noble microbes, have little chance.

In such testing times, Life freely consumes critters and people for exploring the extremes. And I note: prize-winners seem prime candidates for such martyrs. Was it for this that the return of the legendary "lost" son was considered worth more feasting than a son never lost? Yet my instinct and my intuition, even my commonsense wisdom, are terrorized by innovation, adaption, and evolution when they consider the success rate of these gamblers.

Take our reproduction in our present crisis of overpopulation. An arsenal of reorientations, mutations, of love affairs with pets, of sidesteps into a world of hallucinations, or into a cult of lifelong adolescents who play as boys playing with defused sex pleasures, all this may be triggered into play to contain our fertility for a while. Online, many millions of children are induced to feverishly play games of war craft for twenty-five hours weekly to relieve them of unneeded virility. For others, a new devotion to re-green the Earth becomes a strangely new, yet timely, way to have a love affair. Sexual pleasures may be reoriented to become an intoxicating glue for the adults' social bonding. Tiny sand critters change their sex back and forth and to the middle, again and again, to manage their reproduction. Life thrives on these permissive adaption games.

These awesome mechanisms for adapting to a new environment stubbornly itch my learned morals of yesterday. Yet my hunch is: every transgressor is paid by Life for being an explorer. That hunch is my ointment for this itch. Take any man, mean or kind. Doesn't Life keep that man alive to honor him or her for some service rendered?

I note, when Life engenders something unique, it also tends to build some fence around her or him, to keep the bias out. It orders a woman to assert a manner all of her own. It takes her off Prozac. Sometimes, this communication break is made of a rare "deformity" in body, intellect or temperament. To engender the diversity of the Amazon, these fences may be made of towering ridges and forbidding rivers. To become creative, a soul might be exiled on an island fenced by jealousy, by arrogance, by blindness or a bipolar affliction, by an obsession, or to an island of the Galapagos. A man so in hermitage may fashion this singular gift beyond the bounds of common sense.

Take a river. A huge slide crosses and dams that good river. Next spring, an arid land to its side rolls out a carpet of exotic flowers. Take sexual abstinence caused by a hormonal slide, or by willpower, or by a cult, or by whatever. That slide might divert power into shy, dormant talents, and they wake up and raise "hell." Take deep anger, that erupting volcano of truths, one of the natural phenomena and deeply moving wonders. Should I control all of Theo's deeply felt angers, and release these mighty moments of power in little trickles through our nice little irrigation ditches?

You want to eradicate polio? Remember, these little buggers gave the U.S. maybe its best president. You want to eliminate tardiness in speech? Remember, this handicap gave us Einstein, the scientist of the last century. Schizophrenia, this outrageous mountain guide, dares to walk some of us right up to the edge above the abyss with its mind-boggling views. How many seers, how many children in all the kinds of arts, has the mother of the bipolar illnesses given us? With people prone to seizures, she gives us shamans, masters in ecstasy. I bow to her with a shy thank-you for her work.

On a mental level, damned frustration may become the power food of the creators. In these terribly imaginative states of mind, emerging ideas compete against each other, repelling, attracting, catalyzing, cooking, stirring and cooking again this unstable mental soup in which many new patterns of insights spontaneously can compose in a whole new way. Add your own list of unappreciated gifts that can ignite our creativity. Find out, for example, how depression can be a helper. No doubt, "sins" are also ingredients of this creative soup so rich with options that Life loves to go fishing in it for new wings, new rhymes and songs.

All this is teaching me that an extraordinary brilliant talent often demands a hidden, painfully darkened side in its man. Cure him, cut out these dark forces in him, and his extraordinary "paintings" become ordinary. Pull out the peacock's extraordinarily vain feather-display and this splendid bundle of vanity may well bleed to death. Pull out the vanity of a vain person. With his pride broken, this brilliant flower-show may turn into a plain vegetable field.

In our great vulnerability, great things can happen through us.

Here is creativity with tears in its eyes. Here, before all, awaits a creative story to be told that turns tearful happenings into birth pains. Are we not the wonderful results of the crime against comfort and against the past? In our great vulnerability, great things can happen through us.

31. The wisdom hiding in a thorn

Our science of Life's morals is still in the same infancy our science of chemistry was in when it dabbled in alchemy. My hunch: every "bad deed" is a mystery of the goodness of Life that we have not yet solved.

Talking about the preciousness of doing harm, imagine a cactus without any spines. Gone, after the first camel passed and found a juicy dessert delight of pure goodness with no sting! Glory to the terrible bitterness of the apple seed; that nifty bundle of delights knows how to avoid roasting in an apple pie, and instead to end up thriving on a compost pile.

Talking about Theo stealing old bricks lying around in a ruin; Buchi, the caretaker found out that bricks walked away. I had to talk with the angry man, a very humbling talk from on my knees. That's how we became friends. No stolen bricks, no friend. Take a finger full of perfection and lick it. It has a taste of sterility to it. When the Chinese wish a man bad luck, they wish him to meet a perfectly beautiful woman. Why is this?

Ah, and my bragging? Do you think I have been fond of this clown, clowning in me? No, I was taught to be at war with it. But I now discover that these peacock feathers are so much part of my nature: if I pull them all out, I might bleed to death. Hesitantly, I now accept this "pain in the butt" as part of my nature. Be patient. I am still on the lookout for what good work the Creator had in mind with this addition. I will fill you in later, though, or perhaps you are a keener observer and you already know. Meanwhile, they say that Theo's gift for exaggerations sure makes him a spicy storyteller.

I also learned that to confront, or to verbally battle followed by reconciliation, is so much more nourishing than to avoid and therefore have no need for reconciliation. My defeats, my setbacks, my birth pains have taught me more than my come-easy successes. And you want me to regret? Don't try to sneak that ballast into my backpack How can I regret learning? Brute success has never taught me much.

There are "perfectly" laid out minds. All at the same time, they can brush their shoes, make love, pick their teeth, and perfectly keep their cool. I am not so perfect. I am of a more passionate brew. When excitedly carried away, surfing a hot thought through thick and thin, I cannot even walk without risking ending up in a ditch. Clara, when playing the piano, cannot go pee without breaking her ecstasy. Some are clean, smooth surface skimmers. Others are dirty well-diggers, each blessed with his own set of missing viewpoints. In the presence of purity and perfect people, I feel in desert land. I am starving in the company of whitewashed souls and walls.

Ah, the valor to risk making mistakes, the valor to drop the niceness costume and play with my "best" and my "worst"! For a mind with a bent to create, there is no one right way to live. But please, God, give me each morning a bowl full of new, nourishing mistakes to chew so I may grow another inch.

Please, God, give me each morning a bowl full of new, nourishing mistakes to chew so I may grow another inch.

In evolving life, isn't it the wealth of mistakes a man could battle through, without being cut down by indigestion, that is his cash in hand? Look at me. I like my life. What bad has happened to me? So many nourishing things have happened to me. So many mistakes have taught me things. I can think of nothing to regret, apart from happenings from which I ran away. Ah, a face with the scars of learning—here is imperfection to respect. Look, even the Creator makes "mistakes." She sprinkles the Earth with "perfect" worms. She puts one such wriggler in Her hat, and, hocus-pocus, out she pulls a critter with wings. Only magicians can make mistakes. Only creative people can "sin."

And now, when nobody looks, I put my imperfections up to a mirror. And what I see makes me now sob less and laugh more. Nothing shows me more than my own shortcomings how we are all indivisibly tied together to make that beautiful raft of Life whole and able to float in the cosmic sea. And a mischievous smile sneaks onto my face, welcoming my part of the boat with my cracks, my planks missing, my shortcomings, my overdone talents, my missing corners, so others may find these missing blanks and can nicely fit into this raft.

No, it is not in some paradise where the stuff for our won-
drous evolution is heated and forged. So-called failed experi-
ments, if remembered, do never fail. I am watching the lifeblood
of evolution at work. Let life's goofs and imperfections work
their magic a little longer and flowers will start to sing.

32. The longest walk

Each critter, tiny or tall, is embarked on her vision quest. Absolutely nobody else can stand in for the cicada on her quest. "Here
is your body, Theo; here is your physiology. And for Clara, the
butterfly, the eel grasses—here are your personal tools for that
quest. The well-functioning of the toolbox for this adventure is
your health."

The wealthy philanthropist and the nifty little thief that licks
on his dripping wealth are also on this long walk; so too the grassland dwellers, the peoples of the ants and those of man, the caribou and the wolf. Each anatomy is the temporary artwork of such
a trip. Each of these artworks is a long, long book of visions—a
storybook maybe three and a half billion years long.

So many different bundles of points of view! Some huge
bundles of visions are woven into most fantastic forms. Some of
these bundles are walking, some are swimming. Others are flying orchestras. Again, others are modest bunches of visions, still
dwelling in mud stuck in a shell made of silicate. Others cling
to granite for life and very, very patiently digest it. All are passionately scooting with their plates toward The Pot for a serving
of joy.

Over there, in the steaming stress of his overload, a formidable
player in the Money Olympics assembles his caravan of underlings
for his vision-trip: his bankers, advertisement agents, brokers, lobbyists and a hundred camels or a thousand kilowatts under his command. Even this heavily armed man is embarking on this happiness

hunt, yet is mostly still shouting orders, stockpiling, counting—with so many camels or accounts to be driven along.

On this epic viewpoint hunt, I enter also my own inner rainforests. I meet my crocodiles, my lily ponds, my unappreciated talents and memories, my untapped dreams and aquifers, and bring them to light. I start to fill that circus bus you may call Theo with actors and clowns from near and afar. And what do I learn? For a dull man, hardship is misery; for the adventurer, hardships tease out of Theo ten hidden Theos. For a man in love who climbs up to a woman's soul, a soul ache, a muted anger, a temper afire is a new rock face, challenging that timid climber: "Take me on!" And so, when I flatly say: "How evil is this man or how bitchy is this woman or that whatever," an old, old voice rises from down in my toes. "What a chance missed! Remember, son, your eyes need a little more polishing before you say more."

What would a man have added to his epic, had he never jumped a guardrail of prejudices with a daring new insight? If he had never peeked over his Bible's or her Torah's or the canon of the sciences' protective walls, and risked being hit and reeled by a reality he has no tested tools yet to take on, and so becomes a puzzled iconoclast to his friends and to his own docile old self? Some of the storytelling in scientific or sacred books may have to go. Yet no doubt, whether high flying or low flying, imagination has proven for Life a fruitful playground.

To leave lightweight footprints on this happiness hunt is the fitness that counts. "Theo, add another antenna, make contact with a foe. Have a word with somebody you walled off with blame. Your neighbor who tucked his eyes safely away in a box of some -ism, have him over for coffee and pie. Tease out an invitation to a Muslim home. Get lost in some far-off culture and tribal land. You can only love what you know. You are what you love. This is the size of Theo."

33. A grapevine in the vineyard buds below its graft, and turns again a little wild. Does it have a free will?

In the realm of physics, we may see the idea of "free will" in our cosmos' mischievous gift for small deviations from the uniform density in the very early universe. This fertile messiness allowed it to form and evolve all its marvelous irregularities: galaxies, stars, life, and quite recently, people too.

In the realm of biology, we may call this gift of "freedom" the gift of mutations. Here, organisms are sometimes unlocked from the locks of genetics' wisdom to "err" into the stormy sea of new options.

In the realm of the spiritual, we are gifted with creative loopholes in our cultural coding so we are sometimes "free" to rebel, pervert, freak out, sin, revert to our wild, inborn nature, or "err" to the South Pole—to see what we have never seen before. It's the option of mutations in our cultural "genes" (memes). Think here of our creative haggling within our hierarchy of commands between our impatient smartness and our deep wisdom, between the quickies of our reasoning and our mysterious emotional intelligence. Isn't it from such adventurous out-of-steps in the good old parade that Life creates ever more versatile animals, plants and people too? When a person's cultural coding becomes painfully at odds with his genetic coding, are not these the contradictory feelings that ring the alarm we call guilt or shame? And so, from such nostalgia of leaving home and the norm again and again along the march of Life, I confidently can infer that evolution is real.

In the realm of Theo grounded in a Christian civilization, does a dog that does not always obey his master go to "hell"? Theo, when nicely submitting to his society's culture, does he go to "heaven"? I am a leashed dog. Society is my master. It has me trained, domesticated, cultured, fenced, and made useful. Yet, I am a critter that's still imperfectly trained, and so I wear my culture mostly just as a makeup. I do not always follow the society's whistle. I sometimes get unlocked from the grip of my cultural policing. Is the gift to trespass, mutate, rebel, and revert to one's wild and rather self-sufficient, inborn nature a gift of free will?

Our oldest daughter Alexandra, a marine biologist, proved for the first time ever scientifically, that no, we are not alone in having to deal with reputation and with our old nature. Through her studies she has found that the cleaner fish, living mostly in peaceful symbiosis with the big ocean fishes, sometimes cheat too. Instead of nibbling off just parasites while mesmerizing the big fellow, that little nibbler takes a little bite out of his dear host. His old nature breaks through. And even the onlooker fishes well remember his outlawed little trick, and will shun him for it. This little nibbler has to deal with "sin" and reputation too.

In the realm of society: Here the assumption of free will has more of a practical than a philosophical importance. The notion of free will is a prerequisite for the assumption of a divine good and bad. This assumption hands the law enforcer a double whip; one is whipping a man for not conforming with the master, another whip avenges his defiance of the will of some god. Is it for this that kings gave themselves the air of the representative of God? Is it for this that the masters of the Inquisition could claim its duty to triple the viciousness of their tortures? Is it for this that the authorities are always the most zealous promoters of the illusion of free will?

Think here also of the glorious strength of a woman who dares to stand on her own, with absolutely no middle-man to her soul. Ah, free to be a slave to her own inner voice. Free to ride her soul wherever that soul is headed, with no master other than God holding her bridles.

As a woman, so an option, so a concept—do they not all respond to their field of gravity, to their personal attractions? Yet the gift to gravitate toward many women, options, and ideas always tempts me to declare myself master of my destiny. It is an assumption of punishing arrogance. Am I free to choose with whom or what I fall in love? Or toward which option I am finally gravitating? Imagine that you are presented with an old stovepipe and with a warm woman to make love with. Are you free to choose? No, you are not.

Any act seems to me ultimately an act of faith. You say you decided to become a scientist. A voice in me says: "Not so. You are a marvelous cluster of particles thrown together by all of God's winds, a crystal of ideas a zillion times more crystal than a crystal. Life, given time, comes up with such miraculous searching, attracting, probing, repelling, magnetic thinking-things. Yet, you have no say in what Life lends you and what Life withholds."

I am a secretive little bag of memories on my journey toward that fabled Lucky-You Serenity Land. On this journey, zillions of other such memory bags, on the left, the right, above, below, and from also inside me pull on my sleeves. Nonetheless, I am not stuck with just my own little purse of memories, thinking, computing, or not to be an inmate of some little god's flock, rather I am surrounded by Life's whole garden, so fabulously rich with options, all calling me, charming me, all competing for my attention. This rich environment gives me a sense of a wealthier slave. As with any highly bred super crop, the more cultured a person, the smaller his options of which of Life's players he can love, and the greater his intolerance become. Some may fly wildly far and wide with God's winds and do well. Others must fall, guided by the seed machine's microchips, straight into the furrow to survive.

There are raw happenings among us that, whatever I think of smoothing them out, stubbornly remain a disturbing hump in my storybook of man. Yet I can sometimes harmonize these offensive humps nicely, when I dare to take them out of the dear frame we carved so protectively, so lovingly, so beautifully around mankind, and boldly integrate them in that bigger storybook of Life. For instance, while on the wild, open ocean, my mind becomes a little freer to gesticulate. I can look around for the complement of these bumpy happenings, which the little manmade stories may have missed. Here I can infer that some trees and animals actually had a thanksgiving party after what happened in Chernobyl.

You grant me the power to sin? Whoa! You grant me the power to be free to mess up the universal law? Did you ever consider that sins would truly be miracles? Thank you anyway for the compliment.

Are we not each somewhere a part of the shoreline? Waves break and are reflected according to the contours of each man's shore. How sweet to fantasize that each is also a tiny bit captain of the ocean waves. No, we are not boats completely adrift in the tidal currents of the outer world. We can also conjure up worlds from within to fill our sails. And soon we may fall for the fantasy that we are captains with a free hand on the wheel. No other species, though, seems blessed with so much leeway to err, to explore, fall in love or over cliffs, to go with baggy pants or with a string outfit.

I am tossed around and continuously enriched by so many new options, seductively whispering to me. I am a tumbleweed tumbling in Life's zillions of mostly inconceivable winds. And then you turn on a light in that tumbleweed. Free to see! Free from the illusion of being an author, or of taking the credit or the blame for what I do! I can let go of some of my fears, of my boredom, of my grouches and my inner lawsuits clogging me. Free of my fences, my regrets, and narrower concepts and feelings of guilt. The illusion of free will is potent liquor. That darn drink tends to make us forgetful, violent and intellectually lazy. Sobering up from this brew makes me not only more inquisitive, it makes me more compassionate. Without this free-will drink, it doesn't make much sense to kick a tree in the shin for growing crookedly toward the sun.

When we grow up, the notion of free will may
look like crutches we need no more.

34. The virtue of help

My motives have motives hidden from me. I am mean, and a hidden hand may touch me from behind, offering me a thank-you and a smile. I try to do good and donate a life extension to a man, or to a tree who starts to go down. Down in the shade of the underbrush, patiently waiting, little voices immediately rise. "Oh no and no! We were just about to see the light and, darn, you put us back into the shade!" There is no setback that does not also flower a smile—somewhere.

We now love to dress up our raw motives with humanitarian attributes. We count on our own generation, deep in self-love, knowing its applause is secure. Now ask our future generations, the animals and the plants of this wonderful planet, what they feel about those humanitarian medals and honors, and about our love-your-neighbor. They sure must feel they are pushed further and further away from being our "neighbor."

Theo, take help stark naked. Ignore its trappings, its grafted-on heroic feelings, its medals and nifty dresses. Explore now its never-to-be-spoken-of deeper motives. Prepare yourself to think the unthinkable. The relationship of the celebrated helper with the helped might start to look more like that of the farmer with what he farms.

And, yes, some of the sweetness of helping comes from the dominance it bestows on the helper.

This "hand to me what you cannot handle of you" is what an extra serving of vitality given to another woman or man can allow her or him to do. Deep down, a helper may be more respected than loved, for, in this friendly war, he certainly can show off that he is superior to a needy man who has run himself into a ditch. Conscious helping, after all, may also be an act of self-advertisement—a potlatch that polishes reputation.

I beg a man overflowing with vitality, "Sir, can you spare a dime's worth of your vitality, please?" I ask him to inject me with a little of his mind and blood. "Thanks again and again for volunteering to take over some of my shaky kingdom." For some, help offered may simply be a comfy bench offered to sit down. For braver people, help might be a loving kick to the hind, a wake up, a match put to a friend's snoring passion, a challenge to live your own safari—to live the life you are meant to live—an inspiration.

A brave boy, becoming a man, takes on the media storm. Like an unfolding flower, awkwardly he thinks on his own about how to show off his personal ideas and colors. Awkwardly he holds onto his most precious gift—the gift of a soul that can stand on its own. How tempting for him, when in his birth pains, to simply plug into the net that is eager to help him to choose between model T and model A? Why battle and stand into the four winds when sweet help, comfort and Google's handheld information-mart is so near his fingertips? Why retreat into solitude and brainstorm with his own deep voices for advice when a patriarch or some sacred book is so eagerly at hand? Uncountable brave people and critters before us, though, could also have gone for a Model T. But, no, they went the long, exciting way, happily singing, "Who are we hurting? Is it a crime to follow a trail other than the freeways the good citizens use?" Three times my thanks to these explorers for choosing their own longer way.

How tempting to join the canaries that fell for help when baited into the well-stocked economy where they must now, daily, do their eight hours of singing. I, too, accepting help, may soon lose my brave heart to live fending for myself—with or without much money—as a king at large.

My friend Chui is one of the few such surviving kings I know who still feels shame at helping himself to other people's information. He likes to grow his own. And so when I helpfully confide to him that the red snappers are south, he proudly, happily follows his own compass, and may head north.

Think about ants. They are brave little critters. They didn't help each other all the way down to one global village. They went for eighteen thousand different kinds of queendoms, each species doing its own survival skills. They went for eighteen thousand backup systems. I see survival strategy at its best. This is what the valor to remain a unique individual or a unique race can do.

Corporate society now produces knowledge to which ninety-nine percent of us can have no access, yet we may be helped and kept alive by it in a completely passive relationship. Global corporations compete to farm mankind. Their media baits us with an enchanting chorus of "We come to help. Buy, buy, buy." And we elbow into the safety of their cage by the thousands to become their customers, their labor force, their farm animals, and their money fields. In this stampede I try not to lose my foothold. In town, I sometimes am barely able to find a breathing hole for my homemade thoughts. Corporations are the shepherds. We are their flock. Peace of mind to the flock of Fox and CNN! Domestication and artful helping may become sisters and brothers when looked at from afar.

When bumming around the Earth, every niche is challenging me: stop that band-aid business! The flood of man is giving the Earth a bellyache. Is this why the mantra of the businesses of the life sciences, "We help save human lives," makes me wince a little, each time this venerated motto homes in on me? Science for stock market gain has broken the law of moderation a thousand and one times. Is not our population and consumption bomb one of its legacies?

The help-culture of medicine has given us also another marvel absolutely rare in nature. While billions of people before us quietly fulfilled and terminated a fruitful life in time, we are now made to expect a time of immoderate second nursing. In an extra ten years of mostly misery, we are made to expect that we should piggyback on the young, while the young try to swim the river of Life. How much of that extra ballast can our children take without frustration or resentment? I am talking about a kind of negative inheritance for our kids. This is what capitalism can do—the invention of the cold storage of our love for a second nursing time for us in later years. To be enthusiastic about some of our celebrated charities requires a deeply cultivated shortsighted-ness. Help, like credit cards, can be a fast-breeding pathogen. In no time it can breed a thousand shameless little beggar hands.

Life has its own way to send help. It will let me die in time so others waiting in my shade may be helped and jubilate. Most of the vital help and altruism we exchange I see coded in our inborn nature. Our inborn, wild compassion is a vagabond. It often likes to cross over the fences of species. This interspecies, enormously far-reaching generosity is one mystery of Life barely explored. And most sacred books are not insistent about it.

Help can be a potent, yet fragile glass of wine. May the glass break before I get drunk on that wine.

The sweetest help may be that of a woman giving life to a child, or my help to the Earth that I die in due time without whining. Or that of a friend teasing hesitant Theo to dream up his personal script and write it on his fridge door—then tease me on to take that one jubilant step over my fears and live the life I am meant to live. Do you know a sweeter act of love? And who does not need a midwife to deliver some of the talents gesticulat-ing inside her or him?

> *Thank you, Alfons. Fifty years ago, you were the only per-son who forked me, teased me, kicked and charmed me to veer off the speedway of a "successful" business career and to start trotting the modest legend I am meant to live.*

35. Here's a story of why wilderness is dangerous company for the mind.

Imagine, you sit comfy in the football stadium, in the church, in the concert hall or on the TV couch while Life hurls itself—with all its branches, hungers, perfumes, joys and advice, with its downpours of tears, with all its troops of lovers—against the locked windows and doors. Obviously, for one man an encounter with a stuffed animal is his fill. For another man, only meeting Life's love beast in person will do. While practical people preach efficiency and monoculture, lovers adventure into their own wetlands teeming with innumerable dangers and delights that do not sell. High on that wild love brew, I unmask myself and I laugh off the reserves in what Theo wants to hear and see. Everything invites me to be brutally, shamelessly, myself.

In the land not yet plowed, still filthy rich in ideas, I open my arms wide and naively ask, "Please, be my drug dealer for today, make me high on a sip of your wisdom which has kept you so tipsily alive, and made you richer and richer for so long." And my learned response to the answers I get? "Oh no, no and no—this cannot be so!" whimpers the wimp in me. I infer that there is knowing that has to be concealed for all but the sturdiest outdoor minds. For a greenhouse mind, cultivated to produce the fattest tomatoes, some of the wildest knowing must be hidden.

Please, Theo, say this with the least offense. I rub elbows with a crowd of nice people. I surround myself with farmer, corn, and barn—a predictable, orderly scene. My mind feeds on ice cream and other highly refined food. Tame ideas rub into my skin. Out in the Tongass National Forest hunting for mountain goat or deer, my ideas start to take untrodden trails. Amicably, this permissive land makes fun of my stern morals. I receive gifts of insights from the queendoms of the ants and the kingdoms of the galaxies. I get advice from the clouds and the streams. Basic truths, from way down in my own sediments, well up to me. Some of the stories this land acts out are way too raw and true for my indoor mind to swallow them. My armor of fixed positions gets hammered. I become less sure that my wrongs are wrong. My thinking becomes more of a weaseling weasel and less of a self-assured tank. The ocean scene surrounding me pounds me with its power and beauty. It infects my mind with icy-hot ideas, inflicting creative wounds on my cocksureness. Then I must infer that I am surrounded by benevolent thoughts in action that have far more experience than the assumptions we have composed in our sacred books of science and religion. This mighty scene produces the "lightamines" for my mind. In the woods, the trees emit many kinds of growth factors that tease my thinking into growing toward them. Spruces and hemlocks arrange a niche in my mind to be their conference room where they can talk over with me whatever they have to talk about. To be with trees feels instructive and good.

In such potent environments, the marvel might happen. I might become an open front door from head to toe. I might become entirely medium, entirely violin.

To be with trees feels instructive and good.

And this land plays gypsy music with me. My trickster voices jump at the chance. They burst into a language quite incomprehensible to the domesticated horses in me. When I look from my pilothouse out at the coast of Alaska, out at the sea, up to the sky, all teeming with their merry communities, many erections happen in my mind. Dangerously simple questions arise. Secrets of my deeper self start pouring out. Here is a spiritual fitness center for me.

Around me, a love story is being told, a whale of a story that has been edited and reedited again for millions of generations. Here a shy dormant seed of a talent may wake up and burst its husks with a shout: "Let things happen to me!" What a classroom! The love story of my culture is to this narration as one fancy scale on a fish compares to the fish itself. Out here, a very durable success through cooperation courts me, a social contract of all things alive—the Song of the Earth, its song lines refined and re-refined to my horizon and beyond, and again beyond. Each critter is a very ancient manuscript, and still adding to itself. There's no way to imagine the wealth contained in any kind of jellyfish. From a drop of a murky tidal pool it brags, "We, the critters who settled in this watery little sphere, we composed a thousand different symphonies and are simultaneously performing them in harmony."

What a playground for those of us in the search for patterns. Here I can become the lucky owner of a backpack full of materials for metaphors. In short, here I become a wealthy man.

Rubbing against this feast of wild compassion, I light up. I start to glow. I rediscover a friendship in me with all animals and plants. I start to be happy for no reason. I rediscover the third dimension of my compassion, which western culture hushed over when it put our compassion on a leash. Without it, our egotistic technology has no bridle, no brakes, and no shame, monopolizing the land. Out here, nobody can avoid this third dimension, this hunch that this is much too dangerous a place to go it alone. Everything must hold hands with everything else.

Everything must hold hands with everything else.

No, compassion is not some trick we recently invented. This is primal law, and as brutally enforced as gravity. This land out here never addresses me as a man. It addresses me as part of itself. It never blames me, never scolds me. It wakes me up from the dream of my grandeur. It makes me gifts of sweetly intoxicating insights. And it loves to poke fun at the "preacher" in me. Here analogies tell me without much fuss, "Look what marvels we do with what you criticize, stuff in the garbage bin, or put in jail."

In town, a warm cup of Life is served. Out on a deer trail, my mind salivates. A full buffet stacked with plates awaits my mind—hence that urge in me to be in a place where human weeding and scheming is kept out—hence my urge to sometimes have a conversation, not with Henriette, not with Jim, not with CNN, but with the Lisa Creek. Wilderness is the place where I am completely sure a very robust rightness is acted out. And I secretly expect that this rightness will rub into my mind and under my skin. Here, at times, the company of a kingfisher may become dearer to me than my kin. Here I am an apple well connected to its stem. Here, the whole rowdy world that has been stored away and is dreaming in me wakes up and makes a racket. Just by myself in this lively land, I am watchful, alert, erect, and greedy as any nifty little thief for the morsels of the wisdom this land produces in plenty.

> *Wilderness is all lightning, and my mind is full of tinder.*
> *"Theo, take off the captain's hat of your intellect*
> *when that hymn is sung." If there is a drug of choice*
> *for me, that talkative silence out there is it.*

36. Observing nature annoys my common sense.

Observing nature continuously nibbles on the seams of my belief system. This system is too tight—where is the playground? From every nook and niche, I hear one more enthusiastic caller: "Look what my strength can do, neither to agree nor to imitate, but to disagree and go my own way to merry-land!"

Away from the intercom of man, I can break my stare into my cultured inside. When I become absent-eyed and my view retreats into just the neat mindscape of mankind's memory, I hear also a young courageous man raise his voice. He proclaims a new love, a practical love highly profitable for man. The promise: Love your neighbor as you love yourself, and fantastic rewards will be yours. And when talking of neighbors, it seems, he meant people, not camels, not penguins, not trees, not children three generations over the hill. A few curious bystanders wondered, "Is the prophet teaching Life a lesson?" The multitude stepped enthusiastically forward, a little like most of us enthusiastically flocked around the smart scientists, who taught us a new love favoring us on account of all other inhabitants of the Earth, a love that gave us the green revolution with its miracle rice so profitable for us.

My eyes go for a walkabout and the curious lad in me wants to know: "Why do so many saintly teachers single out the neighboring people when they teach me how to distribute my allowance of love? Do they mean Betsy and Bill, my next-door neighbors? Or the crowd on the street? Do they include Fidel Castro and his team, or the Muslims from Kashmir? Am I to monopolize my love and only give it to mankind, who is marching up and down the Earth right now? Are the sparrows included in this lucky clan? Do our children seven generations up the hill qualify? The crabapple trees, the pussy willows full of bees, the misty Gilmore Bay in which I shall drop my anchor and which will be my companion for tonight, are they also included?" And the great global air streams, that breathe life into all, pat me on my shoulder. They want to be mentioned too. Ah, and there is Netsik, the old, ringed seal in the kelp bed. He pops up his head. He wants to know whether he will be treated as a neighbor too. The zillion critters without shoes in the procession of Life that walk generations in front of me, how much should they be considered neighbors?

This roll call becomes endless; should I include about every creature that glides, wriggles, tunnels, slimes, and swims about with us on this blessed Earth? Are they not all composers, singers at our side when the Earth sings "Amazing Grace"? For advice on how I should spend my ration of love, I listen to this chorus of croakers, singers, whistlers—and I weigh it against what our sacred books have to say.

And the curious lad in me pulls me by my sleeve. He wants to know who I will take as my guide. On the one side, a brilliant thirty-three-year-old man, who dared to spend forty days alone in the desert, fasting, to find himself and his prophetic gift. Maybe he also learned from loving a woman, maybe not. In his desert land, few animals and plants could talk to him. He was a man extraordinarily familiar with the sacred books, a man so young, with the exceptional courage to be his own guide. On the other side, Theo, seventy-eight years old. I have been places and learned from Life at large. Maybe five thousand nights and days alone, mainly fishing on the ocean, and then in the taiga and the sierra hunting and bumming around—all this has been giving me some insights.

Am I ready to be my own guide? Yes, and I thank that
charismatic young man for his inspiration. Don't be a fol-
lower. Be your own guide—if you are up to that call.

37. More notes from my serenity quest

The terrible forces around me, are they part of perfection?

To take cheap drugs? I would feel like a burglar. I didn't work for
this high, so it always schemes to run away.

A talkative night sky told me a secret. Every act that you or I
give hell to or regret opens into a mystery, which knows the heart
of a thankful beneficiary of that cursed act.

I love to fish fishes. I love even more to fish for a worldview
with a stage so wide that all the capacities of a woman and man
can show off the use of their niche. After all, each of these talents
is still alive and kicking, and must have proven to be an unbeat-
able survival skill.

And so I cast my net and haul in a set of questions, questions
like:

As in the cataclysmic movements of the elements, does great
violence in human societies also have its place as an act of God?
Do such heart- and society-shattering movements not break the
unbreakable, weld together the unweldable, move the unmov-
able, and speak out the not-to-be-spoken? Continents are shifted.
New countries are built. Outdated, insoluble constitutions are
dissolved. The storm mauls the grafted fruit tree on "high heels."
Its crown with its smart fruits gets knocked off the trunk. After
this violence, sturdy old wisdom may shoot forth again from its
rootstock.

In the great confusion of great violence, the veneer of a cultured man may crack. Wild creative helper wisdom, older than

Starbucks-man, may again break through in that un-veneered man. Life turns that torn-open greenhouse man into an earth moving "Burning Man" into a Genghis Khan. Unforgiving terminator of the stale, mother of radical new starts.

And so, in one of my shattering moments of wild vision, a madman heading a torn, frustrated Germany might turn into a culture- and law-shattering lightning bolt from a supercharged European sky, a catalyst for breaking routines and hearts, while it transfers and reorients super individual energies. Mind-boggling cruelties hold mind-boggling secrets.

In such a wild vision, the terrible "a-dead-Indian-is-a-good-Indian" conquest of the West may show itself as a tectonic plate that in a tearful time of wild creation rams into its new neighbor. Out of lands dotted with tepees and settled in routine, herds of mustangs rise, fantastic space stations rise, new varieties of trees and animals rise, the human genome project and the highest twin towers rise. Endemic subspecies of culture and of greens battle their uneven battles with invaders.

I think here also of a thousand disoriented puffs of wind, of angers, of frustrated people who find their attractor and form a "hurricane." I think of momentarily similar tendencies locked up in many, many individual hearts that find their primer in a supercharged man who discharges their fear and frustration in a culture-shattering explosion. I think here of the possibility of natural disasters in the mindscape of man. In great instability, full of fault lines or critical masses, it might become possible for a strong woman or man to strip him- or herself of all these wonderfully grandeur-boosting exemption myths. These beautiful masks may crack. She becomes the child again that sees mankind, the "emperor of the creation" with no clothes on. He sees human tragedies the same naked way he sees the cataclysms of the land.

A giant spruce comes crashing down. A shortsighted moaner may see death and decay creeping in, and not much more. A spectator on stilts may see this calamity as a time for timid celebrations. He sees seeds germinating, pale little branches hungry for space reaching for armfuls of openness, saplings happily stretching their necks, gorging on mugs of sunlight. She sees the sun and the rain sending out invitations to the molds and woodborers for the banquet soon to begin. And she may see comparable feasts of happy expectations happening when ripe, old Theo will finally bend to the ground.

To me, such shattering mind-openers, moments of awesome mental abandon and courage, are the only possible ticket to a better world. I hear a voice from all the way down my toes. "Don't shoot the waves and the storm." It is also behind such terrifying clarity that my terror of implications looms. Lightweight grief may threaten to move out. Other mental sufferings take more mental banging to give their secrets up. Some of my earlier grief would make a pig fall over laughing.

Here, my not so cataclysmic menu from the last week: an explosion of sarcastic laughter, a spitting fit, the spare anchor of my boat stolen, my fall into the septic hole, a show of quivering, overripe thighs begging, my black cod long-line from four hundred fathoms down on the ocean floor comes up parted, a lucky raven finding my barbecued chicken, a fuming disappointment, jubilant joy that celebrates an enemy getting hurt and out of the way. Here, Theo, are some less spectacular ingredients of Life. You promised to explore how they may snuggle into the beauty of Life. And leave the grading, whether they are good or evil, to those who are afraid to leave home.

To make my peace with the stingray that stung through and permanently blackened a very big hole in my left leg, nearly killing it, was a modest hill to climb. Yet it is with such little snorts of peacemaking that I sometimes bag a shimmer of serenity. I think of giving malice, thievery, grief, rotten apples, and unloved talents a more lovable aspect. Who knows, even vicious cruelty seen from a high enough balcony may turn into some long-term medicine. I think of the enormous satisfaction when love goes on the warpath against hate with a huge floodlight. When the magic hand touches my blind eye with its "See!" vistas fogged up with fear may clear.

Yet, don't get nervous. Soon enough some new indigestible nuisance overcasts that shimmer of light again and I will be down on the docks of Crescent Harbor, banging and scheming.

Against all good advice to be practical and to swiftly lock out anything mean looking, I feel I should be brave and leave a door open for some of these rascals I learned to leave out in the cold. A man can stretch his soul and stretch it again, and so accommodate some of the "monstrous" qualities of Life, rare trace qualities without which the Earth may soon turn pale.

I think of the enormous satisfaction when love goes on the warpath against hate with a huge floodlight.

Maybe my writing is meant to be about this mischief, about thoughts that sing me out of my gloom, about winds that drive on my night sky clouds—and—whoa: silver moon breaks through. The gist of it: to become more alive and less of a grouch. Thank God that my learned expectations have mostly been ignored as the amazing mystery story of Life has taken me on its trek. Life can be much more fun than we are told to expect.

Please, do not judge me too harshly for thinking these illegal thoughts. I opened that prohibited door a crack. I peeked out and I thought I made out a serenity land so outrageously forgiving that saints don't need to wear auras to work. Hell's shovelers of coal are promoted to clear rubble in our experimental gardens where the storm has passed. There is no need for heroic quests. No need for cooks who cook and serve misery, cooks who serve me with plates and more plates heaped with reasons why I should blame her, fear him, rebel, or go on strike.

Blind, sometimes, with unforgiving anger, my fighting spirit needs a new approach.

132

38. Cures of a species

When I think clearly and historically and biologically, I know that mankind now needs cures that are shocking. My whole rather idealistic upbringing can only revolt against what the history of Life is telling me in this respect.

A whack with your ax, and oops, you get a splinter under your skin. Watch well, and not just your insurance policy. Watch for the teaching story that will be acted out for you.

That darn splinter hurts. Infection and pus rot a hole into your skin. A fever might make you lie low. The splinter lubricated with pus is slowly squeezed out through that nasty hole. The hole is healed and again sealed. Ah, thanks over and over for that wonderful healing process.

Think of that teaching story when a society goofs and catches a splinter in its soul.

A people get obsessed with shameless success. It balloons into thin air. Genetically, that people "knows" its cure. It chooses its misleader. Those downers fight the losing battle with indebted money, stimulating more spending. They do a good job. They open that wound. They slowly bankrupt and deflate that drunken, unsustainable success. They humble the empire. The stupefied crowd is given time off in a depression, to scratch their heads, to reflect and sober up. The lost population, sucked up into thin air, is brought down on its knees and to the fertile soil and Earth again. This humbling is the pill. It will be well. It will be a little less feared and more loved. Thank you for the cure!

Think of a powerful, new, yet quite unproven idea that catches the social norms with their pants down, meaning they have no immunity yet evolved against this strange splinter of a thought attacking them—confusion and epidemics of frustration! The many of us who barely have ever been trained in mental self-defense become the ideal tinder and underbrush that help such wildfires of pathogenic ideas to become super-spreaders. Our legislators and judges, meant to be our everyday healers, get sick! The gravitational pull of such a mass of infected people soon distorts the whole social web, creating an eruption into a riot of badly nourished, virulent thoughts. The scene is sweating profusely and continuously mutating, crying for new pathfinder stories and solutions. Hot war can spread like wildfire through such a charged thicket of interwoven men. Here is evolutionary process in action with tears in its eyes.

At times it takes a generation or two, and a big segment of an overcrowded people to pass away, to provide the opening to get rid of that malignant splinter and begin the healing. To help that society again toward The Way, it might take a delirious fever, a complete breakup of routine, a retreat to asking questions during a depression, a soothing salve made of pain-killing drugs, a string of quite disorderly, amoral, and unappreciated reorientations, a collapse of the morals that caused that drunken success, a reversal in the sequence in importance. In this process, defeat might turn into a salve, perversion into a tool of adaptation, a stock market crash into a reintroduction to basics. A brake might accelerate. A shortage of energy or of work might become an ecological blessing. Chaos might be needed to topple an outgrown constitution. In a very overcrowded species, Life may trigger a very smart idiocy or even insanity, to bring it down to the Center.

An obsession with porno, draining inoffensively our virility, may be the prayer of all the fishes of the oceans fulfilled. "Please give the peoples of man more of these infertile sports and fewer children so we, the fishes, are not all dragged from our home sweet homes by a flood of fishermen and dropped into frying pans!"

Life whispers such advice to a greedy species when that species must finally do things that do not help that species, but that help Life. Then Life is much more than the sum of its Legos. A species is much more than the sum of its individuals. There is more to biological communication than we think.

I also note that Life asks many of our so-terribly-many on Earth to spend themselves now in a farewell-bash of consumerism, instead of raising children. To consume, throw up or away, and to consume yet again has become the government's approved narcotic for a species that needs to revert its growth. Romans needed their vomitoriums. We need our city dumps.

Have you also noticed that when a crisis corners us, we tend to turn into herd animals, becoming conservative and nationalistic? Shoulder against shoulder, we form the defense ring of the musk oxen. A crisis fosters prejudice. Honesty and shame in the individual become luxuries. The scenario for stampede is never far away. In times of great stress or of not enough going around for all, we may be switched to auto-cannibalism. We consume part of our own soul or body. We do as some migratory birds do to fuel extreme journeys.

To stop that great flood of human successes, the menaced environment may trigger in us a condition comparable to autism where the neuropathways for exuberant fertile compassion are not triggered to grow. The love of our species for its children is replaced by smartness and details. A kick-ass philosophy with a sweet frosting may spread. A generation against the wall may proudly sport their bumper stickers bragging, "We spent our children's patrimony." When spring love remains frozen over, iPodding may become a high tech way of hibernating—a den not made of willow twigs but of music.

Yet when in a trauma, Life has to put us under the knife to doctor us back to health and harmony, Life is no brute. She clicks us into all kinds of sweetly intoxicating torpor modes.

Our psychology is always changing, as the logic of microbes does, always adapting to present conditions. So I infer that if a person is of a narrow or of a compassionate egoism, it has little to do with personal

Life is no brute. She clicks us into all kinds of sweetly intoxicating torpor modes.

decisions. It is a symptom of a general life situation. We are causing now, not only in the Earth but also in the minds of our children, consequences that will painfully puzzle the old guard.

Theo, try to say this with less arrogance. Remember, out of the grab bag of gifts, you pulled yourself a privileged life. The world now has little room to accommodate such lucky-yous. You watch life in action. Be prepared. "Amazing Grace" now has to perform some unpopular cures.

My little finger tells me that the "body" of a species functions, on an upper level, as my body does. When hurt, it patches itself up, using our genetic policing, with barely any conscious instructions or decisions from the individual. Is it possible that what seems a breakdown in the logic of the individual can be a healing process in the psychology of a species?

I watch how Life, with its mind-boggling self-maintenance power, heals other species that are in comparable situations to ours, and I do not expect that the old logic I learned in school is up to following this awesome healing process with joy. The little ego of Theo might well defame that cure shouting, *foul!* Yes, I expect there to be a loosely charted way, laid out in the mind of the Earth, for how to defuse our overconsumption and overpopulation.

What is my "crime" in thinking this way? I explore a health and a health care that does not start and end with the individual, or with one generation, or with one species, as my upbringing had in mind. Yet to bring to light this larger health logic in Life gives me unexpected confidence and joy. To explore this hidden form of health care helps me to better see how compassionately Life cooperates.

Who applauds the ways a species heals itself? Not the economists, not the moralists, not the politicians, not the priests, not the bankers, not the police. So it will be me who applauds Life for these cures.

To launch ideas that counter gloom in extraordinary times is the joy of the poets and of the merry light-makers among the scientists. Grim poets, as well as grim scientists, are an absurdity.

39. Here, a story of worms

One very happy day, one very lucky worm tunneled furiously up and up and up, and, like a breaching whale, suddenly he shot right into a world flooded with the shine of the sun. A blue deer to the left, a very long snake, a snake at least thirty generations long, in front, many strange and huge life-forms that rhythmically pulsate, never ever seen or felt or imagined by these tunnelers before. "Oh, I see. I see. I see!"

And a long, dumbfounded stare! "Who of we tunnelers would have ever guessed that those greedy sucker-roots we meet down under construct such luminous flower-things on this other world flooded with light?"

And that breaching worm was struck down flat by this insight when it dawned on him, "But in this sea of light, there is nothing, absolutely nothing to be seen that seems in need to be accused, forgiven, redeemed or called a dummy. All seems to be one single perfection that grows and grows. Nothing, nothing evil can happen to anything in this enlightenment out here. All this time we down under must have been the laughing-stock to all those blessed with eyeballs."

In this enormous shine, that worm grasped that the worm-pulling blackbird might also be a guardian angel of the worms. "This sure is not like I dreamed it to be. This very surely is not."

Like that worm so used to living in the safety of his dark tunnels, Theo's own whimpering little intellect also became used to living safely inside some weather-tight mental construction—a kind of permanent sleeping bag for his mind. When I busted windows through these constructs, a new world, flooded with light, burst in. No more thinking in an egg! Endless territories never explored before, with beasts fifty generations tall, with green forms fifty species wide and never before described come into sight, seasons lasting thousands of years, debts changing uncountable hands before they are paid back, winged compassion that skips neighbors while flying away to lands with far-off species in far-off places and times, justice made over a million species, miles and years.

Some of us became so excited from peeking outside that we became ready to trade in our conventional wisdom for a new open-ended model—never mind that our curious minds now risk being pelted and shredded by the four winds. We suspect that if we are meant to survive our daredevil follies, unexpected answers and help will come in view with this tremendous paradigm shift. We expect that a greener, more friendly philosophy to help us on will be in these thought-lines we started to explore here. We are such merry, curious fools. There is no illuminating lightning without the long, pregnant build up of enormous positive and negative energy fields.

There are acts of Life that are of an incomprehensibly larger generosity than those celebrated with a Nobel Prize. They belong to the class that gave us the composition of photosynthesis, the seasons of the climate, the tectonic shifts of the Earth crust, the ebbs and the floods in the working of our love.

40. No intellectual construction has made me more of an intellectual couch potato than the comfy notion of evil. Innumerable hard questions are swiftly covered up with this tool.

Take the most heartbreaking happening in human history you can think off. Don't take this story lightly at its surface value. Yes, it has become a crime to even *think* about it as one sentence in the long, long, wondrous Life story. It has become common

sense to remain uninvolved, and simply contain those heartrend-
ing happenings within the bounds of the notion of evil. Here is
intellectual comfort—a soundproof pillow for tender minds that
has proven a very, very successful mental survival strategy.

Yet nothing has stunted my mental growth more than this
cherished old notion. It put my mind on a diet of white thoughts
and white bread—no sweat, no indigestion, guaranteed. For goodness' sake, Theo, don't yell at the rain. Get a raincoat. Visualize
what sunny days can do with this downpour. See the corn sipping.
See the watercress smile.

A night sky told me that "sins" are acts we must still demonize in order to put them on hold, for they are too hot to be han-
dled intellectually by indoor minds. Life offers such playpens and
keep-off signs to our tender minds. No wonder we have become
the experts at demonizing. We may be the only species to have
invented the idea of hell, evil, and jail. We also discovered that
this notion can nicely foster hate, and that a soldier loaded with
hate is worth ten loaded guns. We discovered that by demonizing disturbing or unadoptable or weird people, branding them as
criminals, we make it easier to simply lock them up without much
heartfelt intellectual pain.

When it dawned on me that the theorem of evil locks out
painful questions—that it is a chastity belt, a curfew, and a part of
the protective confinement for my intellect—a cataclysmic crack
opened in my view. When I peeked through this crack, I peeked
into an openness so darn rich, my thinking first nearly fainted
from anxiety at all the new options to justify and to forgive that I
saw. What a menace to my mental security.

By and by, the credo of evilness has become our indoor minds'
most cherished old coat. Nay, it has
become the permanent survival suit
for tender, highly cultivated minds
in need to live safely indoors on high
heels. Out in that dangerously permissive openness, the wild universal

*Did you ever wonder why
nobody pulls weeds in the
wildflower fields?*

mind homes in on me—uncountable dangers, pitfalls, an ocean of uncertainties—and I am still just a beginner swimmer. Outrageously forgiving, shameless, unbearably patient, relentlessly provocative ideas pound the island of my intellect, ideas that are terribly alive and kicking, and soon are surrounded by offspring. That's why a wild mind never gets fat. And did you ever wonder why nobody pulls weeds in the wildflower fields?

Yes, I definitely start to see more rewarding viewpoints for looking at what an indoor mind calls evil. And in this permissive reality, any boat made of pure reasoning must ultimately capsize. Only holding onto deep faith in life's goodness will keep me afloat on this safari.

The belief in evil has become for me a convenient dumpster for all the Creator's mysterious goodness that still refuses to allow my intellect justification and answers. This belief serves me well as sunglasses. It disposes of the aggressive clarity when meeting Life as it is, which can be quite blinding for an indoor mind. This concept also justifies my moan, and encourages me to work for a tamer world. And the more I become an expert and specialist, the more I need this helpful notion. There are many parts of Life's goodness that are way too large to cram them into one narrow niche or into one species to show off their merits.

To wean my intellect from readily taking refuge in the idea of wickedness, so I can learn to better confront the wildness of Life with just my native clothing of the mind on, has become high adventure for me. This mental rock-face climbing gives me a high. All of Life's gifts are beyond safety. So I must choose my place between safety and danger. I choose how alive I can afford to be. And I promise not to whine when, braving the Creator's outdoor thoughts, my mind catches a cold.

There are many things that we desperately want to call evil and keep them under lock in that other Pandora box. They are the Creator's aphids, nettles, wasps, hailstorms and tsunamis, Genghis Khans that we do not want in our beautifully manicured flower shows. There are many thoughts pertaining to the mind of

Life that have to be fenced off, or warehoused in dreams, so that a child may not have to live with unbearable anxiety. Think of the sea of angry fists from all the florists if a dandelion were declared as noble as their elegant greenhouse crops, and also declared part of the beauty of God.

Criticism has been instant ice cream for my mind. To find the beauty of what offends, my mind may have to first trek a hundred miles alone to get its fill. May evolution help us to outgrow the notion of evil, and patiently free us from this psychological beginner's need.

Yes, doors are opened into the unknown at great risk. An iceberg may float right through my home sweet home.

41. A religion fit for the outdoors

Many people expect their organized religion to be for their minds what the Cadillac is for their bodes—a vehicle of comfort. No climbing over logs anymore. No confusion. No lying. No risk of getting lost. No driving on either side of the road. Their souls become proud inmates of a fine road system carved into their psychic wild land. Others see in their religion a great cruise ship, beautifully furnished with all taken care of to comfort indoor-minds. These people like to devote themselves to one sacred book. They like to have a formula classifying everything—no doubts, no wondering, no growing pains, no creative fevers, no driving on the "wrong" side, and no weed thoughts for them. Organized religions were probably our first attempts at monoculture. Their commandments facilitate neat cultures of thinking, just as herbicides facilitate weed-free agriculture. Weeding out "sins" has comparable side effects on our soul-scape to those side effects the application of herbicides has on the land.

Others, we are God's stray dogs. We are antsy to go on adventures. That chance for a mental safari might never come again. Meandering, we make our own trails and our own commandments. We are comfort-dodgers. Happily we look for trouble and wade through creeks. We like our minds unencumbered by traffic signals and by conclusions. We love to sneak out of those manicured gardens where reasoning cultivates its safe, scaled-down and man-serving logic and we go nuts with exuberance. Yes, we do sometimes step in mud puddles and gopher holes, and fall over logs.

The Christian view of the world was the beautiful garment of my intellect that later felt a size slightly too tight for me. It taught me to focus my love more and more on less and less. Some of Life's very large beauty just would not quite fit under that tight fitting coat of a soul. Much had to go to waste in some garbage dump, jail or hell. Many components of Life's very, very stable constructions became illegal weeds. My thoughts stepped high, my thoughts jumped far, and a seam of that coat seemed often to tear. How difficult for a mind dressed in such a fine credo to think wild and jump a fence. Try to fit into such holy doctrines, a gay man, a weed man, a perfect storm, a protective lie, a storm of a man, a dandelion, a Muslim. That beauty under a dome might have no room for them.

Yet, is not our species' cash in hand our phenomenal wealth in the recordings of our trespasses and "try-me-outs"? Still, many of us are more faithfully married to some safe belief system than to our spouses. Women and men who seriously study the sayings of one master, or of one of the many manmade gods, may soon fall for the illusion that they know it all. But is their sweet gift of curiosity happy with it?

I have always felt reluctant toward a guru, a savior, a patriarch, a lecturer, who teaches that a man can find himself and his credo only with the help of a master or a mentor. This certainly is not how the Earth got blessed with ten thousand different kinds of grasses. Many organized religions have proved quite helpless against being infiltrated by the power psychology to dominate others.

I dare to become a little deconstructed and wild. I step on my staircase to the rooftop one tipsy step up. Wow, I realize I am more, much more than a man. *I grasp that there are things done through me not done as a man and not for man.* Life works through me, and mostly in a mysterious way. I realize that Life does things through rabbits that are not for rabbits but for Life. Ms. Rabbit, for example, keeps up a four-star eatery for her neighbors, the coyote and the fox. I grasp: if there is a creative power we may call God, this enormous generosity has more to do with wildness and less with the leash laws of all our "you-should-nots." I grasp that the idea of paradise, of *our* Great Society, of a smooth united world economy, is a huge underestimation of the beauty of Life. This popular assumption had misled my intellect to look and wish for beautiful parrots in a cage or people, cows, machines, pigs, corn, and sunflowers in a farm.

I grasp that there are things done through me not done as a man and not for man.

A hunch has infected me that does not want to heal: beyond our western worldview awaits an incredibly forgiving and generous reality that for its wild truthfulness the patriarchs protectively made vanish in a mist of "shhh! Do-not-think-or-talk-about-it."

Yet Life keeps on lifting her skirt teasing us with her "peek at me! I am more preposterous than any sacred book has dared to talk about." Here the eighth day in the creation story of my intellect has begun. Here my reconciliation with the beautiful, carnal, feverish Earth has begun. That old coat for my soul needs to be knitted a little roomier, a little more accommodating, a little more like the coat of God.

A stink bug and a grain of sand, the Creator made them in His own image. Each is a mirror of the All. Every critter nurses all creation a little. The wolf hunting a caribou comes out as an act of compassion,

That old coat for my soul needs to be knitted a little roomier, a little more accommodating, a little more like the coat of God.

and the mosquito as a protector of Life. Name any act of Life, bitter or sweet. It has a deep experience behind it. Our written moral's history is the latest tentative little sidestep in that experience.

I note for example that the most exciting game of cooperation is not going on among the individuals of a species. It goes on among the species as a whole. The Earth is far too dangerous a place for all species not to hold each others' hand.

You and I, when confined to the history of only mankind, would we not appear but scattered, chaotic heaps of virtues and sins? Mankind contributes a minor up or down in the circus show, with not enough room in humanism to lay out and reveal the enormous beauty of the act to which we contribute. Science, through hints on how we ultimately rhyme with that much larger Song of the Earth, can make us forgiving, trusting, and laughing. Science can tickle us to shout, "Life, what an ingenious recipe to keep adding new numbers to that Greatest Circus the cosmos might ever see." To make us spectators yell and applaud at this circus, now here is a good deed of our sciences worth a Nobel Prize.

Laughing Water tells me that if you can appreciate when a person is born, and when she dies in all her fall seasons' colors, you are a wise and colorful woman or man. Laughing Water also spilled to me the best kept secret in heaven: ugly ducklings, ugly spiders, as well as ugly people and acts, need not be redeemed or pardoned. If hugged and loved in the arms of a huge heart, they reveal to us their beauty and their perfect niche in the grand beauty of Life. Fall a little in love with these defamed spiders—up to five million of these tightrope walkers per hectare! Forget the birds. Without these daddy long and short legs, the Earth would be knee deep with insects by year's end.

Climb high! That fantastic view might be generations beyond the hills. A sweet friendship among all things becomes visible above the mist. And the tears and laughter there are sometimes quite different from those of the nice people who advise me to stay down home and fight shades and phantoms, fears and worthless pains. From up there, the two thousand four hundred kinds of mosquitoes may look like as precious guardians of life as are our dear corn and our dear cows. A sea of sleeping lava awakes and suddenly erupts into a terribly violent outburst. Eons later, you see that pressure cooker opening its hand, and here are your diamonds. Up there, Attila, Buddha, and my sneaky friend Ramon are all Life's sons. Theo, the viruses, all beasties are all words in The Song. Christianity, Islam, the atheists, all species of religion, the social systems of the bees, and on and on are its mental flowers—some in yellow, others in shades of blue. Together they produce the joys of this one life force. Is that good news? And here I imagine from you, "but what-about-him-or-that?" Yes, from this high a view, even in the most terrible him or it we may start to note a first shimmer of light reflected.

What implications! What mind quakes! The shell of my commonsense morals cracks. The guesthouse of my mind needs to be re-engineered and widened to accommodate so many outlandish guests that for fault of imagination I had to turn away, some to be spray-killed or to be roasted in some hell, others to go to waste in jails. Think here of Roundup (glyphosate) and Clearfield (imidazolinone). They are our global chemical weapons of mass destruction, meant to nicely wipe out all plant life except our crops in an enormous genocide, a hugely successful war with which we cleanse millions of hectares into quasi-deserts. We mutilate zillions of living things each season for their simple "crime" of refusing to cook food exclusively for man. Yet many religions still have a mute heart for such holocausts.

One blessed, cataclysmic day, it might dawn on us, that in ignorant good-naturedness we proudly have also been cleansing our merry souls in a comparable way. And so, as Buddha did, I sometimes leave our civilization in order to become civilized.

Popular religions are great fashion houses offering clothes for the mind, catering to the large crowd. It is quite true that these religions have never claimed to be the forerunners of our mental evolution. Every courageous woman and man I know could grow out of this fashion business and undertake to tailor their very own style of garments, loosely fitting the contours of their generous and gesticulating minds. *But remember, we all do need clothes for the mind.* Who, after all, likes to be completely naked and shiver with numbing anxiety in the vast and brutal goodness of the outdoors?

The most precious contribution to Life's celebration that religions produce might not be their saints, after all. It might be their daughters and sons who ultimately outgrow their teachers. Think of the survivors who pass the religions' initiations, with their exercises of "self-discipline" and obedience, spiked with dangerous apparitions, terrifying suggestions, testing privations, retreats into solitude. Daughters and sons who measure up to their patriarchs and the many curfews imposed their defenseless flock. These courageous pupils learn from their teachers, and add to their teachers' knowledge new growth rings. They keep these mental plants alive and flowering. They turn these challenging "gifts" of hardship into their own shaman's initiation. Some break in themselves the unbroken power of man—centered and small thinking. And to be surpassed by his pupil, could that not be an educator's sweetest purring joy?

Laughing Water tells me of a religion with absolutely no need for evil, no sheepdogs, no landmines of guilt, no fear. She tells me of a science of pure enlightenment: a science that does not pile even more favors on us. A science, ultimately, which the rivers, the animals, and all the photosynthesizers do not have to fear.

For seventy-eight years, this world of the laughing waters has discreetly, directly been instructing me on a deeper level than sacred books could translate for me on what to do, and what to let go.

> *I dream of a religion that does not just bring an*
> *anesthetic relief; I dream of one in which skepticism*
> *and doubt are commandments, and a stagnant*
> *mind is not allowed. To gently turn on more*
> *streetlights in a mind is religion for me.*

42. A man takes a vacation from his narrow alphabetic world—a woman puts her mind on a fast of no words.

My mind is an eternal baby. It cries out for the Mama. It wants to feed from her huge, mysterious breasts, overflowing with the organic wisdom she cooks and distills in the genes of every one of her critters. My mind doesn't do so well when it only nurses on some formula, bottled in books.

Nothing has seduced me more to become a refined-minded humanist than our written word, our printing press, and the mental fast food from our electronic communication. Here is exquisite language, exclusively processed by man and for man. No tree, no bird may listen in and comment. Critters with no shoes or hats are up in arms at being left out of this conversation. Our technology of communication has become a miraculous multiplication of our daily mental bread. Take a finger full of my mind and taste how shamelessly practical it has become. The internet has become irresistible ice cream for our minds. The general practitioner in my mind is starving for whole food.

No wonder so many of us have lost trust in our personal memories, as these memories are mostly no longer backed by self-made experiences, and so they are not our property. Our memoryscapes, born to be uncommitted rainforests and waving dunes, are being turned into a monoculture, are getting pale from the lack of "lightamines" (messages of awesome complexity that flood our mind) and limp now a little from too much manmade input. Are we becoming disconnected little bundles of selfish thoughts, loaded down with many blind, negative assumptions? Are our memories becoming a lost caravan and undernourished, like fellows who have gotten to eat only toast and eggs for life?

Out in the free land, I am on a visit with my deeper past that offers more nourishing gossip than what's found in the little collection of memories we have stored away in our books and surface minds. A memory that is not tied to a farmer but is roaming beyond fences gets the "lightamines" to grow many generations tall, many species wide. And there is less need for mental lawsuits to clog Theo's mind. When so kept whole, it can make a cheerful everyday shaman of her or him.

An addiction to a strictly verbalized communication has turned our species into a secretive and egotistic enterprise. It made me an avid collector in practical knowledge. Here the ideas of Life are butchered and cut into their parts—eyes, testicles, thoughts and all—to be sifted for what can be profitably sold. I became a market of manmade ideas made in who-knows-where. I buy, I sell. Some of my memory's items are made as cheaply as gadgets from Taiwan. My poetic memory has been harshly wallpapered over by sellers and buyers with countless sweetly intoxicating propaganda slogans.

An addiction to a strictly verbalized communication has turned our species into a secretive and egotistic enterprise.

The picture language of television has now become the global language with which mind-farmers farm the mindscape of their customers. This phenomenal one-species affair in communication, this exaggerated inbreeding of our own species' point of view, so rare in nature, makes me quite physically semi-blind and semi-deaf. Silent goes the universal identification-hum, the universal exchange of signals, where every critter tilling the Earth advertises her gifts and her needs. How fat with words, how chauvinistic the printing press has made my intellect, how exaggerated my consciousness! How swiftly it is turning now our minds into a monoculture field. In such a quarantine, a man may now spend his lifetime without the slightest curiosity to ask the skylark that sings the morning glory for him: "What is the good morning news that would make you fly a mile into the sky in delirious joy?" Who knows, this little singer might just wish that all the Monsanto farmers as far as it can see were sent to heaven. Such might be the good tidings that shy little companion may be praying for. Our memories store now fewer stories of animals and plants than ever before. "Where is the bread, the car, the check, the sex?" Is that all we need to know? A grotesquely muscular, purely humanistic mind is crowding out the other songbirds in my jungle mind. Prescription stimulants can now focus a mind even more in this way.

Think of a quite ordinary stag beetle obsessed with dominance that goofed and developed his antlers to ten pounds, or of a mind that has completely committed itself to some split-expertise, or a mind that has been tied to a lawn mower on a golf course for life.

Now, look around. How undesirable it has become to remain a general practitioner or a hermit who do not plane themselves down to qualify for a job or tie their mind to a stake to become an expert. Think of the low esteem for a woman who in our epidemic of practicalities laughs off a job to remain a full-time mother to her children or who turns into an open guesthouse to all things that sprint, crawl, green and smile, who loves to gossip with her geraniums and the neighbor's kids. (This must be Clara in me, talking here.) Yes, this heart in here tells me with every thump, that it is meant to beat for something richer than just food, sex and job. No man is further away from becoming a poet than a fine specialist.

I am done living with my mind fluttering in a safe cage, in the promising thought-bubble of some -ism or in the spell of our high tech mass-mind-production machine, suspended in an immense silence, endlessly listening to our own echoes. Now, what do I do with my life—for whom, for what—now, that we are about done with raising our five children? Now, that I should be done with the esthetic arts and other safe toys and with competing to be one of the best experts in fishing?

You want to be safe? Stay aboard. I do not want to be safe. And so I sometimes go overboard.

While intellectuals haggle about professional expertise and perfection in one niche, we lovers of the outdoors train now in extended social skills. To explore the hugely complex relationship among all of life's sciences is our safari and our ultimate work of art. Some build their big or little boats to float around in a pond. Others become the ocean. You want to be safe? Stay aboard. I do not want to be safe. And so I sometimes go overboard. To do so, solitude seems to work better for me than narcotic helper weeds. "It's time, Theo, to be again a hermit in the Dry Pass cabin for a week, and let your mind go on a walkabout. Spend again a week during which you do not talk, you do not write or read, you leave your rifle at home, you do no fishing schemes, the next neighbor twenty miles away. A week during which you are not a shopper, not a fisher; a week you are an observatory from head to toe. The company of talkative trees, fishes, rivers, mushrooms, and the fleets of clouds will fill your days. Go, have a telephone conversation with the Earth! You need a detox week."

Recently I was with Clara out to the hunting cabin, going through these essays, line by line, haggling, discussing, laughing by candlelight and the woodstove, talking. What you have here is what she reluctantly let me get by with.

43. All I am aware of—that's me.

If I am just aware of pork and beans, then pork and beans, that's me.

When I become a better listener, you can rub a little into me—and I may become a little you.

While plowing the *Onyx*, my fishing boat, into a stiff westerly, pulling long line gear for halibut offshore in Southeast Alaska, the thought strikes me: so many of the creative people I meet, I read, love, and am inspired by, had quite a strict religious or cultural upbringing and grew out of their tight children's shoes, like me. I think of my Catholic upbringing: the fasts, the confessions, the retreats, the rosaries, the Latin chants, the Sunday rituals, the fantastic teaching stories, the vegetarian Fridays, all my exercises in willpower and self-control, the training in obedience, the guilt and the conflict creating beliefs tattooed into me. All the other punishing fences to keep me safely inside the compound— the holy communion in which we ritually became one with all people, all penguins, all trees. Ah, and my mental chastity belt that was of such good quality, it kept me a virgin you would be astonished for how long.

Many activities in this initiation were not planned by my genes and were not "natural" acts. Instead they were idealistic, "heaven-bent" acts that have more to do with a shaman's initiation. I had to invent and learn strange, far-off things, compensations and learning experiences exclusively reserved for souls in curfew.

Born a happy oyster, my culture wedged little pebbles of difficulties under my shell—many kinds of dos and do-not-dos my genes had never seen. Quite naturally I made "pearls" out of these difficulties. When others cruised the freeways, when others remained free to live their nature—eat, sow their wild oats, laugh easily and make manure—I was ordered off-road as an experiment to live on new, unproven recipes. My way out: I set my heart on observing and learning, and got hooked on it for life. Should I have regrets?

Here are some side effects my long way out of this initiation had on me. I had to become a little more than the usual shopping cart of memories. I became a little your memories, the leaf-cutter ants' memories, and that of the willows and that of Mona our cat's memories. And of the memories of sundry other rascals too. New stars started to twinkle, shining their light from where for others their night sky remained unexplored and mute. Old convenient convictions got spotlighted from strange viewpoints. And some of my "moon's" shaded sides came into view. Dark, "evil" acts and people started to lift their black skirt and give their brighter secrets up. Sections, set off-limits by common sense, opened up. And I learned to recruit that cussed self-discipline forced onto me as my personal helper. And, yes, this addiction to observe, to learn, to become aware has become fun, so much so, that I do not dream anymore of just cruising the freeways of my genes. And there are many viewpoints still hiding in my deeper self, awaiting Theo's viewpoint quest.

All this makes me think of microbes that among our armies of antibiotics cannot live their normal, old selves. Yes, many simply comply. They give in. Yet a very few daredevils make it. They become creative, stronger, and more complex. With a brand-new string of rebellious side steps and insights for defense, they outmaneuver us and survive. These lucky ones become resistant to our old tricks. They know something good old "natural" microbes do not know.

And so, I too might have got to know a little something that "natural" people do not know. Life's amazing grace uses negative things to bring out positive things. When Life wants to force-feed and prodigiously develop a splinter skill in me, it handicaps or dams off some of my old-hat talents for a while. Great energy may build up behind such dams and finally it might surge, and pour into that dormant seed of a skill.

A strict cultural environment can be an enormously powerful wave of the psychology to have protective power over others. That wave may carry a young man nicely and safely along, out of his responsibility and control—until that non-swimmer learns to swim and surfs that power wave. Trained in self-discipline, he uses that workhorse for himself and starts to live his personal legend and not an imitation of you-name-who.

A boot camp in obedience is a test. If that test does not succeed in bringing a man down to the height of his boots, it makes him stronger instead. And he or she will know things that the natural tinkers and the Noble Savages cannot know. She may become a Blue Lake halfway to the ocean, while others remained a stagnant frog pond further up.

In the awareness game filters open or close according to a life situation. When you are sick, your caretaker sends away all but the dearest guests. In a frozen ocean of love, filters shut, culminating in hypothermia, the most austere and protective egotism of all. On sunny days flowers open—a feast of awareness.

When blessed with summer time a man or a woman may then wonder, "What is it like to be born as Irene or as Paul, or as a Muslim, or as a wolf? Her inner voice replies, "Visit them. Have them over for smoked salmon. Take on their identity. Imitate their qualities and the holes in their qualities with your own modest kind of ecstasy." Is that not what the professional shaman does, when he imitates the voices, the movements, the longings, the hang-ups, and, with his mask, the looks of these people and animals he wants to explore? This professional observer taps into what their clients feel and hear. You and I, we may be amateurs doing the same. We walk the tightrope between soberness and being high.

On one side: our domesticated awareness diluted with filters and our exuberant imaginations tied to a stake. Here the chestnut tree in front of your porch might be a foreigner to you. Here mothers with strollers, hikers, commuters, and runners are plugged into their dear iPods. They are on the pill that protects them from fertile intercourse with the wild world at large—a gentle condom made of sounds that repels disturbing awareness.

On the other side: my inquisitive child awareness, still with no filter and no shame, burning for a trip to far-off people and places, or into the ecstatically wild, still fingering anything with its hands and mind. With my hesitations about what I want to see and hear gone overboard, I am free to meet whatever gifts Life gave you to compose your world. And is not each head a world? In your world, different continents, fears, boogey-men, mountain slides, loaded fruit trees I have never seen, flocks of tropical ideas I have never met, maybe tracks of impenetrable permafrost in your love that did not freeze over in my world, tenderness that my physical wiring does not allow. Knowing you a little more, I soon step a little less on your heart and your toes.

Ah, to give in to life's unending siege of our walled-in safe harbors, to be teased again, by curious anxiety and doubt, out of the Comfort Express that heads to some stacked Safeway. To be lured by our prodigious curiosity into the nooks and crannies, the realities and hearts of other people and into new worlds to find out! Conventional wisdom might get a little too tight and that old snakeskin of Theo may split. While the whole Theo gets vigilant this way, like a cat without aiming bounces on a prey, his questions bounce on their answers. What a sweet, unfashionable treat!

After my first reorientation in which I rebelled so much against my upbringing, these are very, very helpful thoughts. They help me to make peace, not just with some sundry shadows, but also with my own upbringing. The gift of that revolt: some immunity against criticism-itis, regret, foul mouth, and a larger toolbox for tolerance. Less complaint from Theo; look, I come out of it a wealthier man. I have spices for my daily bowl of happiness that easy-goers may not have.

44. To be in reason—or to be in love

My heart is a thousand-stringed instrument; my reason is a four-stringed fiddle.

Look to your side when you drive through the corn belt of the United States. You will see endless fields of F-1 hybrid corn plants, all identical—no birds, no butterflies, no flowering weeds, thanks to Monsanto and to the Haber-Bosh process that fixes nitrogen. Here is land not in love but in reason. It's converted to our beliefs. It's force-fed, sanitized and well behaved. It's blessed, blessed but once, with corn, corn, corn—an awesome exaggeration of corn. In the corn belt, I am in a kitchen that feverishly cooks food exclusively for the huger and huger clan of man. It's McDonald's land. Few animals and plants come to live here, where it's just hamburgers and fries on every acre every day. Agro-businesses can produce such high yield sad lands. As you see, reasoning is the quick and short-term scheming that Life gives us for crisis times.

Paddle way up the Amazon or trek the trails of Yellowstone. Pagan land, land that makes me think the unthinkable! Here is a system of intelligence at work in which my reasoning may get indigestion from the rich diversity Life acts out. Here is a basket heaped with unappreciated blessings. Wherever I look I see generosity that puts the puny humane generosity I learned into the shade.

I paddle through land that's not in reason but wildly in love. When I look at its results, I must infer that every act here is a good deed. The Curious George in me peeks excitedly into a kitchen that's vastly less uniform and sanitary than McDonald's land. Millions of cooks here, some with the most outrageous hats, all peeling, stirring, chewing, brewing, simmering, pissing, ruminating food and inventions. Here millions of different dishes for millions of different clients are served, with one goal: keep that motley clientele healthy and diversifying for another million years.

Here are countless busy little bugs, each thousands of times more complex than our latest fighter jets or Pablo Picasso's works of art. Each of these little artists has its own show of creativity, each homing in on my mind with its own kind of growth factors hollering, "Look at me! Grow toward me! Count me in!" Here also each one of my organs is a cell community. And each healthy cell is completely compassionate and altruistic, doing its best for its holder, most of the time. Take your hand. Move it. Look at it. What a tool—what a free-for-all! Countless cells are doing the fishing for Theo—indescribably more obedient and coordinated than the American Navy.

Here everything around me is motivated by something much more mysterious than my simplistic reasoning is, which is, after all, only my toy box of the few Legos our consciousness assembled to experiment with. And that wonderful something rubs up on me. I am in a university that has remained our pillar of free, wild learning.

In town, that learning institution has mostly been bought by corporations, castrated, tamed, and put to work. Here, a mare is pulling a plow. Out there, the flying mustang of the mind.

And don't think for a second that the shrews, the bats, the armies of worms under the mud flats along this great river of soup do not also care for whoever gives them yummy food. Long before us, these delightful bundles of selfish genes have learned the trick of compassion—the good-gardener principle. (Think of all their mirror neurons that help their instinct to practice altruism.) Long before us, they made agriculture a joint venture, nay, a potlatch where species very selfishly outdo each other to be the fittest gardeners and givers without going bankrupt as a result of their generosity.

Life has a Nobel Prize for organisms that are fit for changing their environment favorably by creating new niches for additional symbiotic friends. Don't laugh at genetics' sixty-four commandments. Rumors in heaven have it that they might just be higher ranking guides on the payroll of the Creator than the tentative commandments of our own sacred books.

Here is land that does not just fiddle on four strings. Here the love-dynamics play a very professional orchestra. Here, it's not just the arrogant voice of some mankind that mostly laments and seldom thanks. Here the rich overpowering Song of the Earth is serenading us. I see economics at its best. I see technology that is totally compassionate.

No highly cultivated thinking can penetrate into the wildness of Life and survive as is. Plant a kernel of an F-1 hybrid corn in rat, fungi, and raven land and see what happens to highly educated Dr. Corn wearing a tie. Without continuous outside help it will slowly regress closer to its root wisdom—or it will be overgrown. When my cultured mind lands on this high plateau, my greenhouse thoughts also soon catch a cold. Cheap, nice thinking, with its manmade love, is no match for the love of the four seasons. Might it be for this, that I am attracted by people with a moderate IQ and still gifted with a high social skill—people who didn't mint their wisdom into smartness?

I, too, started out as an acre of this wildly permissive Earth. Some of my deeper tracks are still wildly in love and filthy rich with options and ideas. On other plots you find now my mono-cultures, the pesticides, the focus-enhancers and steroids, the moralists, the farm police, the plow, the economist, the profes-sional fisherman. In my cultivated mind, the glorious variety of my Amazon is simplified to a monoculture of some expertise. Here land in love with its billions of options is simplified to land in reason with its limited options. Here our life sciences are embarked on their celebrated genocide of our incorruptible quality controllers, tiny and big, like pathogens. On these neat tracts I am brought down into hard reason. Rationality, that emergency gift of handy nearsightedness, has built its farm in my mind.

When I melt down the mustang into raw horsepower, when I melt down my wisdom into raw smartness, I will sure be more feared and probably less loved. A planed-down and simplified heart is needed to be practical and smart.

Land in love reminds us of the logistic of the four seasons. It teases us to indulge together in a heart-made psychosynthe-sis. Shame has no chance in this wonderful healing love-folly. Wildly permissive streams of transmissions go back and forth in this outdoor therapy. We get a taste of communion. Out here, when the left hand gives the right hand a "hand," it does not expect a thank-you. I notice, when by and by a woman and a man become one, it is the same. A thank-you among us would then ring an alarm. I also notice: when a woman and man compete, their relationship starts to bleed.

My task: To make peace between the analphabetic voices from my deep and my loud reasoning, between my dark mysteri-ous and my strikingly obvious in my hierarchy of communica-tions. I need them both. No need for them to roll in broken glass, fighting with each other.

45. A species whose associates can become sick remains a guesthouse for Life's zillion artists to chisel on her and him—welcome in!

Life functions and evolves well when a pinch of malfunction or defeat for the individual is included in the recipe. Ask around, sickness has been around for a long while. So I infer that sickness must be part of our deep genetic wisdom. Our interaction with pathogens reminds me of the deep friendship story of the arctic hare and the fox, helping each other to evolve. Here is a tool for interaction, exploration, and learning at work that is older than our eyes or our system of arms and legs, a genetic tool that opens us to compassion. Sickness periodically involves us in confrontation and reconciliation, a discreet learning process we want to know little about.

We meet opponents that know things we do not know. Take sickle cell anemia or favism. These nifty little tricksters from other species know how to protect against malaria. Cystic fibrosis knows ways to protect from malaria, typhoid fever and tuberculosis. People with autism have incredibly keen eyesight, seeing almost as acutely as birds of prey. They beat me a hundredfold in picking up details. Autism knows something I do not know. Many genetic diseases turn out to be complex evolutionary blessings. Their pains also seed our garden with many questions, and later engender the answers. Here we go to the Olympics with the athletes of other species—and we learn from them new treats and tricks.

No doubt, Life without our games of sickness would be less magic. In these routine breaking shake-ups, eye-openers, new know-hows, shock revelations, and many kinds of genetic additions can happen to a woman and a man that will not occur in an undisturbed life with no such feisty interactions. We are a brave, wonderful cluster of wounds we learned to heal.

A science obsessed with righting all these "malfunctions," or game management here in Alaska that wants to shoot the wolves to be "good" to the caribou, seems a science groping in the dark. Think of an unlucky porcupine clan that gets obsessed with a blind science. It only dreams of how to give the porkies more quills, speed, poisonous fangs, claws, a vaccine against any foreign guest or a warhead in each of its quills against its dear, sundry nibblers, chiselers, teachers, and foes. Wouldn't that clan of munchers soon turn into a cataclysmic wood chewing machine, munching the great boreal forests into one single pile of manure in no time? Think of a rhino clan that went mad and got engrossed with a blind rhino science. It labors in the steamy sweat of the rhino's brows to grow their horns a hundred feet tall.

Dear adventurer, think now for a moment outside your commonsense frame. Think of a mankind that comes down with constipated hearing. It can no longer hear the long, wonderful song of birth, bullfights, pathogens, glorious victories, tests, and the march home. We become obsessed with cures, with drugs, herbicides, hygiene and safety, with pesticides, with mouthwashes, with vaccines against hunger, against creative fevers, against solitude and retreats into depressions, against the allocators of death, against high temper, hyper-activity and hyper-vision, against ecstatic seizures, against the sweet timely forgetfulness of old age and against the frosts in fall. To skip the test of a drought, we swallow and get high on credit cards.

Are we becoming a species stuck in a mania of stockpiling the arsenals of its financial and chemical medicine with every imaginable anti-so-and-so, turning the environment all spic-and-span and truly sterile? Tell me, is clinical medicine trying to save the non-swimmers by bailing out the sea?

Tell me, is clinical medicine trying to save the non-swimmers by bailing out the sea?

We may see diseases as weeds, pests, and enemies in a man's inner landscape. But the history of Life tells me that these rascals are Life's tireless long-term helpers, and therefore we must learn to live in harmony with these tricksters, to better watch the law of moderation and enter with the family members of life into some arms agreements.

Yes, as the land can be "gloriously" farmed and medicated toward death, so a medical and a drug industry can slowly medicate, tame, and erode the health and resilience of a species toward death. Sometimes I see one of our sciences that fell down into a well-shaft and so has become endlessly angry with Life. I see a science motivated by fear instead of admiration, and therefore out to steamroll through the merry, permissive circus of life with the most power and mass. Sometimes I see a science with its head stuck in the mud and proud to know more details about this pile of mud than about the mind of God, ever scheming to censor the Creator with one more cure. Why try so hard to cure a species of all its sicknesses and deprive it so of its most proven remedies? Sicknesses are the commodity market for the genes. And why cure us of the pains of quality and population control? Why seek a cure for evolution? Have not these little buggers since eons doctored us back into harmony and higher health? And these routine-spoilers can shake the shaman awake in a woman or a man. Deficit and hyper disorders can be door openers to creativity. They can acquaint us with other worlds.

Look at this Earth, this wondrous basket heaped with life, heaped with the gifts of these magic interactions where even the "mean" viruses are now finally winning applause as devoted ferrymen for genes and wisdom.

By stepping into the ring and arguing with these armies of nifty little opponents—isn't that how I learn? Pathogens fertilize the workings of my mind. And they sneak to me the chance of an audience with the emperor when he has no clothes on, or with a friend who is too sick to think straight or to put his niceness-mask over his face for my visit. They are the key out of an impenetrable health that locks me into a yawning ring-a-round of stasis.

Aren't also these "persecutions" bringing out hidden ghosts and resources in us?

Now that I am at the end of my eighth decade, and I am getting a little sweet and ripe and less driven by the messy fever to provide and provide, I can reinvent my mind away from so seriously working in some niche, like the one on how to fish ever better. It's time to play a little with my neuroplasticity and to unify my mind more with the mind of Life.

Each critter now alive has mastered the art of walking the sky-rope between vulnerability and defense. In biological terms, to remain vulnerable, to remain open to sickness, to remain compassionate, these three are probably all close to being synonymous—three different expressions for sharing Life among critters big and small. The sickening assumption that sicknesses are our archenemies begs for a mental cure. Sickness deserves a better story than the one we are told. That better story will be the gentlest painkiller yet.

> *Sickness deserves a better story than the one we are told. That better story will be the gentlest painkiller yet.*

A lightning bolt, please, to light up my obscured relationship with these discreet little helpers that tease awake sleeping talents in me, that fling open doors in my routine and in the fortress of my genes.

And wow, I see, I see. The cure is here!

46. In and around me: the cosmic song of signals!

In and around me: the universal Spirit and caller of my thoughts, my moods, my body, my deeper sense of orientation, of my protests and angers, my genes, my chores, my "everything." The signals of each molecule in the cosmos, of the ebbs and the floods of each wave, the signals of each mineral, each critter, each memory and the joys of every crybaby and star combined, they say who I am. These countless pathfinder stars in and around me point out, "Theo, not here! Try there!"

As the nucleus of a cell is a part of that cell, and each of my cells is part of Theo, so I see also Theo as one cell of something much, much larger than Theo. Continuously, I breathe, eyeball, and filter in huge amounts of information. Millions of different molecules in one breath, uncountable different waves and growth factors go in and out with one sight, each a signal that keeps my genes and your genes informed. No, a gene set does not fend for one individual. It fends for an environment that helps each little ticker to tick, kick, and survive. And only God knows what all other helpers my soul is provided with. I am swimming in the belly of that cosmic whale of compassion with no way to get away from this godly net of "lightamines." Virtuous or vicious, builder or wrecker, my yesses of today may be ordered to be tomorrow's nos, creative constructs of the cosmic mind that come and go and have no permanence in a cosmos that runs on and on.

Today I may be called to be a drummer with a sledgehammer, you a singer, she a hole in the caller's flute, or an asshole, whether we get the meaning or not. My resonance is best when every fiber in me is on the loose and vibrates to this universal discourse. Be antenna from head to toe, Theo, drum loud from the top of City Hall!

Everything curls and loops in its own way toward the light. None is free to grow away from the sun. Everything, mean or kind, stands with its plate in line around the pot for a serving of joy.

47. Our networks of beliefs, they are our hammocks and artworks of thought, comforting our confused minds.

No, I will never again ridicule a person who in this awesome sea of confusion and no answers creates an island or rents a seat in a boat, or weaves her own hammock, so she can feel a little safer and at home in this storm. May we all be free to shop for a mental kind of mosquito net against the piercing questions continuously buzzing around our minds, a net fitting each the span of his or her soul.

No man can live without a skin and without some kind of custom built mental shelter in which he can do and think his "whatever" without being continuously menaced by the pounding sea of awesome truths.

Does it matter that the great elements of truth lick and pound the shore of our manmade credos, ultimately breaking up again into rubble any such refuge, sturdy or not, if not continuously reinforced and improved to be yet finally sunk again in a harmony more powerful than all those mental artworks of man?

Does it matter that some construct their shelters from the revelations of the world of our sciences, others from myths and legends of holy women and men, others again from their local materials like the spirits of trees, of frogs and eagles, the fertility of the sun and the sea? And that others prefer to compose their credos from mathematical constructs? Is that diversity a blessing?

Some need a battleship to ride safely out the terrible seas of towering questions and few calming answers. Others are happy with a canoe. The duck makes do with a feathered survival suit.

The golden toad in Costa Rica's Monte-Verde Cloud Forest could not take the rapid change when the heating of sea surface temperatures within years lifted its perpetual cloud above the peak of the park. They died to the last. Changes in our mental climate can be equally devastating when triggered too fast.

Noah built his ark. I am building my own, so not to drown in this great sea of mysteries and confusion. I can use materials we've lately found that are a little sturdier than those Noah had at hand. I see in Christ for example an extraordinarily creative boat builder, building such a barge for billions who had no means to build their own. No wonder, though, that with so many different floating devices circulating now all over in our overcrowded sea, all of different shapes, models, steering systems and crews, some of these ships bang into others.

For most of us, our sheltering belief systems and their myths are the only artworks that follow us around, day and night, and are meant to give us a sense of having a home here or yonder.

48. Thanks over and over for my ignorance.

How could I step even one single step on the green carpet spread underneath the woods if I were totally aware of how infinite a work of art just one bundle of moss really is? How could I step on such an artful canvas? So, what a flute player has to know first and foremost when playing his part, is what holes have to be held closed. For getting a specific job done, Life does to our awareness the same.

I shop for a little wisdom—just a little—lest I freeze by the wise man's curse that turns him into an uninvolved spectator. Blessed be my little crazinesses and the wisdom to know them to be so. Thank god I am not God.

Is it true that my pleasure strings and my drums of pain, when caressed and drummed, never neutralize or become flat, thanks to my ignoring some of the complementariness of the sad and happy happenings that are played on the shaded side of my moons? Thanks to the holes in my knowing, my inner music is not dull, but has its ups and its downs. No "bad" deed goes "unrewarded" just as no "good" deed is "forgiven" its debt. Is that not the gist of harmonious music?

Great wisdom and folly are lovers that meet in the bushes. Take a woman in love. She throws all our clever talk to the dogs—more impossible to hold her back than to dam a swollen mountain stream. Yet, it is not our cleverness, it is her wise folly that has been keeping us on our merry march since our ancestors first departed from the mud flats.

Take the neat cleverness of our agronomists and what their work ultimately does to the Earth. Take the "chaos" of the Amazon where a million species do their trading in a way that seems brute folly to us, and then compare the endurance of their success with what our cleverness does to the Earth. Theo, take your writings of fifteen years. You paid a publisher a bundle to give that tome mostly as a gift. These "follies" are your domesticated ducks that remember and do their ocean things for a treat, instead of doing cleverness, science, money, and fish.

To cleverness, my sweetest deeds do not make much sense.

49. I saw our new manmade goodness cry.

When I read the history of Life, in its economy "good" deeds are debts, "bad" deeds are savings accounts. Both will become due, one to be paid back, the other to be spent in a giveaway of fresh opportunities. When a flooding Nile plows the land, Life salivates with expectation, anticipating: so many new options to plant! When in summertime it is all fruits and greens, again Life salivates, seeing so much to take under and nourish the soil!

Bumming with Clara through Ethiopia, I learn with anguish how the smart goodness our politicians or our patriarchs invented plays tricks on us.

For eons, this country's human population has been kept vigorous and slim with some good help from its periodic droughts. Without much fuss, the animals, the plants, the people contributed with a sacrifice when the rain did not come.

We, the children of a new practical goodness, decided: too expensive for us! And we rebelled. We pitted a new manmade goodness, an inexpensive imitation of the real thing, versus the Great Goodness whose quality never comes cheap. The grain ships are being sent in, the foreign aid, the wheat convoys, the bales of secondhand clothing, the Coke, the vaccines, the Medecins Sans Frontieres, the technologists, the consortium of power planters, the enterprises of do-gooders, the World Bank, the Red Cross. Within sixty years, a population of fifteen million flooded to sixty-five million along with twenty-five million cows, and a bigger herd of sheep and goats nibbling nonstop in between. And that flood is rising fast.

And again, I see this fantastic success in Ethiopia swollen into an uninterrupted checkerboard of fields for the thousand miles of our walk and truck-about. These voracious fields indiscriminately engulf the steep hillsides of this country, scraggly flats, baked rock piles, and the runoffs once lush with woods. Ninety-eight percent of the forests had to lie down to make room for our new, practical goodness' success. A couple of lonely trees per mile are still confused, holding hands. They still try to withstand that tremendous flood of human activity. Look! Our success has swept away everything that breathes, yet had no name in the yellow pages of our telephone books. This is how we help these people to cheat and avoid their share in the sacrifice.

So burdened now with survival, this has become the scenario in which a people ultimately may turn to thorns, leaving few flowers, few birds, meager kindness and music, no gaily painted houses, just bare mortar and bricks. This scenario soon leaves each soul withdrawn in a tough callus of self-defense, an epidemic of misleading, with a swarm of starving flies ever ready to descend on a crumb of spoil. This is what the motto "love your neighbor" or your own generation or at best your own species, can do to a land.

This country and its beautiful people tell me that it is our smart new goodness on a leash that is our most efficient pesticide. It silences the songbirds, the lupines, the laughing waters and the laughing women washing in the creek, the singing leisure time, the howls of the coyote, the butterflies, the lively soil which for long have all cheered that people's land and hearts, the gentle song when people contentedly die in time. That new ethic ultimately spreads a silent spring interrupted by sobs, video games, or the roar of big rigs packed with UN rice and guns. The heat wave of this runaway human activity dries and erodes now the very soul of that land.

On the other side of the Earth, I meet another child of this same simplistic goodness. Indiana's giant Gibson power generating station spreads three thousand megawatts of that goodness' comfort. The boilers of this technological marvel gulp twenty-five tons of coal every minute, releasing fifty-four tons of carbon dioxide into the air every minute, along with sulfur dioxide, nitrogen dioxide, and mercury. Here is a celebrated fart that ultimately breaks all table manners. The side effects of this offspring of the manmade goodness make now a zillion earthlings lose their good breath. Our manmade goodness makes the Earth cry.

From this cataclysmic lesson I learn that in globalization, it is not only the different strains of pathogens that exchange their secrets of combat, enormously strengthening their virulence. In globalization it is before all mankind that enormously enhances its virulence. Different strains of technology and of science can become informers. Worldwide and with the slightest shame we now inbreed our strategies of attack to hammer the whole living Earth into submission. This is what the sciences of technology are about. No wonder that, apart from all the highly enriched uranium, enough plutonium now lies around in forty-six countries to build an additional one hundred thousand nuclear warheads.

Combine the speed of the cheetah, the venomousness of the rattler, the cunning of the coyote, the strength of the elephant, the echo night vision of the bat and you have a living tank that is just too overqualified for considerately circulating in the Garden of Grace. With such heavy footsteps when dancing to the law of moderation, a scenario of feast and bust soon prevails. As a plow, so does the touch of our humanitarian interventions, it leaves a people and their land irreversibly changed.

Think of mankind, or bear-kind, or any species that one day would become in our sense all "good" and truly live according to our new sacred goodness. Think about such hugely "successful" living. I promise you, you will soon start to pray for impracticality, for weeds, mortality and "sin."

Our softhearted humanitarian interventions, the miserable life extensions sold by our medical cartels, when wisdom tells us we should be strong-hearted and not casually intervene, show up later as our most saintly, most persistent follies. Wherever I look, Life teaches me for example that a measure of child mortality is an asset for a species' long-term resilience. Founders of big-time charities may like to ponder on this while having the "stones" for their "pyramids" amassed.

Back to Ethiopia. Prick up your ears! Do you hear this land cry from the wounds of our many good deeds, from all the endeavors of earning prizes and medals promised by some committee yonder or here? Heroes who are of weak hearing and cannot sway to the beautiful song of the four seasons are prone to revolt when a people or trees are periodically shedding their leaves.

I had to see it to believe. I never even dreamed that our new strictly humane goodness could have such a cataclysmic effect.

As in a population explosion the lemmings get disoriented, we too in such a situation, get from Life a gift box full of confusion, and for good reason. Disorientation is the first tool for reorientation. Look, just last week we awarded a Nobel Prize to a savant who initiated the pouring of, by now, four million in vitro babies into the flood we have become. And we started now to proudly send these terribly overcrowded countries of Africa low cost in-vitro fertilization clinics as part of our aid. For commonsense people this still may look like honorable help. Others, we are confused. We start to see the pain such uninspired help is causing the Earth. How I see it depends on how much I dare to peek over my lazy old common sense.

The manmade goodness I learned at school seems still an awkward imitation of Life's awesome generosity, like the little shoes of a child's little soul. No wonder I get blisters when I still wear that childhood goodness as an adult.

The September song sings to me, "For goodness' sake, please stop bragging about saving human lives. The boat is overloaded with human cargo and sinking. What are you trying to do? Stop the march of the seasons?"

Just as it does to quit smoking, it takes courage to give up sweetly intoxicating thinking.

50. A mind also can get obese when gorging in a McDonald's land for the intellect.

An antelope scratches a living in a thorny savanna land. All of a sudden this meandering muncher faces a so, so juicy alfalfa field. This field is so soft, so uniform, so rich, with no ticks, weeds, thorns, completely ideal and green, a feast not seen before, even in dreams. Is it a trap? How could that beast not go for this muncher's paradise and join the other happy antelopes wading chest deep in favorite food?

Laboriously, a man fends for his mind out in the jungle of complex designs and ideas, always moving, back, up and forth, nibbling on all kinds of raw information hanging his way while swatting sucker flies. All of a sudden, this subsistence hunter stumbles into our media circus—the freshly baked news, the TV, the cell phone, the GPS, the evening paper, Google's information mart, the Walkman, the CDs, the libraries, the iPod—the informer's paradise! What power over the have-nots is awaiting him here! How could he resist?

He lies down, plumb in the middle of this banquet of information, feasting on that McDonald's food for the mind, all ready to become an enthusiastic inmate of it. Here, information is served that has been selected, pre-chewed, sorted, alphabetized, thoroughly cleansed and refined, completely humanized, and sold at a bargain price! Here is monoculture of information, all of it exclusively from and for man exquisitely verbalized. This banquet is more seducing to a starving mind than glittering Broadway is for a man in heat. Here a surplus of mental calories can nicely fatten a mind. Plugged into our latest kind of god, our glorious global information mart, soon he cannot help but dance, dress, think, applaud, condemn, opinionate and vote to its pictures and tune.

Yet to learn deep social skills, do I ask a genius? Do I go to Picasso school? Do I ask an acrobat how to walk safely through a long life? No, I don't. I ask a man who hasn't tasted applause.

Yet, do we not tend to celebrate a man for spotlighting with his love a splinter skill in him and keeping his other "children" starving in the closet? And I wonder here: is it for such implosion of information on which we focus our attention so shamelessly and efficiently on the affairs of man, that we become so awkward in Life's social skill?

Did you notice how the media, that ruthlessly effective global power tool to re-engineer our minds, rapidly transforms our good old democracies into *mediacracies*? Imagine: very professionally, the media chefs cook and stir what goes into our amazingly plastic minds in order to remodel our minds to the taste of a client we barely know. Eventually, the viewers' minds soften and take on neuropathways favorable to the client's demands: a little hate or fear here, a spoonful of wishful thinking there. Eventually, the spell takes hold. One broadcaster yawns and fifty million viewers yawn. Soon, one burns to vote for that media-fabricated hero. One of the factories where whisperers produce minds made to order is Washington D.C., with a team of forty thousand lobbyists, seventy thousand lawyers, and twenty-five thousand public relations specialists.

To visualize this feast: Imagine, many night gnats find a streetlight. Mesmerized by this bubble of blinding visibility, they excitedly, irreversibly swarm and rampage into it. Outside this luminous bubble, all the dark and mysterious goes black. Unbelievable! One gnat breaks out of this magic luminous circle. And, with all her antennas out, she heads again into the mysteries of a rich night. Here is power to respect!

Now, watch that unfashionable man. Unbelievable! In the middle of this magnificent feast of information, this maverick walks out of the range of the media. He shuns the huge enthusiastic crowd milling on our global information mart. He connects with the Earth in a different way. He chooses to live more dangerously, triggering his mind to produce its own opiates. He might become a part-time hermit and think out of our control. That will be his "crime." Yet, Life might reward him for his feat with a high all of his own.

By far the most dramatic loss from living in an entirely manmade environment might be the loss of mind nourishing likenesses. A change into a wild environment massages my brain. Its plasticity gets back in shape. I am, for example, animated again to take lessons in sharing power, or to become a practitioner of sustainable populations, lessons our technology and grand charities skipped. In the clarity of this cathartic land, I give my mind a bath. My brain's plasticity gets restored. Like the geneticists who can coax a fully specialized cell into a stem cell again, I think about how to create an environment that restores a mind's plasticity for a creative while so to coax a fully specialized mind into a pluripotent, childlike thinker again.

I realize that this generous land with no leash laws is the only shopping mall for designs and ideas large enough to deliver the answers for my anxieties in a way that uplifts my heart. It is my classroom for the science of generic. Similarities are the guides and night-vision goggles for when I probe in the dark. They are the prize for sneaking out of the swimming pool and plunging into the deep ocean of thinking. Likenesses are the cobblestones to cobble my way to Serenity Land. They are my think-helpers that furnish me with prefabricated, approximate solutions for problems we share with other times and species. In this permissive land, I can see all of my rowdy self reflected. And I see no need for shame. I recognize in it all my qualities, beastly or not. None are stigmatized. All are amusing, all welcomed guests. No need to belittle anybody. That's why I feel well connected and at home in this raw, "messy" information mart whose product we mostly do not verbalize.

All this is to simply say that my deeply rewarding thoughts have seldom arisen from human language. They have risen from richer situations, places where words and discussions stop and my feelings combine unspeakable forms to a reality beyond common sense.

Two gay people tenderly feel out each other's faces. Drunk with adrenaline, Theo rides home his boat *Vienes del Mar*, surfing the first breakers of a storm laughing on his heels. The sweet blue Mistral brings me the scent of pines freshly baked in the noon sun of the Provence. Things re-engineer my thoughts that are vastly too complex to be verbalized or computerized.

I have a nest of eggs in my deep volcanic mind
that no human language can fertilize.

51. Nature is my chest of remedial likenesses.

Nature is my huge magic mirror-mirror-on-the-wall, where I see myself reflected.

I see all my talents, my vices and my body parts reflected in likenesses by this mirror. I see my pimples, my shadows, my little crazinesses, my overdone talents, my bragging and my missing corners, my counterfeits, my sun spots, my lying, and my kindness and compassion. Even the most defamed vices, there they are all equals in the toolbox Life uses to finger, squeeze, bend, mill and chisel the granite into this fantastic bio-fantasia that now gives me sweet company.

What I loved to hate in myself and in others, there, in that mirror, it is reflected in likenesses. And I love what I see! Instead of being a grim man at war with a bunch of sundry presumed enemies, bad men and with myself, I start to fall a little in love with Theo and other sundry rascals too. A voice in me whispers: "Polish your awareness. Visit your shadows. Be kind to them. Invite them over for barbecued venison. Ask them what spices they add to our dishes! Keep accumulating your 'medicine bundle' of metaphors. Lick with it your pissed-off-ness. That's how serenity is cooked and served. Absolutely nothing but your awareness needs polishing."

Absolutely nothing but your awareness needs polishing.

No, I am not made only of dust, and to ashes I go. I am winning great respect for Life and for Theo. Awareness is the door to my guesthouse. "Theo, be up and out early! That place wants to get filled." Yesterday, it was defamed prejudice I invited in to stay over night after I noted how this guardian spirit keeps the marigold and the bluebell from mixing their colors and turning grey. Each new-welcomed guest is one more piece of Lego for my imagination to play with.

So, don't ask me to be your counselor. Ask me to be your mirror, a mirror I am polishing three times over for you—no veils, no politeness and niceness, no sunglasses, no guards, no ornaments, medals, titles and regalia, no non-entry signs, no mudslinging and advertising, no droppings of flies. A mirror shined so stark naked for you, it makes you shout, "But that's me!" And lo! In that mirror you might recognize vital talents you have never before dared to give thanks for. Unwrap and enjoy using them.

52. We are each drunk in a different way. How rich in drunkennesses we are!

Don't tell me you are sober. You would have dropped dead on the spot. We are all drunk, each of a slightly different brew of what each has touched, heard and seen.

The dandelion, surprised, greets the iris, "Oh! How exciting, you are drunk on a different brew of memories than I. How beautiful you are!" And what if everybody in town starts to look down the same tunnel and channel? The same cocktail of public education and TV shows, the same drunkenness all over, a global sugar-cane field! Is this our wish for how the world should be improved? Consider the fourteen thousand kinds of ferns in the family of ferns—fourteen thousand kinds of drunkenness!

The huge global troops of man migrate through life to who-knows-where. A freak wind, a malady, a gaping crevasse right through the middle of his love, a whatever, that special godsend whirls a man right out of the orderly commonsense columns. Out in his unique solitude, that hermit learns to survive on new, unproven food, on uncensored pictures, ideas, and acts the commonsense pilgrim of the caravan never needs to taste. He learns to live with a love that is not subsidized by the crowd. This rare, exotic brew of love makes him spirited in a marvelously different way.

Theo, drunk with the teachings of the West, gets teased out of his cozy commune by an urge, an accident, a who-knows-what. Ah! and by Irma, the first woman he loved. High up in a Pakistani hut of sun baked mud, he sits down with a "Muslim-drunk" between goat manure and firewood; greetings, fabulous stories, tea, and excitement about so much common ground. Their "drunkenness" gets richer and richer and more colorful by the day. Their stiff minds get worked over. Streams in their neural pathways change course. New synapses form in these two brains, steering thoughts into more wholesome rhymes.

> *Whoever you meet, whatever you see and talk to, these*
> *liquors stay with you. Tell me what you have seen and*
> *I will tell you of what drunkenness you are.*

53. Fall season of a man

Each of a lifetime's seasons has a moral and a dimension of its own. In our September Song, the greedy leaves, the penis, the flowers turned into seeds, all start to make little noises. They want to work less and to curiously look around more, after they have wrapped up their summer clothes.

The mind of the fall season pulled on my sleeves, and now also pulls on my hair, asking: "What's this outdated business of competing doing here in your quiet season of sweet, red berries and yellow leaves? Theo, trash the businessman in you! Your five motives have matured, and have their own motives now. This is your liberation time, your time to become a new kind of apprentice. Here is your license to become an aged, merry vantage fool. Laugh off and out those ghosts that at your seventy-eight years still try to sell you toys!"

A mocking bird in me wonders: "I hear squeaking. What's this juvenile proving of yourself doing here, in your time of turning sour into sweet? Do you want to remain a firm, sour plum to a sour end—or ripen to a sweet, merry man all anxious to be nibbled on?"

I have to come to this again and again. I am an old racehorse. My dream of hay-meadow-land has been too long in exile. I am so used to digging in my hoofs in the racetrack of our economy. I am still talking myself into jumping that fence and leaving that outdated competitor riding me behind. Imagine, I am well in my eighth decade and am still looking for some wine that unties me from my pledge to work hard and to measure my worth by how much better I fish than other high liners do. I am still chased by the hounds that my culture of the economy-idolaters has turned on me.

Theo, have patience with Theo. The spirit of the fall season is sending you help. Note that lately you depend a little less on applause from the neighbors and bystanders, and more on the success of your heart. Note that your preoccupations are not so much your reputation, the economy, or the fish prices anymore. Your short-term memory is becoming less of a tyrant. Pain relievers and sedatives in your mind are waking up. With a shift in vision to far-sightedness—details start to shut up. Soon you will have finished the plates of pleasures your hormones have been cooking and serving you, and you will be full. Note, even your penis starts to sputter and complain, "Why always me? There are a thousand jubilant ways of lovemaking you have not yet given a chance." Isn't it time you enjoy a drink of the primordial innocence that you distill from the murk of dualism brewing inside you?"

Early on an elder gave me a hint, "Careful, young man, when you ask one of us for wisdom. Obediently, he might have spent his lifetime unlearning knowledge that proved too deep for his shallow roots."

It's fall. The dead leaves are not dead. They keep on running and singing their joyous stories through the woods, the genes, the children and the streets. Theo, keep alive your memory of how to die in time when you become a burden. Learn from cells. They remain compassionate to the last. When a burden, they instigate apoptosis, taking the genetic "suicide pill."

When Theo migrates to beyond, may this book
make great compost for minds to come.

54. I promise you never to ask you for a promise.

You could have leashed him with a promise. But you didn't. What generosity, what a gift! You trusted your heart to be creative and beamy enough to keep him in your love, wherever, whatever changes of course and appointments missed it takes him to fulfill his dreams.

And lucky you, Theo, who may change your course a thousand times and stay in her love.

Do you think it cruel to ask a snake to live in the same skin for years—or to ask a human her or him to see the world in the same baby way after they have tripped together three times around the world? Do you have such low expectations of her that you expect her to ford a creek at the same iffy spot as ten years before, or that she will love you for the same few reasons in ten years as she does now?

Stonewalling in conclusions sucks opportunities.

Promises are for old maids, crying, "Please, no! No! Spontaneity bewilders me!" Promises are children of the terror of change. Sometimes a promise is a simple tie up rope. It paralyzes vitality. It breeds envy. Stonewalling in conclusions sucks opportunities.

Here a hint: I run with my empty basket. I run and run through rain and hail trying to look straight. I get lost. Where,

where is the farm of the farmer from whom I promised to buy ten pounds of apples? In the corner of my eyes: fruit trees to my left, my right, all loaded down to the grass, enormous fruits everywhere and spilled on the ground begging for a taker. Green, red, sweet, purple, a yummy carpet of fruits, a banquet with clouds of rich apple perfumes. Free, free, for the taker. We are rotting! Yet Theo is in his tunnel. Theo made a promise. Soaked with rain and cussing he makes it to the farm. And the farmer is not home.

Think of your daring times. In that glorious excitement of all promises forgotten, every door flung wide open. You are invited to a feast of vitality, a time for serious encounters and responses! No hand rails, no fences. Enormous sparks, lightning of spontaneity. Don't postpone, here chances are as rare as sparks of iron! Think of the infidelity that finally broke Clara's pledge to her very structured religion. Opened, she became vulnerable to the tremendous flood of insights from all the mysterious and all the new—and her tolerance grew big. Saved from being an inmate of her baby shoes, she entered in the spell of the sensuous again.

Theo, I wish you a life of few appointments. In such openness, every minute teases you with a thousand invitations, unlimited opportunities—a kingdom for you that is filthy rich in options. Ah, the strength to remain inconsistent, playable, adaptable to every "now." Ah, to remain fit for a road system as rich as that of squirrels when you chase after that "lucky-you."

Spring promises: I will be back next year. Ah! God willing! Theo promises: I will grow toward the sun, Inshallah! And when the soft spring breeze sneaks up, caressing and melting that old snowfield in you, be ready. The spirit of betrayal is reaching for a higher truth with crocuses, fireweeds, the warmth of May, while that old snowfield has promised you more snow!

When looking back, I was a sheepish hoper and wisher. It's just hilarious what I learned to hope and wish for. I learned for instance to hope Theo would become some loaded CEO. What heartbreaking success I was taught to applaud!

Ah, the gift of spontaneity! A day with no dates, no expectations, no hopes, and no safety measures, a day I improvise, a day passionately uncertain and alive. When I squeeze a promise out of you and after ten years I expect you to still live within the limits of this promise, I am not your friend. I am your prison guard. There is a trust that does not need promises. There is a generosity I did not learn in school.

To never change his dear old self—what a misfortune for her or him!
No vows anymore for Theo. I am too dumb to read God's mind.

55. Imperfection, the good mother of tolerance

How could I fit in with you if you had nothing missing?

When I walk this permissive Earth with a by-the-book believer at my side, with any expert in goodness, with a world improver, I get an itch that I walk with a limousine passenger in an impeccable suit. His model may tolerate but the few freeways carved in bleeding straight lines through the soul of that man and through the soul of this wildly permissive Earth. It is said that his secure, well patrolled, well structured road system, with its many traffic signs, brings him or her with no growing pains, unharmed and unscarred swiftly to some no-hardship land yonder or here. Not much chance here to lock arms and to ford a creek together.

Now take a spontaneous man. At sparkling risks, that turn-any-way-you-please man remains a dangerously-wealthy-in-options man. Any fancy of God is a crossover for him. A log, a Golden Gate, a boulder, a pitcher of wine, a neck of a giraffe, a bear swimming, a well-placed lie, a wink of an eye, a Muslim, they are all options for him to cross a creek toward serenity land. Walking, that merry walking man makes his way, never quite sure in the morning how Life reshuffles his mind for that day, never quite sure what the Creator lets seep into his loose dogmas riddled with opportunities. So, meandering curiously along, holding onto the voices he hears inside him, that adventurer, ennobled with scars of learning from mistakes, risks bringing to Life's circus show a hocus pocus all of his own.

To make us tolerant and kind, is that not what making peace with our weaknesses, imperfections, missing talents and answers, the holes and the pliable morals in our character and our over-done cookies can do? Ask a rosebush: does she want a diamond or a dung pile for breakfast?

*These cracks and missing or overdone faculties in our charac-
ters allow the root systems of others to penetrate our hearts. So
rooted together we can stand into the winds and ford the creeks.*

56. We are walking boxes stuffed with gifts. We bow to each other, congratulating how impeccably we are wrapped.

It is inexpensive and easy to like a nice woman or man; I only need to like her "clothing."

Ah! But in a moment I am drunk with courage, I might get spirited beyond common sense and my eggshell of politeness breaks. I might overstep those keep-off signs. For this festive visit, I give my shield of politeness the day off. In this open sesame, a woman and a man surrender to each other. We drill test holes into each other. We look for wealth to add to our relationship that sur-face bonding cannot reach. And soon we bake together another cookie of love. Adventures begin! Wow! I find myself in her inner rainforest: orchids, tigers, snakes, chameleons, and ten-winged butterflies! Beyond her niceness every minute a new find! The jubilant chorus of a whole new jungle day awakening welcomes me in. Floods of aggressive light, rising and rising, terrifying the night dwellers and the nursery rhymes in my soul. Wildly permissive talents step into view—tipsy qualities she could never have brought to light in a prudent climate of niceness. And yes, many of our talents are still snoring. Once that beautifully embroidered night curtain is flung open, old, proud little starlets of common sense simply evaporate. What a reservoir of energy and intelligence starts heaving and rising from deep inside us. What a he, what a she!

With this outbreak, here I stand, in this packed storehouse that is you and me. Everywhere I am surrounded by yummy food for my deeper mind, piles of happenings we dream in movies about, that could feed our day nicely, still packaged and untouched. The prospect of a nourishing day!

From every niche Life laughs: "What? The survival of the fittest? In what? I am the fantastic Christmas tree. I invite the most productive guests and givers to linger a little longer at my feast. I am no stock exchange. I am an exchange of gifts. Every of my named and unnamed crawlers and wrigglers, the feared night dwellers too, are all laboring for me. Here, stealing or a sting is a welcomed gift. There a pot of honey is what I need. Even the part played by a man and woman in bed, cuddling, laughing about what music a joint meal of beans can produce, is needed for my show. Wait till I take off my mask. This opening of eyes is of the joy that sparkles in the children opening their Christmas gifts. See, your little Edens and your perfect democracies and your tea gardens are grotesque underestimations of the beauty of Life!"

Here I stand, in this garden lush and bursting with irrational wealth. How could I discard anything here offhand as a crime? Take any woman or man. So many muffled voices pleading from their within to become shouts, begging, "Let me live, let me run, hummer my husk, plant me in the sun!" Voices that are muffled by commands of "You must work! You must be nice!" When they are too long stepped on, they make her temper burst into flames. So many talents kept sound asleep, master strokes still waiting for the master, seeds that need to be cooked in the gizzard of one specific bird to sprout! Pine cones that need a forest fire to see the light and explode into pines. You talk about independence? There are thousands of latent talents in a man that only a brave woman can tease alive! Imagine, all these powers in wait—and still she bashfully plays Barbie, still he modestly chases a ball. So much treadling of exercise machines, while out there masses of fantastic ideas, ingenious designs, undiscovered friends burn to be chased down to play with her or him. "Theo, one step beyond your fears, and these adventures are yours. And whatever new steps and curls you add to your relationships will be your work of art."

As a woman so a man, we are such a wonderful gathering of seeds—
so many works of art in heat that want to copulate with you and
me and bring children forth in our hearts. Here waits our chance.

Theo, don't be so darn shy. Go, unwrap today
another of your gifts. Lick your bashfulness.

57. To be humble costs little and gives so much. What a bargain!

Do you like my mischievous passion for sniffing out likenesses from across the fence when we play together the game of questions and first answers that come to mind? Did you also note how our learned arrogant state of mind often squats forbiddingly right across our trail of learning, which winds up and up to confidence and serenity served by the rooftop view?

Think of our grafted-on notions of dualism and of idealism, of our punishing exemption theorem for mankind, or the punishing illusion of belonging to a god-chosen people. Think of the burdensome idea that we can be in bad hands and can wreck the universal laws with miracles and sins. Think of our maddening phantasm of free will, which is a horsefly that sucks our chance to completely forgive ourselves, and others too. These dead weight notions do not help us to fly high.

Chosen roosters kept spoiled and isolated in beautiful cages become smart, discreetly vicious and extremely competitive fighting cocks. I notice that people kept isolated in some glorified cage of elitism, in a god-chosen people, a superior race, or mankind rounded up in some exemption myth or some -ism, tend also to become such aggressive fighting cocks. Watch any people caged in such a deceiving notion and see whether I am not a little right. This "we-are-better-than" has turned out to be a nifty ruse of some ambitious patriarchs.

So many hints and likenesses point to this: "Look, we all are firmly in the good hands of the universal laws." I am finished with these gamblers and their fighting cocks—no cage anymore for that rooster in me. May he happily join the happy hens on the compost pile.

Yes, this exemption theorem for man turned out to be a sturdy placenta for my adolescent mind. It kept many insights, too rich to digest for little Theo, from seeping in. And it made me a willing follower. Here my thanks for doing what it had to do. That watery cushioning had to spill. It was this letting go, and what I must now face and see, that humbles me. In this initiation, doors are flung open. Whirlwinds of awesome wisdom might blow right through my living room—many leaks in the roof, the "frosting" on my life gone! I step out into a net of social skills so darn far out, it rough-handles my body and boggles my whimpering mind. Here is no doubt that the forces that move a madly cresting sea, the stars, the tyrants, the weather fronts, the forces that move the fingers on the mad Gipsy violin and very, very gently settle the morning dew, are all of the same Force that moves me. They compose my feelings, my thoughts, my everything. Sometimes they transport me into a clearing and tease me, "See, see, see!" Sometimes they blow a fat cloud into my eyes and delegate me to do some brewing or some wrecking job. Is that degrading?

How now not to be sweetly humbled when realizing that with each footstep, careless or with elegance, I step on countless critters, each outdoing and out-enduring any of our works of art. I see myself as no master anymore, but as a lifelong apprentice and observer, still unfit for any serious, moral judgment or complaint.

A man humbles himself, and he can learn from mistakes and successes not only among us, but also from among any family member of Life. He can start his collection of metaphors. Later, scientists can use these collections as guides for their research and their gentler technologies. Here is where creativity starts.

I like that such creativity may cause a soft landing of the paradigm shifts when these insights first take off from poetry. Science tends to crash-land such terrifying news onto us.

My faith that we are not orphans but rather taken care of by the mother of all laws, my faith that Grace cannot be broken, that no good or bad miracles can happen—this persuasion has become my catalyst to make peace with my shadow. For me, here starts the only possible better world. Accepting a greater organizing force than us some may call God, others whatever, is fruitful, humbling, a psychological masterstroke that gives tolerance and forgiveness a roomier playground.

Yet, humbleness is a risky place. It may reveal more than we can take. Whoever cannot swim in the wild wisdom stream yet does not hold on to some kind of log or raft of faith is going to sink.

58. The good news: There is only Good News!

(The dear old critic in me will have fits reading this news.)

Always haunted by the desire for certain "good" news and for certain "bad" news, according to what team I joined in the match, yesterday, out of the deep blue, a voice rose up from inside me: "No more taking sides! Left-winged birds and right-winged birds do not make good flyers. From now on, there will be only one kind of news: good news. 'Bad' news, like 'bad' deeds, are the experiments that tell you: 'Not through here, try there!' They reveal to you the poisonous mushrooms. You remember their advice. For this they deserve your thanks. Whatever you hear, smell, touch, meet, see, the newscast on TV, from now on, it's going to be simply revelations, bit by tiny bit, of the unbelievably wondrous affair Life has with the Earth."

This affair has remained mostly beyond comprehension for me. So I fret and kick. No, no, and no. This has to be bad news, and that murderous bad man too! Yet that blue voice insists, "My dear little boy, you joined a lesson in Life's biology. Be patient, this is good news for adults! Follow Life's news story back and forth. Whip on your imagination a little more. Don't insist that the story must always keep a human face—or justify itself within your garden fence. Soon some joyful face with whiskers or a beak may also pop up behind that fence while you fret and blame. Joy in confrontation, joy in holding hands, joy in welcoming your pains of learning, joy of swans winging south, joy of children in the monsoon flood splashing in the street. All your motives have motives hidden from you. You try to be mean? Theo, be patient— soon a hidden hand will touch you discreetly, maybe from far away, offering you a thank-you and a smile."

It's these kind of tricks my faith in the goodness of Life plays on me. It is also this faith always tickling me that has become my North Star to find my trail out of misery.

Now, when I listen to the news, I am a little cocky when I can resist the temptation for a while to take sides and smartly bash, bang or shuffle my money into some pocket in applause. Her Holiness, the North Wind, added hints for me to see light in that darn secret of Life, telling me, "All living things wish Life well. We are all slaves to the highest of moral codes." I am still struggling at the feet of this haughty point of view. To realize beyond repair that to decry any act that Life ever tried out is a sacrilege, what a devastating blow to my dear troupe of blames. How much of my expensive armor would become worthless with such a truce!

And the consequences? While you have an angry, menacing night tossing you around, I might not be able to share your anger. I would have to sculpt thoughts that are good news for you instead. I would have to fashion little notes that are a fresh sea breeze waiting in the morning at your bedside. My heart would become all Gipsy violin on which Life loves to play the wildest, sexiest music for you. What would I not give to become master in this trade?

And here is the best news in the long news week of the cosmos: A little pile of mud started to blink—and see! This good news, by and by, has become you and me.

Left-winged birds and right-winged birds do not make good flyers!

59. Indoor and outdoor justice

Hints toward a wonderful paradigm shift.

Wild justice is made in the bushes, hopelessly out of the reach of my reasoning, which does not like to go far from home. Out there, countless players, generations, and species amicably play together the justice-game. No way to keep a book of all the bills and payments that crisscross the Earth in one single day. Only blind faith in the goodness of Life can save me from getting completely hoarse from shouting foul of what I see.

The dear compositions of justice we create in our books that should sound sweet and obvious to us are still just playful sandcastles made from mental scraps we pick up here and there. The next big wave or calamity sweeps them away. And how many times have we ourselves kicked in these buildings in pursuit of a sturdier concept? While we demand to see, smell and know God's justice, resisting that humbling faith, no wonder, we must put up with seeing so much wrong in Life and are bogged down with needless lawsuits, heroism, anger, and revenge—until we give in to this faith.

In a curious lad that takes off for scenic viewpoints, by and by, some designs that are less uneven with knots of injustice may assemble in that adventuring mind. He becomes less upset about Life's justice. Broken-off ends start to find their way and hold hands. There is less need to send in truckloads of food where the good spirit of fall already clears that land, pays back some debts to the soil, and makes it rich again for a new crop. To be a basher of God starts to look more like squandered time to this lad. A sip of serenity has seeped into him.

In this big world of countless mysteries, in this world in which my nearsightedness often makes me angry because I can see only a man's crooked share of love, I make one step up the staircase to the rooftop. Surprise, surprise, up there some of these crookeries and angers might join and bake into a pecan pie for angry, hungry Theo! Thank God, I can think of a woman's pregnancy and her nine months of unpaid labor. Here is "injustice" within my scope that I can easily adjust. Or I can think of a violent pressure, up and up and up, with no relief. Now, millions of years later, the Earth opens her hands, and lo! Here are your majestic peaks of the Himalaya Range. Life has pregnancies lasting millions of years.

We are ranch ducks that pledged allegiance to the farmer's rule. We waggle and haggle with the farmer about our provision of corn and his provision of our meat. Yet, we still sometimes do fly over the fence, go on a fun errand, and dig for our own kinds of worms, instead of nicely, justly, munching "free" grain for the meat we provide.

The long philosophy of Life reads: *Earth-Justice*. Imagine here a courtroom where every species has a member in the jury box when justice is made.

The short philosophy of our mind-culture and our agriculture reads: *Less for them and more for man*. With genetic engineering, we now infect the very genetics of other species with our crooked justice. And they must comply. (Think Newleaf potato, miracle soya, super salmon, Monsanto corn.) As you see, we too have mostly become the garden-variety do-gooders. But wait, we are learning! Our new fascination with Earth First! justice is our latest step up to this upper room of justice.

And so we listen to questions like that of a young inquisitive stand of spruce, living along the Lisa Creek, that wants to know, "Theo, how many of us would you deem justified to be cut down to keep up a frail child, ready to lie down? How many acres of grassland would you gladly, justly pave over to speed up a man who has slowed down, ready to go home? How many hours of labor could you justly demand from your children to secure a life extension for a setting man? How high a wall for stopping a setting sun?"

In a telephone conversation with the Earth, she told me that last century we passed the tipping point of our sustainable advantage grab and are now maxed out on our credit cards with the Earth. She told me that Life has a clearinghouse for compensations, where claims are settled. And we must expect to pay compensation in a way that will break the backbone of our old commonsense justice.

Take courage, Theo, from the fox and the hare. These players got creative to overcome. They found their way to harmonize the relationship they now enjoy. They adapted their breeding and their table manners. Our Earth-First! people have learned from the foxes and the hares at great political risk. They have started to talk with the woods and the oceans on equal terms, and include these players when justice is made in our courts. Yet what outrage in our little jury boxes, which are nailed closed and full of obscure small talk, when a hand touches their lid!

Life is good. When my mind gets burnt in one of its very hot justice-games, one of our own little constructs of justice can offer me a temporary indoor swimming experience and a fresh shower to top it off. When a species is caught in an extreme situation, Life can arrange such indoor games. She lets us, for instance, create our rest stops made of music—a brief manmade tiny island of obvious, perfectly harmonious justice fitting nicely a whining intellect, a tea garden of sounds, a brief relaxing isolation with the illusion that nothing needs to be done. She accommodates Nanuk, the great white bear, when winter tells a story too cold for her. She provides her with a den to slumber in. If the daisy demanded immediate justice from the tectonic pressure that pushed it up and higher up to where it caught a cold and insisted, "No and no! Don't you do that to me!" then I would never wake to the glory of morning when the awaking sun paints the glaciers behind my house with all its magnificent blues and reds.

And now, when I burn to get even with her or him, or have the lawyer do the job for me, such muffled hints have become loud and welcome hints again. They can soothe my angry "not-fair!" with a massage, give me a back rub when I am among cheaters, hose me down when I am on fire with revenge.

I heard tell of a judge and his accused rascal who both became fascinated with telling each other their life stories. When they realized that all life stories ultimately become the threads woven into Life's beautiful quilt, they became so excited about their common work of art, they forgot all about the boring business of guilty or not.

Theo, don't look too close to the early Greeks or to early Christianity for inspiration for Earth justice. Theirs was a local, humanistic justice, a justice still in its egg waiting to hatch. Their mental model of Man-first-Earth-second is now overdue to hatch.

Here my thanks for the brave legislators who laughed off Washington's teams of puny professional whisperers and put aside protected areas of this gifted planet where Life can do its very large things without being continuously pestered by our puny sense of justice.

60. The ocean experience

Great fishes are fished in the ocean. "Theo, don't fish in your aquarium. Fish in the ocean!

"Great, proven ideas are not fished from the little bag of your own memory. This bag is reserved for your experimental garden. You transplant a few promising ideas to this experimental plot. You manipulate them back and forth, with no success guaranteed. Here are your tinker toys and your Legos. Theo, take heart, go for the ocean experience. For a Sunday treat, stop that tinkering, that gardening, that inner gurgling, that reading, that scheming, that department thinking. Fling windows open in your stuffy memory, with its dead furniture. Take that deep breath of looking outside. Watch a spider weave. Watch the raven at their sky acrobatic parties playing against the winds. Follow the mighty currents of the oceans powered by the mighty winds bringing life-sustaining circulation, serving the ocean people huge plates of food. In short: become aware. Go for the zillion-synapse experience. There, among uncountable bundles of lively, delightful memories, crawling, flattering, sprouting, singing, your own memory's synapses are just

Take heart, go for the ocean experience.

the few sheep corralled and grazing in one single brain, some goldfish nicely installed in a bowl."

A man visits a Muslim land and is invited in. Wow! So many exotic mind forms he has never seen! Some sting. Others are so, so sweet in a Muslim land. Here tenderness and lies wear different coats than in the mental climate of a Christian land. There are different offenses, different hugs. Here sweet gentleness may not be made of honey but of sugarcane. The visitor from the United States gets a little Muslim-drunk. Then a man gets drunk of all he has touched, heard and seen. It is these encounters that brew the liquor for his most persistent drunkenness.

Or think here of a very large soul who overrides all the departments of a university. He unites all that is cooked in these orderly kitchens of mental food in one single delicious banquet for his friends. The chef of each department is ordered to bring up and serve his best plates of food, gets his applause, and is sent back to his kitchen again for cleanup. At this very merry, very undisciplined feast, the dean, the administrator, the security guards, the canons of scientific thought have no place and are given the day off. At this merry feast of generosity any fence would be considered an offense. This is what a great poet does.

When Theo sails in this way out of himself, he submits himself to a vision larger than his latest memories. Lost memories talk to him again. Memories are retrieved in their powerful originality, not substitutes cooked up by the media. That ocean fishing has a sweet, therapeutic effect on a fisher of the beauty of Life. The fisher gets involved again in greater things and forces than mankind. In such a volcanic moment a spell may break its hold on him. His power from deep down rises up again to stretch his imagination so darn much that he can for the first time clearly picture the consequences of his padded, "non-negotiable" lifestyle on his mindscape, and on the Earth alive.

Just now leaving the angry open sea behind, white rollers still on my heels. My boat, the *Onyx*, runs me on autopilot through Sergius Narrows bucking a five-knot tidal current, the Chrysler-

Nissan purring like a bee. Hoonah Sound lies ahead. The quietness of six hundred square miles of inside water awaits me, with the Tongass National Forest surrounding the scene. I will set there and tomorrow pull my long line gear for halibut, the same way a Kalahari woman smoothly dib-dabs, jar balancing on her head, back from the well. What we love to do turns into rhymes and becomes beautiful.

What we love to do turns into rhymes and becomes beautiful.

For living my own life in such fullness, I do not want to consult with the crowd. If I had done so, I would be probably some mediocre CEO by now.

May others enjoy the safety of tennis courts, the swing, slide, and playgrounds, the beautiful wooden play-fishes, the gyms and the concert halls. I feel alive and well when I am on the wild, full-blooded playground of the sea. This older brother continuously tells stories to me.

61. Welcome to the glorious world of contradictions. Here is room to spare for every imaginable Yes and No.

On the ocean beaches, young vacationers are sunbathing, laughing, worshiping the sun, and yet are also weary of little clouds far down the horizon. Barely noticed, a fleet of vapors silently lifts from the ocean and heads loaded for the hills.

On the other side of the hill: a long expectant, sunbaked silence, weary of no clouds! No clouds! And then the tremendous downpour. Children in Rajasthan are splashing in the flooded streets, celebrating. The rice is drinking, the monsoon is providing.

Life is a wide and deep river. Some of us are happy to wade merrily along the familiar bank of spontaneity with no self-discipline, no denials and stress to bother about. They feel confident. They surrender to what comes naturally and what is proven, and they are having fun. Others, in somber dignity, on the opposite bank of that great turbulent river, roll up their pants a little and very, very seriously tiptoe along that opposite shallow shore roped off for non-swimmers with grim self-discipline, hoping for a reserved deck chair in some yonder merry land.

A few, don't ask me why, are a guesthouse of many spirits. We need it both ways. We dive in and under, swim, wade, surf and skim. We commute between spontaneity and self-discipline and we also do and think all kinds of fun things right in the middle of that great stream, like catching deep water fishes and deep ideas that we are not supposed to mix with the catch of those fished in the shallows. With so wide and deep a river of options to play with, what a treat! How could we resist becoming a little creative? Here our spiritual impulses get their elbow room to go wherever they must go to assemble their work of art. And we do not forget in our equations that half the streams discreetly stream up and away from the sea, that hate and love, repulsion and attraction, honey and thorns are forces Life combines, stirs, and cooks into all kinds of delicious jams.

A love for spontaneity together with a love for firm self-discipline, here is sweet contradiction. When young, I learned to pray, "Please free me from temptations." Not anymore. I found the duel between my instinct and my reason to be one of Life's most fruitful tools to create high voltage and new situations. It's a catalyst for creativity.

A Gipsy guitar, please, that wakes up the ten thousand
birds in my roost of sleepers, and makes them sing!

62. Caterpillars metamorphose— so do we.

A ripe, fat caterpillar retires from the crowd of munchers and crawlers. Solitude! So preoccupied with munching leaves, she barely ever noticed before how the great forest is hugging her. After a long silent retreat, a loud relentless urge. Metamorphosis starts tremendous transformations in future Ms. Butterfly. And then the rebirth. Gently pumping and pumping, she inflates wings that flutter her up into a high from where she sees a world she has never before seen. Nothing unnatural. And don't think for a moment that metamorphosis is the privilege of just those little munchers.

A humanistic mind has also munched and haggled for advantages and run back and forth its share. Stuck up to the neck in a pile of men and their work, that future flyer has barely ever seen the vast work and the vast laws of the outdoors. One full moon, a long quiet incubation comes over her or him. People behind his back whisper: but he has become weird! Yes, in weird tremors, cracks appear in what he thought he knew for sure. In that metamorphosis: confusion, confusion! All of a sudden a gaping split in his comfy, softly lit cocoon woven of humanistic paradigms! A tremendous burst of light is hitting her and changes her dim view beyond repair.

And is not each man drunk on whatever she or he has touched, heard and seen, making him stay low or get high? Soon, out of that cracked cocoon wriggles a completely re-engineered, bewildered mind that rubs its eyes and rubs them again. Liberated from down under, that mind unfolds wings, which wing that new-born flyer tipsily high, maybe clear out of sight and comprehension of his fellow croppers with their feet on solid ground. In this upper scene, beyond a world made for man, our law books become rather insignificant children's compositions on how to order the Earth. The great Laws of Life become visible and want to guide her or him. Vast devastation in the commonsense way she used to see, to value, to condemn, to applaud! Many fun camaraderies and warm feelings belonging to the folks' well-grounded disconnect. Short-wired connections burn up. Goals get trashed. Yet with an "oh-I-never-guessed," painfully lonely ideas unexpectedly start holding hands in this new visibility.

There is nothing unnatural in this kind of liberating divorce. It's just that life reorients some adult souls to do other jobs. People down under want their wine. Up on their platforms in space, the gang of poets and seer-scientists are drunk enough on what they see to brew the sweetly intoxicating ideas that sway into confidence the croppers who labor so hard in their offices, their sugarcanes, their mines.

And now it's getting time that my good old fisher's garments should not be mended anymore, so I can fly a little above the fleet of fishers to simply have a conversation with the Earth and become an apprentice again. So when my old fisher's way of seeing things tells me mean-spiritedly, "Ball your fist! Clench your mind!" I may also secretly be a little amused.

Theo, when you are caught in a crowd and you get that itchy feeling that you are out of step, don't get nervous. You are not alone. Caterpillars metamorphose too.

63. To forgive—or to annihilate the need to forgive.

I tiptoed along my whole repertoire of steps. This cannot be said without stepping on old feelings. Does the caribou need to forgive the wolf?

I forgive. Again I did not rise to the challenge: become creative; find the brighter viewpoint for this unappreciated happening in

Life's working. Again I stuck with the crowd of blamers who manage to repeat but that old, raw and hurtful story for this demonized happening and to repeat that hurtful story again, over and over. With my arrogant, "I forgive" I evaded that challenge. I made the cheap deal with myself: to not bother to ever enter deeper into the mysteries of Life—or to not ever talk about and explore with her her wondrous inner wildlife refuge. I missed my chance to make peace with one of my shadows. Figuring out a more accommodating story for that ugly duckling, I might have come up with a beautiful swan and incorporated that mischievous bundle of joys into the vast beauty of life. And gone with it my need to accuse and to forgive!

Take courage, Theo, think of what we lately did with the vicious story of the viruses. To forgive them? We now honor some of these nifty little rascals for being expert ferrymen and vectors of genes! And by the day they take on more cheerful colors. They became the darlings of genetic engineering. We discovered that without their help, Life could have never embroidered its carpet with such a profusion of beautiful designs. Remember, when you put her down or blame him: instead, create a new, more accommodating and amusing story of her, him or it. Do this instead of calling them discreetly an asshole and later haughtily forgiving them; this is first-class creativity.

Life is a story of breaking camps. Life gallops. It leaves the forgivers with their unimaginative "don't-you-do-that-again!" behind. We are on an expedition into thin air, up and up toward what? Toward making of hell one more lovable place! Toward giving mud a set of eyes! But that's like stealing the fisherman's good old coat! Nonetheless, that's exactly what that fairy tale of the ugly toad turned into a royal swan tells us. Is it an offense that a mind seeks to produce less garbage and less need for garbage dumps and jails? Is it a crime that a man wants to get rid of his sack full of "I-forgive-you" that he has been dragging along?

Did you ever hear in Blue Blossom Land anything that sounds like "forgive me," or "I am sorry" or "I blame you"? Does Ms. Moon need to be forgiven for being lazy and getting up, each day, a little later, or for not paying utility bills to Mama Sun?

Imagine, we could go beyond merely becoming good at forgiving. We could completely outgrow and forget about this minor's need and throw away forgiveness, like our baby shoes. Be done with accusations! Let every encounter be a safari! Isn't that what a grown-up heart can afford to do?

A better world or a paradise seems to me not a grotesquely peaceful place but a fantastic state of mind where nothing, absolutely nothing, needs a pardon. This hunch pursues me. Whenever I am mad and get ready to degrade you with my priestly I-forgive-you, this hunch pats on my shoulder. And I get a little less sure about being mad.

Clara, you have always been reluctant to simply forgive me. You do better. You rather tease me to tell my unedited story with ever more hidden details and lo! some ugly toads in our relationship have taken on colors, becoming lovable and beautiful.

And now tell me: how could I be kind to you if I never learned to be kind to myself and to honor my own crooked, curly love?

64. Inbreeding of the mind

Imagine that you parachute into the heart of the Amazon. Touching down, you are surrounded by millions of signals—love calls, magnificent forms, critters, exotic colors, perfumes, all whispering, shouting, begging, "Read me! I want to be seen and heard! I am full of strategies that want to mate with your strategies!" Gorgeous clusters of wisdom and designs, all hot to make love with what you know. The land drips with generosity wherever you look. What a place to rejuvenate the flexibility of a mind. Yet in this magnificent place of power and beauty you plug your mind into your iPod, or bury it in a book while waiting to be again picked up. Now would that not be an incestuous mind?

I wonder here: Does the love affair we have with the written language, or with the digital natives of the screen have comparable effects on our mind to what lovemaking with siblings has to the health of our body? Such inbreeding may well engender a highly focused yet sickly imbalanced mind that soon catches an anger in a weather front and loses its foothold, while the emotional intelligence gets a little paler by the day. The reason why our root-nature discourages us from becoming such shameless informers exclusively among ourselves is one of the darndest secrets of Life that few of us explore.

Now think of the opposite: of a hermit, a man who leaves our society for a while to become more widely social, a man who chooses to breed his mind not just with mankind but cross-pollinates his thoughts with the thoughts of the bats that swarm in his evening sky, or asks the dragonflies their opinion on how to fly, or listens to the silence of the night for advice. He is fascinated with wondering how other families of Life deal with the problems we face. Think of what forty days and nights of solitude in the company of the desert song did to the mind of Jesus. Did you ever promise yourself not to read for a week? Is it our illusion of grandeur and of being the purpose of creation that seduced us to become mentally so elitist and so incestuous? Is it for the lack of mental variability that we find ourselves now so stuck in a meager pile of self-serving alphabetic thinking? Creation myths have consequences on the endurance of our good relationship with the land. Slowly I have been opening up my elitist belief system of man's stewardship to one of participation. This downgrading is such a relief! Back home from a thousand years of loneliness!

65. The stampede syndrome

A man never walks quite as aware as when he walks alone.
A lone buffalo never runs over cliffs.

Just walking together with a friend can trigger a little carelessness, even a seed of mass-hysteria, to germinate in her or him. A crowd is such a lullaby. It is said that a buffalo that runs alone never runs over cliffs. Also a man is never as sharp as when he is all on his own. Maybe five thousand days and nights alone on the oceans, fishing, has taught me to prick my senses and be aware.

Take a team of ten creative scientists. They might be a little less creative than ten individual creative scientists each working on his own. That group feeling lowers the team workers' guards. Likewise, twenty individual countries and cultures are each probably more responsible, more creative, more on their toes than when lumped together in a European Union. Our ancestors were more aware of the hermit effect and valued the advice of their outpost people.

In groups and teamwork I hold my pee. I hesitate to swat a horsefly bothering me. It's harder to say that firm "no" and rock the boat. Mistakes love us in groups. They get their way more easily. For instance, mass murder seems less of a murder for the milling masses than it is for a man running alone. For a crowd, atrocities seem less atrocious, a cliff less of a cliff. When in great numbers, we become less responsible, a little dumber and more complacent. Compassion, the highest intelligence, gets narrowed down to smartness. That timely mental affliction makes a man so darn self-conscious, a strategy for bare survival. That emergency high-voltage thinking allows him to burn up one gallon of his inner energy to bulldoze one mile through the thicket of man.

In a population explosion, whether among buffaloes, lemmings, arctic hares or men or in any monoculture, a species surrounds itself densely with copies of its own. Buffaloes drowning in buffaloes! A boat, please, for my solitude! I am drowning in a flood of men, of the same legs running, of the same minds in synch thinking, same needs, same internet gossip. Clouds of parrots imitate each other, commiserating. Clouds of loose leaves, driven by some fashion wind, obscure my view. More of the same as far as I can see! Think of the internet. How not to lose your foothold and imitate in this most enormous and most contagious of all our gatherings? It's poor soil for creativity.

Emerging new ideas are quite defenseless babies. They need some kind of placenta or other solitude to fend off criticisms while in gestation. Caught in a sameness cloud, how am I to stretch my neck high enough to remain information rich?

What I deep down love is outshouted by the shouters of our economy. In this steaming mass, drunk with the brew of too much man, in this irresistible scenario for our extraordinary talent to imitate, how to avoid being stripped of my individual responsibilities? The wild, vast world, mother of my inspirations and my personal orientation, so full of ingenious designs and advice, this compass and search engine for my deeper mind, becomes clogged with men. In this impoverished environment the wise old weeds get out of sight, the mocking birds, the green runners and creepers, the great contours and the morals of the great seasons of the Earth get out of sight. The eloquent quietness of the night, the wise environment beyond the city of man, which is meant to be my GPS to keep my love on track, gets jammed.

Ask any captain—he knows what a five pound wrench mislaid close by his compass does to his sense of orientation. That's what the five pounds of my learned smartness does when I let it overwhelm the compass of my deep, emotional intelligence.

This meager visibility crammed with men is the scenario for stampede. It gets harder to hold on to my own will and steering power, Far-off things start to happen that in unhurried times I thought just could not happen. At great sacrifice, life looks feverishly for new options—epidemics of prodigal smartness, collective egotism, dumbness of the hearts, confused orientation, stern humanism, a messed up sequence of importance, idealism, blind politicians and bankers turned to legalized robbers. This thundering sameness crowd can sweep my meandering curiosity away. Rushing along with the stream of rushers, my deeper sense of orientation loses its waypoints.

In this hectic scenario, our deep need for continuance in our relationships, so they may take deep roots, does not do well. (Transplant a tree three times in one year and it will die.)

I am thinking here about an unnamed epidemic spreading in a worldwide flood of people that reminds me of a gentle form of autism—the struggle to read and interpret emotions of others. When ever busy with defenses, our neural pathways to mirror other people's needs and feelings may remain underdeveloped. Mirror neurons become luxuries. Stress-related hormones, like cortisol, do their work. And so, for getting advice, our forebears have been more trusting of their hermits than of the storming, steaming troops of some mediacracy.

But wait! This enormously routine-breaking happening might not be in vain. There is a very, very precious residue in its fallout.

We are not alone and not the first. It is said that for example in some rodent population explosions a comparable correction happens periodically to these nibblers. In such extraordinary times, Life starves also in these restless animals their sense of orientation. It's their genetic policing that makes them aimlessly err around and brings down their numbers. But wait—and lo! A precious few, groping far removed from their bare-nibbled home sweet home and routine, finally climb through thin air or fall over cliffs and err into new valleys, new environments, new options to create new homes. The most creative among our "lost" refugees refuse to be lost. Spontaneously they may take a sad child, a sad stand of trees or a sad coral reef by its hand and call it "mine." They nurse and make good where we failed. It's their new way to build their new family home.

Thank you. Yes, in this present mental weather front that wonder can happen. I hit a clearing—and I step over my fear and cussing right into it. Wow! This doesn't look so discouraging! I make out in Life a strangely benevolent feedback system with a dose of corrective self-destruction at work. I see how Life helps a runaway growth forward to a new moderation and to the center again. I definitely see help I never learned to applaud. This gets exciting. Call this discreet helper "environment dominated genetics," call it "The Holy Spirit," call it whatever. Here is hope for a grim mind angry at Life.

I need now a different drunkenness than that of a crowd ecstatically drunk by the thundering mass spirit of a soccer game. A mug of solitude, please, for him, her, or me who needs to see beyond a thundering global herd that stampedes to does-any-body-know-where.

Lucky you, who could remain a straggler left behind
or in front. Lucky are the stray dogs.

66. My relationships are my lovebirds that are passionately alive.

Before she cuddles into her night blankets, her guardian spirits want to know, "Claudia, did you feed Ery, your parrot, did you water the geraniums, and Kelly your darling dog too? And now, what yummy plates of food did you serve today to your relationships that want to dart to every hidden talent a woman or man is able to grow?"

The moment a relationship does not move, change, grow, or reach for the moon, it's dead meat. Every instant our togetherness wants to be fed bits of energy food. And we are way more nourishing for each other than we dare to think! Thousands of dark niches, secrets, hidden resources, huge untapped aquifers, riddles, passions in hiding, underground fires of anger needing to cool, shaking hands in the open. Golden talents buried waiting for a miner, seabirds that need a job on the ocean, broom handles longing for a broom, stupendous enthusiasm skipping uncontrolled in high waves in need of an anchor. High temper is looking for a mediator, eggs that have been dreaming sperms for years. There are her thunders and lightning that tell of an imminent spring rain ready for a beggar to beg it down. A grief is desperately in need of reconciliation. You cradle it in your warm hands and out of this love in tears flies a bird of joy! He begs her, "Give me your eyes, so I can see what you see." And what does he see? She cradles seven dreams in her heart that he has never before met, and they are so desperate to become true! For years her neck, her shoulders and her seven secret talents have silently been begging to be touched. These are the plates of food a relationship wants to be served. This is the clay we thumb and knead into our beautiful relationship that becomes our only works of art worth their sweat.

May many chances for reconciliation happen to me. Each is a precious gift. Theo, for your luck's sake, grab it, quickly! Add a new balcony to your relationship.

You and I, we are wagons full of beggar artists, all begging, protesting to be let out and onto the stage. Yet, people everywhere are stumbling through storehouses loaded with piles of delights still wrapped in boxes. And these bored people moan, "What is there to do?"

You look at me. Instantly pictures of us two light up and swarm in front of you. The sum of those pictures, that's you and me! May your memory have many, many pictures to light up, so you may never have to step into a dark alley when we meet, so that you and I may be a large and bright mosaic.

Yet, look. He settled for life in the same dull, comfy notion of good and evil, the same old slippers, the same macho talk and heroes. He is sleeping! How can it be that he still wears his baby shoes?

The gist of it: to live not a single day without breaking an expectation, a promise, a routine, one of yesterday's goals. Go; crush a fat boulder into my fortress wall! Make me the gift of another window in my common sense.

In winter, tulips curl up underground. In a drought of adventure and love, a relationship does the same. Go hibernate, live on your reserves while they last. When the rain does not come, a toad may retire in a ball of mud for years.

Each morning, The Book of Changes wants my yesterday trashed, so I enter a new day without ballast. Ask the kernel of a cherry how the bursting of that husk feels, the husk that was so dear to that little curled up tree when snow was here.

Are we not all eternal kernels playing that husk-and-burst-the-husk game, over and over? On one side: my terror of change, inertia, barely more than a chick in the egg. On the opposite side: Life, that Gipsy queen, a true vagabond, always out for a grand bash and ready to leave home. Don't expect her to be made of just potato chips, niceness, eggs, Kleenex, soap and sex. She is an Amazon!

No, our encounters do not need to remain as crude as the broom handle that finally falls in step with a broom!

67. My wealthy thoughts are my vagabonds. I give them my blessing: Go and trespass!

As a monkey so a thought, they do not like to be tied up, to be put to work, to perform. It's their joy to be passionately alive and go as they please. Their monkey business with every critter, opportunity and mystery are their love affairs. Exuberant thoughts do not want to be confined in domains and bottled in conclusions. Any interruption is a gift for them—a precious new rag to be woven into their wisdom-quilt. In an environment of manic objectivity with structured lessons, structured writing and loving, structured homework and thinking, these laughing, shining thoughts risk becoming lame plants pulled out of the ground, good only for processing. In my world, everything has become part Theo, part of every other domain, part of the universe.

You have a young, adventurous mind sitting down to write a thesis: "Stick to your subject; deliver a conclusion!" What a grudge you have invented for that inquisitive, freedom-loving lad! Life will give you ten lashes for this crime! Yes, this is how we lasso a wild mind, corral it and break it in to perform or pull a plow. Yes, this is the crime needed when faultless usefulness is bred, making a spontaneous, wise mind melt down and be minted into coins of smartness. When, per chance, a thought sneaks again to the surface for a rich breath of a sexy multiview—"Down with that shameless spontaneity; concentrate! This is not a place for poets!" Swiftly that "misbehaved" thought, just curiously peeking about, is ordered back into line. Soon a mind prevails in which every dimension but practicality is suppressed. Experts are expected to build cages for what they think they know. For adventurous minds, though, to father a fruit bearing thought has remained part of their sex lives with its very own joyous *zim-bum-tralalalas*. Lucky you, who is not an inmate of a highly structured lifestyle!

Awareness is a quality of passivity, with no scheming, no mulling fish prices, no judging, and no blaming monopolizing the screen. I sneak out of mankind's own little garden of memories that is a narrow bird cage for my awareness to fly about with mostly just crumbs of highly processed food for the picking. All gates are open. Welcome out! Here begins the "crime" of inclusiveness! I shake hands with that motley crowd of enemies and friends, of deserters and disasters, weeds and unsellable sights, ideas and things. "Sit down, please. Be my guests! Tell me your story!" Land that is still wildly in love gladly pours affluence into any soul that is thirsty and willing to drink. This is Sunday or Sabbath, a time of absorbing and learning, a soma sacrifice—truly, the time of surrender. During these gatherings my polarity is given the day off.

Once upon a time a very inquisitive little bluebell turned iconoclastic. Slowly, clumsily, battered by many errors stretching its neck, it turned itself into a bluebell tower never before seen, and it gave itself a new name. In a creative hand, this is what daring to be different and absent minded can do. This is what not just to fish in the aquarium of one's own memories can do. These are the marvels that the tools of disobedience, disagreement, irreverence, and impudence can create. Life seems to be fond of these kinds of adulteries and divorces.

Interspeciation has proven more fruitful for my interchange of ideas than our own species' global internet. With so many more ideas on the market, a more nourishing soup is on the stove waiting for me. Mankind, even on global scale, is a small fishing pond for ideas.

As I see it, it is a thought's acquaintance with every imaginable culture, subject and species that gives it its resilience and its breadth. The gist is to ask Life all around, "How do you sculpt out of all these shreds of obscure, often offensive ideas, such bright bundles of joy?" And what I am shown makes me a little tipsily high.

68. On my way to make peace with an old, old shadow in my heart, I look left and right to fellow species. I note, Life sometimes asks of her sons and daughters a painful reorientation.

In the "crisis" of the bare and cold winter, Life asks the badger: go and hole up deep underground, to slumber and dream safely. In an extremely dry and scorching desert season, the Good Mother begs the Palo Verde and the Ocotillo to literally strangle and shed their meager crop of leaves (apoptosis): "Go, celebrate a season of bareness and retreat! This is the help I need from you right now." Here is love and goodness at work; here is a moral at work that commands a change of morals.

In a cataclysmic change of climate or in the explosion of a population, Life force-feeds a species' male qualities and stifles its female qualities. It may enhance aggression, egotism, cannibalism, exploration, consciousness, perversions, inventiveness, creativity, daring, reasoning, and mutations. Anything goes that puts a brake on reproduction. In short, in Life's wonderful play of evolution all morals become subject to adaptation.

As a child I sometimes got carried away, gobbling unripe cherries and plums. Life induced me to throw up what I was not prepared to take on and digest well. Life commanded Clara in her youth to simply faint and lie low when a situation was beyond her physical or mental capacity (like a long church ceremony on an empty stomach). In a mental confrontation that is beyond what a man can take on and digest, Life may help this helpless man to clam up in some fundamentalism, or hole up in sarcasm, or in arrogance, or to nicely gobble up potato chips in front of a TV show. In a great flood, the Good Mother may confuse my dearest routines, maybe making me sleep in a treetop or on the roof. When Susi, our neighbor's dog, lost her litter, she did the forbidden and nursed our orphaned kittens. A pregnant tigress falls into captivity or a pregnant stingray gets hooked by Theo the fisherman, and their souls cry, "Oh no, not now! This is no time for birthing." And they still-birth their litter! When sick with too many men, the Earth gets indigestion and starts to lose its colors. Life, with its magic toolbox of genetics, whispers some of us into becoming sleepers, activists, druggies, poets, shamans, singles, video gamers, playboys, digital girls, Earth First warriors. Anything goes that is a stick in the wheels of a runaway population growth. The bravest of us Life may ready for creativeness and to err into new options.

When I watched the Universal Lawyer laughing good-heartedly, amused by our dear self-styled commandments, when

I first watched her outrageously flexible wisdom at work, my own little bag of strict morals got me all angry and confused. Unimpressed, her sharp blade kept on cutting down what sprouted too far into the season of fall. It must be saved underground, maybe sleeping in roots, in tubers, maybe turned into tasty compost. In her October Song, every minute zillions of seeds, still barely sprouting, barely broken out of their husks, are cut down, abiding the Lawyer's blade. Out of a hundred pregnancies, out of a thousand eggs, out of a billion spores, just a couple mature individuals! Out of one cherry tree with a carpet of rotting cherries underneath, just one new mature cherry tree every fifty years!

Did you get wind by now of what serious mischief I have up my sleeve? I am confusing my old common sense of what is right and natural. And for good reason. Dandelions, gigantic sequoias, Theo and Clara, we all abide by that Lawyer's blade. I am about to make peace with a seventy-seven year old shadow in my heart.

An ailing or stress-torn or unprepared creature may be asked by Life to abort a future child. Plants and animals everywhere are asked to make this sacrifice when in a bind. I met a bat species in the highland caves of Borneo that puts their pregnancies on hold when food is scarce. If good insect times do not arrive soon they readily abort. An ailing or unprepared mind can provoke its holder to do the same. A society that has stumbled in managing its growth may be asked to make this sacrifice and hold back for a while with its fertility, and wait for gentler times. Life is good. It wants to bring back such stumblers into balance and to the Middle Way again. Is that a blessing?

With so many encouraging hints and likenesses in the Great Story acted out around me, a brighter story for abortion can be composed than the tears and punishments some sacred books tattoo into our hearts. Think of the glorious October Song, the colorful whirl dance of leaves decaying in the tree of Life, a celebration of abortion and retreat that gladdens our hearts; for on the horizon we also see its good intention peeking.

Sometimes a life with ten children can be a hell life. Sometimes a life with no children can be a tree loaded with sweet heart-warming fruits. With a doctorate in marine biology, Alexandra, our oldest daughter, cares for the Great Barrier Reef. She feels that these reefs need a mother more than the Earth needs more children. We are so proud of her.

Don't kick me in the shin and run! Not yet! Wait! This here is my awkwardness at its best. This is just a start of the anatomy of this hotly disputed act that soon will be more forgivingly told. I believe with all the natives of America that it is our wonderful gift to make peace with our shadow. And Life tells me that it can be done with elegance.

69. The frog wanted to be so, so successful and so, so big that she ate the pond she was merrily paddling in! Where the pond was yesterday, there, in the empty mud-hole, now squats one huge belly of a successful frog from shore to shore. And now what?

Take a deep breath with me so this loaded thought may not sink our boat.

I learn from observing patterns in nature. In a mania for power and success, a species overdoes its gift of aggression and defenses. It goofs. It gobbles up every victory in reach, and its neighbor's victories too. It forgets to cool its aggression with compassion. It slips and oversteps the law of moderation. It forgets its table manners.

In his evolution, the grizzly bear, one by one, bravely outdid his opponents. Excess in braveness was his "undoing." Left without the help of outside moderators, this visitor to my backyard had to turn inside for the help of quality and population controllers. Each year, the big males must now take out a part of the newborn bear population. In grizzly land this has become a good deed, an act of compassion.

With our therapeutic culture and its mania for safety, longevity, personal eternity, we also have developed a disproportional arsenal of aggression and defenses. Think of our obsession with hygiene, vaccines, our litany of every imaginable anti-so-and-so, all our technological defenses, the warning systems, the fly and mouse and you-name-it traps, our rodent killers, predator eradicators and painkillers, the brave Medecins Sans Frontieres, our food supplements, the crops genetically engineered so that they must become guesthouses for none but us, the tsunami alerts, herbicides, pesticides, nasal, anal and mosquito sprays, our production of millions of tons of toxins, our "cures" to relieve us of our ripe old age when our nature wants us to mature so in a gift spree to finally give it all, our clinical medicine's enormous army of brave troopers. Extraordinarily sensitive and vulnerable people who are not standard models are carefully doctored back to the "healthy" and the ordinary. So much of our brainpower is bogged down in our personal eternity industry, searching for ever more personal cures.

Take our heroic effort to save OUR world with biofuel. To feed all cars with biofuel would require ninety percent of all the arable land of the Earth. Consider: it takes 2.7 lbs. of corn to produce 1 lb. of ethanol. It takes 4.8 gallons of it to replace the energy of the three gallons of gasoline the average car may burn daily. That is a hundred and two pounds of corn that corn-fed car eats daily. At eighteen hundred calories per pound of corn, Mr. Car serves himself the daily food in calories of sixty-five people, by my calculations.

To make the Earth one garden city of man, our applied sciences have now become our stingers that are a million times more deadly for all the draft-dodgers of the human enterprise than all the scorpion tails. Is there a free animal or plant left on Earth that needs not tremble from our mighty armament? Is there an animal or plant that can sleep in peace? Will we ever make gifts to other species again?

Now think a moment of what we give up for being such feared dictators. Think of a not so sanitized, dangerous, vulnerable and fertile lifestyle, of an environment that is wildly adventurous and infectious for body and mind. Think of a world with fewer people and of many plants and animals. Each breath of it yields a million different gifts; each sight of it yielding messages from a million different companions, each one a creative writer in genetics. Each acre of land free of our control provides a banquet of food cooked by a million different chefs. Every minute of it is a news-arena where millions of very different artists meet, exchanging recipes and advice on how to live well. Zillions of encounters! A feast of inspiration! A feast of illuminating hardships and mind-altering challenges! This exuberant environment is a continuous mind-altering drug for us that beats cocaine.

No, an illness for example infects us not only with some dengue; it infects us also with mischievous break-ins into our routine, with creative rest and bedtime, with experiences of compassion, with reflections, with bangs that shock sleeping talents awake. Our artful suffering is a chance for an extraordinarily fruitful apprenticeship. Hardship seeds our flower fields of insights, whereas raw victories engender mostly enmities. A euphoric triumph soon reeks of a place of exile. In your relationships, did you find out what tastes better than victory?

Yet what body armors! What an army of exterminators! Are we becoming the species entirely covered with thorns? And there are so many scientists scheming how to make us even more impenetrable, rendering us even less sociable among all species and more victorious and hostile. Think here also about our arsenal of herbicides and pesticides. No other species beats us in cleansing mass destruction. Are we becoming the dumbest species in social skills?

So many of our knowledge miners are now cramped deep down in some niche! Few surface from this heroic underworld so to become seers, poets and other obsessed seekers and light catchers, concocting for us "medicine" that makes us tolerant, trusting, vulnerable, giving, lusty, serene. May we become blessed exuberant scientists that do not just "cure" but are passionate about opening our minds, lead us to critical, long-range thinking, infect us to become enthusiastic learners, make of us excited listeners to all our neighbors: people, animals and plants.

It is this imbalance that gives me the chills when others still so unconcerned celebrate our "heroic" business of saving human lives. We can sink from an overload of advantages. We can sink from an overload of saved human lives. We truly can!

Ah! The gift of vulnerability, the invitation to all other organisms to act on us, to be artists and chisel on us, bestow on us gifts of their genetic memories, the gift to remain open to quality controllers.

So, may we be safe from another "cure" that could add another billion troops to mankind and make the plants and animals even fewer.

In a time in which we squat so heavily and wide on every niche of the Earth, may we be safe, for the time being, from myopic scientists who for example still heroically figure out technologies to force physical fertility on women and men who are by nature physically unfertile. These special people may be meant to be fertile in a new and more needed way! Or do we want the scenario for auto-cannibalism in all its mean details to become even more compelling? Will we let clinical medicine grow into a crowdedness and meanness-breeding business affair that develops ever-bigger guns to shoot our way to a hundred years of loneliness?

In the spirit of the arms agreements among us, a mature science can contain the voracious accumulation of human biomass and opt for a non-proliferation arms agreement between our research in clinical medicine and our other life partners.

Did you ever consider how counterproductive in the long term an exaggerated human life saving industry can be on our gift of self-maintenance and personal resilience, on our long-range health and on our niche on Earth with limited seats and resources and how a tie-up rope for this sacred cow could benefit us?

And so, some of us dare now ask that simple question: "Is it a blessing when now more people die than are being born?"

I wish us the gift of moments when nothing needs to be done. I wish our life sciences a meditating retreat, an adaptive reorientation, a symposium that is less preoccupied with cures and more to lighting streetlights in our minds. May these gifted minds help us to a poetic interpretation of our life situations in storm and in sun.

70. The fear of learning; the terror that the sky comes crushing down while our pillars of knowledge are being moved to higher ground.

Fundamentalists may be crabs that molted and are not quite ready yet to molt again to enlarge their creation myths. Scientists may be somewhat older crabs, or another breed of crabs, that also need their shells, their assumptions, theorems, creation myths, their canon, sometimes as strict as the credo the church has tattooed into my juvenile soul. Out of a black, empty hat, hocus-pocus, the magi of science pull out a fantastically big bang-and-a-puff. And the universe, endowed with its unimaginable spectrum of possibilities, has now been thirteen billion years in the making. This is a little longer than the Bible-God's "working week" of long ago, but not so much, and, yes, more detailed. How to deal rationally with a miracle?

Scientists, too, dream bad dreams of being kicked out of their safe nest of assumptions by an updated, better theorem. The Bible creation story, the Buddha myths, the dream time myths of aborigines, the big bang theory of the big savants—some poetic minds need a creation story in which Life is one single super-organism. Even the slick, waterproof survival-of-the-fittest story has become to them a crude garment for their mind from a time when men wore animal skins. No wonder, every government builds its own umbrella against unsettling news, sheltering its flock from unrest, creative fever, anxiety, the fear of novelty.

These mental constructs and safe-harbors, so fantastic and diverse, are they not our truest works of art, art made of local ideas, pictures, time scales and materials at hand, all filling in with beautiful designs the mysterious void in our view into how the world came to be and where we go?

Each little bundle of joy holds on for dear life to his very own brand of that mental carapace. No egg wants to be without a shell!

When the terror of learning and changing, of letting go and molting rattles your soul, take heart from the oak. Look at how this courageous companion splits and splits again its bark every few years to grow a roomier bark around his roomier world.

How vulnerable and confused a man becomes in the between-time of old-shell-new-shell. Think of a man who hides in the bushes just to change his pants! Nobody wants to be caught with his pants down, and least with those of his mind. In their nakedness, when molting, crabs retreat into the deepest, darkest crannies and nooks. Think of grandma who crocheted all her life her beautiful designs only to be told that her designs are out of date and a waste of time. A dear routine comes to an end. A bigger world has to be taken on. Think also of wild, mixed metaphors whose teaching-stories could degrade a humanist and knock down his crown.

It takes great courage to learn! It takes courage to bring to light painful, sunken memories—and make peace with them, graduating them to our teachers. Scientists greater than most of us refused to leave the labyrinth of some doctorate and look through Galileo's glass and see Jupiter's moons. Truly, I talk about the end of one world. And nobody is exempted from this creative trauma.

No wonder only reckless souls lifted anchor in Europe-sweet-home and sailed over their horizon for the New World, never to be sure what of the new they will find goes down well and what new they find will leave them helpless with new infections or a constipated soul. Some cannot digest milk; they need a soya formula. Others need a special formula with no sugar explaining how the Earth was built.

Yet creation myths have consequences. Consider the placebo and the painebo effect of our expectations. Some creation myths reinforce in us the notion that our morals are in stasis. They make us complacent. They make our minds lazy. In such an environment of see-nothing, hear-nothing, doubt-nothing, our mind and body chemistry may lose their capacity to build up our tolerance and to churn out adaptive proteins and ideas when needed. Our neuropathways become stiff. We become a mental couch potato, unable to jump a creek or a moral fence six feet tall when in a bind. Some creation myths may never prime the neurochemicals in a child that want to grow him into a spirited adventurer but instead let him be a puppy for life. Some creation stories foster in their flock a reckless attitude of we-give-a-hoot for this yeasty, seedy misery-place down here, for we are on the fast track to some promised yonder merry land. Other creation stories became so tight and stressful to what we now know, they produce much friction and stress hormones that strangle the pathways for our exuberant thinking.

Other myths keep us on our toes, always teasing us on to evolve, to adapt, to peek over the horizon in the great contest of love, never to be certain about the menu of tomorrow, and to be cocksure of whether to look for a shelter or go for an adventure.

Take heart. We are not alone with this nostalgia. Look at the growth rings in a clam's shell. Don't tell me our views of the world and its morals are less alive and less growing.

71. The merry Seed-Scatterer

Any life situation, meager or fat, She swings and opens her full hand of seeds toward it: "Go, figure out a new home-design for this new situation!"

I get dizzy from seeing too much generosity when I watch daring Life so freely scattering her seeds. She fills a cruise ship's garbage bin with papaya seeds and empties that bin again only when the North Pole is near. She plants a young man, not in a sweet, cozy Muslim or a Christian home, but into a life situation equal to the South Pole that is nearly guaranteed ruin. Frostbitten, yet that lad may survive in this love-forsaken land and brings back a pack full of vistas I never dared to get to know. She plants a common talent into autism or a bipolar disorder, and yes, once in a great while, this messed up environment grows that talent into a wonder-talent.

To a cockroach she gives a litter in a sunken submarine. Fish eggs she sweeps high into the shade of palms: go find a new way to hatch and wriggle in the sand! She makes a camel eat melon seeds and to scatter these seeds on a Sahara dune: become creative; tease out of this wasteland something beautiful! She lets a woman give birth in a concentration camp, or in a back alley with nothing but rags and drunks—and only God knows what Life had in mind. She transplants a tiny tip of a coral reef into an empty oil tanker's water ballast, or into the stomach of a whale— go home shopping around the world! She parachuted a dandelion seed into the hungry mouth of a lion, and nobody can remember what marvel or misery happened to this adventurous little seed. I am dizzied by all this seemingly wasteful generosity.

Salmon are more generous than we are. They don't lament the high mortality rate when they spawn their eggs by the thousands into the worldwide atelier of the Creator, which resounds with the chip-chop music of his chisel all day and all night. All this seeding into ruin to sift for this one speck of a precious chance to compose a new design!

No, wait! All this passion of Life also to cook for her children in her fertility rites a nourishing soup made of all these chip-chop flakes from when she sculpts her work of art: the greatest give-away of food, the greatest potlatch ever, where species compete in generosity. Every player ecstatically cooks heaps of berries, or fries eggs or grows steaks for it. Everybody is having fun fighting to contribute the biggest pot of food to this feast and to brag about his virility.

Life laughs at our standards, codes and building inspectors, when she wants to build one story higher. Or do you think an Earth with no "wasted" seeds and scooped up, tasty little ducklings, with no deserts, or failures, or tsunamis or holes in the shoes, or sunken options, washed up fishes and "failed" people or continental rifts and shifts, or miscarriages, or seagulls feasting on salmon eggs, or dictators, or banquets cooked of waste would be a wealthier and more high rising Earth? Consider, if Life would follow *our* ten or hundred commandments, what would happen to our so sexy, so permissive Earth, ever-ready to lift her skirt?

Ah, the logic of creativity! I see it as the investment of one's surplus love into playing with apparent senseless, teasing the hidden options out of the forbidden, the unhealthy, the perverse, the poisonous deep sea vents, to seed the badlands, the bleeding wounds, the deserts in our love or to sneak a lantern into a heart that blacked out. Go, play with ruin, juggle the secret options out of this potent mess—make a tasty pudding of that waste. Go, walk the edge between cooperation and rivalry. Befriend a prison inmate; ring out what Life had in mind for this rascal soul. Create of this awkward prison visit a memory for him and you that makes both of you jump up and down with joy. That passion of Life to play creatively with ruin, waste and pompous giveaways instead of being practical and produce one cherry to replace the old cherry tree might also be her dearest, most ingenious tool for quality and population control.

I come to think of art as that wonderful new need of a woman or a man to express her or himself beyond common food, manure, and sex, to create a brand-new way of making love and offspring and of making a living in a new environment. New kinds of sunflowers may grow of it in our mind. I come to think that it might after all not be the healthy boys and the model girls or the saints, but the near failures, the weird and the mad, the exiled, those parachuted beyond the last frontiers that are the shiniest cash in evolution's creative hands. It may be the "misfits" for which psychiatrists with tiny eyes could only invent but sickly names, the phenomena in man's psyche that push our limits of adaptation like cynics, dominators, braggarts, dreamers, flirters, hedonists, egotists, gays, messiahs, loners. Obviously, Life laughs off the tiny names-callers among us, for it keeps on producing such specialists, for it is madly in love with creating new flavors. And so, may these "martyrs," who walk for us the hairy life situations on the edge of the impossible and ruin, also be rewarded with a keg of the Ethiopian honey beer so mustache-licking good.

Next time, Theo, you meet a wacky, uneven man, or a beetle that landed in your coffee cup, remember what you just have said out loud. Those sunburnt, love-burnt, struggling, frostbitten explorers of forbidding options may contribute more to Life than you with your fishing. Just look at Life's seed scattering and our idea of meritocracy sinks to the bottom of the sea.

Through a sunlit window of our tame, anesthetic art shows, the Earth tells me, "For Life, nothing is wild enough!" If three billion years ago Life would have got stuck in an ideal life situation, it might still be healthy bacteria from top to the bottom of the Earth, nothing more.

72. The giving of names. I bring to light juicy morsels of my inner wildlife refuge.

My inner land is full of wild horses, yet still I go on foot. No saddle, no spurs, no reins, no names. That whole crowd of spirits, muffled voices, still down in my deep well, are a chorus of untranslated languages from beyond. And I can barely understand what I hear. All the hours I spend looking from my pilot house out into the open sea, random fragments of these voices rise from my depth and dance in front of me. I decipher these voices in me. I assemble them. I write them. I give them names. This is the creative act of "aha!" that is what they wanted to say all along.

This is the act that puts the rope on my bucket with which I bring these helpers up from the well into the light. Up here it's springtime. They may grow leaves and flower answers with names. With that bucket full of names I nourish and make my visualization grow—and I become more alive. With that bucket full of new names I design thoughts that are a fresh sea breeze in a stale mind, stories that are health food for a mind constipated with anger, thoughts that point to a beauty so great, it overflows any garden fence, thoughts that are streetlights spotlighting goodness hidden in the night. I formulate exciting new questions from these thoughts. More and more of the world's broadcasters come in my range and so become part of Theo. When the sunshine is right, reassuring answers grow out of my richer soil.

This naming and roll call of the many weeds, wild fruits, beasts and other unrecognized helpers in a woman's jungle land brings to light all those fragments of her hidden wealth and adds them to her personality. I meet an ever-new woman I can get all excited about! A meaningful relationship, rich, resourceful, sexy, and awesomely fertile, can rise.

I see artists at work that light up a landscape waiting at dawn. In darkness and black thunderclouds of fear, these artists are a rising moon. From misery, they ring out smiles. They do more for us than bankers do who open their vaults and shout, "You poor and miserable, come get your fill!"

To say it out loud is an act of courage. Naming is meeting, is seeing. No escape anymore into the safe cave of I-do-not-know. This is the power of confession. I am the confessant. I am the listener of my confessions. I give birth to my ghosts. I create my troop of advisers. They pat me on the shoulder, or scold me when I fail.

73. I climb out of my window on a twisted bedsheet to come to tell you what I should not.

Fifty years ago, in Paris, a young Swiss executive in the making met a young Belgian concert pianist in the making. Both shared a nagging doubt that they had embarked on the life they were meant to live. There a wonderfully confused and fruitful season started for us. And, yes, Clara, you so generously said, "Wherever you want to go, I want to go." (I, an uncarved block of solid driftwood—and she a carver, deciding to cling to and do her carving on it.)

Ah, to wake up in the morning with Clara and the sun peeking on my side. Springtime warmth is melting us. I open her wish list. And my own litanies of petitions and complaints with God might also fetch her smile. That's when together we take the world apart and put it back together again the way we fancy it should be. We are such merry fools. And so we visit together our deeper self, taking a safari into our inner jungle land. Amazing things and more amazing things we bring to light: orchids, snakes, papagayos, misery, generosity, betrayals, and our beautiful counterfeits. All kinds of lovemaking!

What you tell me is the light stuff. What you do not know how to tell me is the heavyweight soul-stuff I am all excited about.

Clara's story: when a teenage girl, your parents locked you up in a convent school to "save" a girl made all feverish by new hormones. How did that feel? Tell me. Ah! And you thanked your dad later on for doing so. Now here is a wound that you healed well and made bloom. And when as a little girl your mom wanted to cut your long hair and you dove into the garden waste barrel to hide for three hours while the whole troop was out and shouting, hunting for you, and you as mute as a little mouse in the company of rotting grass and goat manure; how did that feel? Even the "music" of a joint meal of beans becomes a welcome component at such a morning rendezvous. Sourness doesn't have a chance in such intimacies.

My culture disoriented and tamed many of my wilder talents, and like disoriented whales they got beached. Meeting you, Clara, I met the incoming tide that surged all under and over me. Floating once more, some of these stranded talents found their way to the ocean again.

Ah! The dark side of niceness! Muted people, terribly constipated with the ghosts of avoidance; for adventure's sake, take off your masks! No, it's not so much the thank-you-honeys and the birthday shopping, it's these wild intimacies that are the glue of relationships. We story-tell from that expanded identity, still dreaming below the graft of the good boy and girl that society has grafted on our souls. Beneath those simple, orderly tattoos, Clara and Theo are a thousand times richer mosaic than the mosaic with which society embellished our souls. I was trained to squat, like a forbidding prison guard, on that incredible beauty. I was trained to keep the gate to that artwork of Amazing Grace under three locks. Not anymore.

Amazing insights become possible when the emperor, when Clara and Theo have no clothes on. Try to open your heart to her or him while you wait and meditate on your toilet seat. For a constipated soul, it's good medicine.

And so, when returning from a fishing trip, I see smoke curl from the chimney and your bike outside, telling me you are home, I become all tick-a-tick dance, and only you, Clara, know what that means.

74. Blessings for the misunderstandings

There is an understanding that loves the tool of misunder-standings to kindle creativity.

What would happen if the sunflower and the lilac had the same bundle of understanding, the same blind spots, the same logic, or were connected to the same internet? Might there ultimately not be just one kind of flower and color? I bow to misunderstanding with a thank-you for adding new dots and strips and curls to Life's canvas.

Hunting for mountain goat, Theo sees a grizzly at the edge of the muskeg. Lightning of excitement shakes him all alive. Tiptoe-ing, he goes back and forth, sharpening his eyes and flipping off the cover of his rifle's scope. He thinks of strategies for defense. Maybe he composes a prayer to his God. Out of a nest of bore-dom, all of a sudden, bundles of activity explode. He watches and watches again this shade of a bear—no, darn, he mistook a rock for a bear!

Ah, to see what is not! The illusion of a bearded God where there may be none. How much art, music, paintings, sciences, all kinds of wars, such mirages have brought forth? How many prayers are composed? How much anxiety created and anxiety relieved? How many exercises to get high and higher to better see that mirage? Yes, and how much learning? A courageous man who dares to see patterns where he risks there might be none is a better observer and survivor than a no-risk observer who needs to see the whole thing before he sees it and reacts.

No, it's not serenity that teases the Earth to evolve. It's our blindness that makes us fumble, probe, invent, move, sniff around, and that makes us bite into anything with the slightest promise of being yummy food. It's my ignorance that keeps me trying to stitch a better pair of boots for "God."

Blessed be the barriers for understanding. Two groups of people talking different languages invent not one but two separate and unique kingdoms. Look at the diversity such non-understandings have brought to the family of the ant species. They evolved eighteen thousand kinds of greetings, of body anatomies, of positions to making love.

Hence one of the darndest mysteries of Life: understanding must not be allowed to become universal.

We do not understand, but we do have theories, truckloads of these most refined and fruitful misunderstandings. Each is blessed with his personal toolbox of Legos. Each is also hawkish by instinct when others try sneaking their fingers into his personal grab bag to fish for goodies, or when Google tries to walk away with another bit of her private information to add it to their information shopping mall.

Look at our economy for what the art of secrecy and deception can do. It adds to complexity. Misunderstanding, the mother of all fear, is also an enormously powerful catalyst for inventions, for consumption, for creating new needs, for a booming economy.

And so, my mental activity is more activated by a secretive enemy, and by all his savory tricks, that I do not yet know, than by a like-minded friend. Each eye, each point of view, each hill or mountain of thoughts, they have their different blind spots, a different understanding and truth, a differently shaped shadow and logic.

> *Each head is a world. The only perfect mental tool*
> *to understand the feelings in dogdom is a dog.*

75. Did you ever consider sickness as a remedy? Make a headstand and try again.

You might think a rat is just a no-good scavenger in the sewer getting fat. Yet a couple nights ago a wise old Mrs. Rat, perching arrogantly on a kitchen beam, was challenging me: "A rat is wealthier than you! Every one of the therapies the rat needs is her property. Ever more of the therapies that keep you going are no longer your property."

Corporate International is embarked on a great robbery. I see healing capacity after healing capacity being wrestled away from the individual by the life science industry and packed away. Step by glorious step our health walks over into that industry's hands and the individual will be begging for alms. Soon our sweet romance with having a child will be defamed as sickly wild, and society will cultivate its future workers on demand and out of our reach on the other side of a fence.

On a clear day, sickness may show itself as a tool of our health care—a cleansing, a learning, a quality refining and growth control process. Seen over generations, pathogens turn into healers. They also turn into creators of scenes for a person's creativity. Periodically, they involve us in a learning and testing process we are not fond of. Yet for a proud man or woman, that ready consult-your-doctor may still have a shy nag of defeat for them.

Cradle for a daring minute sickness' family of wondrous little pathogens in your arms. Give them a moment's tender consideration. Give them beautiful names. You cradle a circus show a billion times more imaginative than any circus you have ever seen. Uncountable actors, each doing most incredible feasts—you are on a safari that could fill a million Discovery Channels. So many of these little buggers are vital to our own health, and so for sure on the payroll of God. All must be in some way beneficial to Life. In fact, it is they who created most of it. Consider for instance that long ago an endogenous retro virus inserted a precious sentence of its own memory into our ancestors' genome that now helps us to harbor our embryos safely in a placenta instead of in a fragile egg. We consider here a process of Life's tinkering more wonderful than walking a sky trope span from the Earth to the Moon. To simply defame these little actors as sickly sicknesses and pathogens is the privilege of unimaginative folks. Viruses, bacteria and fungi are Nobel Prize winners for helping to shape our evolutionary history. I have a hunch that these little buggers are dearer to Life than our super corn. Life's magic at work!

Pains are like children. They want to be held and gently listened and talked to, not battered and cussed. They do better this way. When so tenderly held, they love to teach us about our needs.

Pains are like children. They want to be held and gently listened and talked to, not battered and cussed.

Why this obsession to collectively evermore bail out and "heal" a battling individual, proudly cheating her out of this wondrous yet poorly understood quality of life—to play with pathogens? We don't need to get the creeps even at the thought of pathogens. I notice that nemesis is a helper coded into our nature, ever ready to correct our slips into exaggerations, ever ready to invite us to a bullfight. I also notice that many of our new medical practices become so costly, they may soon only survive in a mankind that practices a system of castes, where a lot of throwaway people labor for a caste of "high priests."

My pillow tells me that on a deeper level, the spirit of life perceives our obsession with clinical medicine and body veneration also as an opportunity for experimenting in our health maintenance, yet "thanks" to this obsession, in the UK death is currently preceded by an average of ten years of miserable ill health. And so, when we stumble in moderation and exterminate too many of her sicknesses, Life seems to lose no time. As a gift to her stumblers, she triggers a new, more resistant malady into play to keep up this creative interplay. Antibiotic resistance tells us so persuasively Life's glorious story of evolution's creative interplay.

Did you note that on the world stage of Life, one of the first survival strategies invented was success management? I am talking about zillions of reconciliations, of weapons and birth agreements, of laws of moderation, of open guesthouses and open wounds. A tree or a man comes crashing down. Critters and more critters are impatiently waiting to move into this wound. For Life, an open wound is an open guesthouse.

You want an Eden without sickness? Consider, Life might well still be stuck in the mud without this precious helper. Species are genetically much more dynamic than we thought. They can grab from and give to neighbors secondhand genes in these creative encounters much faster than we expected. It is said that more mutations, sins, more lawbreakers and encounters with pathogens equals more tickets in the lottery of the adaptation game. You want an Eden that is perfect? In such a place, wouldn't Life fossilize in a yawning stasis?

Here is another hint for how we could give sickness a more lovable face. Think of a man who is overheating from inner friction (and what man does not at times?). Life might give him time off in a depression, providing him with a retreat to depressively and honestly analyze himself. He gets a chance to come out of this retreat as a more cheerful man who knows more about himself and the world. Beware of simply getting drunk on a pill. You might kill that insight-giving ailment and your chance to encounter yourself. May we allow ourselves to consider depression as a cure?

Our bruises are our signs of learning. And when have we not felt pride in our scars?

When I see you and me in evolutionary terms, I also come to feel that our last few thousand generations have been living in an enormously privileged moment of evolutionary time. Imagine, for two people to be able to self-procreate with no outside help, to self-maintain their bodies, to self-think, to self-invent, to so profusely sin, mutate, revolt, play with deficiencies and excesses, yet survive, to get stranded completely alone in no man's land and do it just by their own wits, to see directly with their bare eyes and to have no middleman or a media baron to God. We are a feast. We are a short, bright Sunday of Amazing Grace. We are a celebration in the working calendar of Life, a celebration so generous it cannot last in the evolutionary push to who-knows-where. There will be another long hardworking week in the story of creation before another such feast in self-reliance can occur.

It is true, our system of self-maintenance is our crown jewel as queens and kings of our joys and pains. Don't pawn lightly that wild gift for a loan of feeling well. Sickness is an important component of health. Sickness has a deep, beautiful voice when the Earth sings its glory-hallelujah to its maker.

76. Stop all the family quarrels when the home is on fire.

It had to come to this. All the so terribly fruitful local competitions and quarrels about what is the best recipe for *our* success—among nations, religions, classes, sexes, races and colors, among all the -isms—they fade now into the background. Buddha, Marx, Jesus, Kant, Aristotle, Socrates, St. Augustine, Mr. Economist, and Mr. CNN, the president of the United States, name any of the ordained messengers for a more successful mankind, all those of us who have been caught in the spell of that intoxicating march music: "Mankind, Mankind over all!" Our inside fights, the differences in our commandments and in our diverse fineries dim in the one common provocation written now over all the oceans, lands and skies. That provocation points the finger at each and all of us with a "You!" The living Earth asks us to accept this difficult change in our sequence of importance. The spirit of Life asks us to create together new, enlightened morals in our relationship with the living Earth and to put this new sacrament first. Spiritual leaders are asked to graduate to a compassion that is bigger than mankind. The success of their initial teachings, with no success management built in, is now growing out of control. Some of our dearest mythologies might have to go. Our spiritual leaders are asked to incorporate this new sacrament of "Love the living Earth as you love yourself" when they preach. And our medals and Nobel Prizes will no longer reward smartness that has no table manners.

The Earth is becoming a tiny bus for seven billion people with their packs fat with stuff. We are becoming feverish and cursers from too much friction—and everywhere nuclear weapons are stacked. An arsenal of those darn things might go off in that mounting friction!

"Become an amateur shaman, Theo." Take on, for a minute, the identity of one of your grandchildren and think with her innocent mind. You may find, that for this little lover there is no gift more appreciated than the thinning out of our world population—if we don't want them to live in some fancy feed lot. If the Earth does not hear from us soon, we ask the living Earth to yell the answer at us.

Afflicted with an enormously inventive complex of superiority, most of the latest cultures made us forget our table manners at this fantastic banquet of food and ideas for the family of Life. Hence, we enforce our deadly superior smartness, with its mental and technological sand castles, and our ticking success and population bombs.

Our great father-figures were pioneers on virgin, "promised" land. Euphoric, they did not see an immediate need to educate our behavior so we would moderate our success. They were practical women and men. In a splendid extravaganza they high bred reasoning, a shortcut department for urgent situations in our layered intelligence. Eureka! This frenzy in mental shortcuts ballooned us in seconds of evolutionary time into a truly fantastic, truly unsustainable success.

Alarmed, we now look around and observe how Life reacts, when other adventurous species get stuck in similar dead-end options, Yes, Life has ways to draw them back to closer to their roots. Nothing lost! Life remembers these precious lessons from such extravaganzas. She hands out her thanks, leaving some fat baggage of luxo-chic behind. A little wiser, She ventures into a more promising version of that same "find-new-delights."

Will we remain creative and be thankful for and learn from our mistakes and give our minds wings and, yes, brush away, dear old habits of thought. Or will we lazily remain "good" and "fundamental" and stick safely to "no wings!" close to the ground where mankind's experiment in love-only-your-neighbor seems to lead unexpectedly, not into some paradise, but into a manmade down-to-earth inferno that is identical for and open to us all?

The most resilient flowers of the meadow and of the mind, including some of our sacred literature, manage to remain humble and disposable and thus partakers of evolution. They can disperse their power, a little like our humble teachers do, whose happiness occurs, when the pupils reach their level and surpass them too.

"Go! Add to my basics another insight, another wing and color, a leaner photosynthesis, one more growth ring. I am no dead-end street."

77. Greed, oh mean old Greed, tell me your story.

In a mysterious way, this rascal must be dear to Life, for She lets him survive, and survive.

In my childhood's model, greed mostly computes to a terrible injustice, a twister hurricane, many broken trees, relations, and loves. I need to invent a bigger stable in my mind to accommodate this wild horse.

Excessive greed is a difficult gift. It's like a man being called to spearhead to the South Pole and bring us back some of its blast-frozen news. It's an affliction like fiery red hair. You can dye it, shave it, make long braids with it, or reorient it, but you are going to live with this over-boiling vitality.

Brainstorming, I begin here my collection of ideas on how to make peace with grouchy old greed. Don't leave me alone with this rascal and run and hide, discarding this irksome ingredient of Life off-hand into some pit of evil or the devil. Help me to compose something helpful, maybe even beautiful, of the debris that brainstorm is flying us in. To know the secret of how that "monster" of an unappreciated gift fits into the beauty of Life is a blessing I miss.

Little centers of high density punctured the uniformity of the very young cosmos. Centers of egos came to be. The whirl-dance of self-centered galaxies came to be. Many kinds of amazing pyramids, some made of minerals, some of cells, others of money, also came to be. All these seem to be children of mamma greed.

The longest march, the highest climb, the tallest tomb, the riches bags of cells, the bravest warrior, the deepest root, the greenest grass, the biggest crystal or brain, the fastest run, the biggest bomb, the scientist with the most published papers or prizes, the bank account with the most zeroes—all are adventures that are a little scary and hard on tender hearts.

Greed of the patriarch for the biggest flock.

Greed of the explorer to bag the coldest cold of the South Pole.

Greed of the seagull to fly higher than all earthbound fliers and touch the sun.

Reoriented greed that turned creative and teases a fisherman away from simply catching the most fish, and toward hauling in the biggest catch of light and insights.

Greed to recruit the biggest army of bank accounts.

Take the magnificent power of grand charity fueled by very wealthy men. Might that showy benevolence not also be a child of greed? Here a man bursting with vitality can take into his hand the health of thousands. He can decide who and who not. He can sit at the head of a table as the provider of thousands and will be empowered with respect. Truly, greed and generosity might ultimately be Siamese twins living together in the dark. The greater the greed in spring, the greater the generosity in fall.

Evolution loves greedy greed. Love of excesses is its darling among power tools. It creates endless new situations, new playgrounds for the games of its inventiveness, high voltage, exotic concoctions for new kinds of pies. A man "cursed" with an obsession of greed can do experiments no humble gravedigger can do. Greed in knowledge has built amazing biological pyramids—look at us!

A greedy greed can dam enormous energies. Unifying the many trickles of laughing waters, it can flood badlands that have never before tasted a drop of rain. The affliction of extravagant greed brings to town the costliest of circus shows.

A modest man may be a gentle whirlpool. Not much of a quality inspector here, but a good friend. An extra puff of a "who-knows-what" accelerates that gentle love eddy and turns it into a world-class shoplifter on Wall Street, into a world moving Genghis Khan, into an enormous international blender of cultures, into a cyclone, sucking into its whirling circle of love the shallow rooted, the gentle hearted, and the dumbed down by fat TV ballads. Name anything that might be easy fodder for a twister-man. Here is a gift that is no friend-maker, but rather a creator of polarity.

Think of the enormous differences in needs among the different species of greed. Here, one spore, a tiny greed still in hiding, stands up discreetly to become a tuft of moss. There, Life commands another such seed, "Go pile up into a giant sequoia tree in the next thousand years." And do not forget that the bigger the taker, the bigger its giveaway later. Different sizes of greed haven't survived in the evolutionary game because they are a bad idea. Name any of Life's beautiful designs; they are grandchildren of mamma greed. Greed puts our outstanding talent for exaggeration to work. There are many willing martyrs here. And, surprise, surprise! Life's ministry of evolution gives medals, thanks, and sweet illusions to those experimenters in excesses for their sacrifice.

In times of great blue abundance there is little stockpiling and much dancing and fun. In crisis times of save-your-hide-if-you-can, everybody is out to grab and hoard, with no time for fun and games. We are in with the squirrels that are programmed by wisdom to become hot with greed, when the coming winter warns them, "I am going to be very, very cold with you." We are in with the wisdom of the grizzlies that tramp in September to the salmon stream to lay on an extra layer of lard when fall knocks on the door cautioning, "Soon there will be no more banquets." We conspire with the ants. They cover their nest with an extra foot of pine needles when their inner oracle tells them of a snowman heading their way with an extra load of ice and cold.

And do not forget that the bigger the taker, the bigger its giveaway later.

232

As we now face the scary "not-enough-for-all" syndrome roaming everywhere among the seven billion foraging men, our good old greed may go on a rampage. Frenzied, we start stepping all over each other's toes while everybody is rushing back and forth to rake in the last acres of the unplowed Earth. So terribly many of us! And, unbelievably, we still try to save so many spent human lives from setting in due time, even while the animals and the plants are so quickly losing ground. Truly, greedy humanism can ultimately bring down our healthy greed with a delirious fever that slowly spreads the paralyzing song with the one simple refrain: "It's mine, it's mine."

For our children, being born into the impoverished environment of an over-population that quickly consumes our leisure and inner warmth is like falling into the Arctic Sea—a kind of hypothermia may soon overcome their hearts. This is the leanest egotism that can still beat their hearts.

The spirit of the North Wind tells me now, "This will be the first hard winter, when your dear old instinct to hoard before the snow invades you, is not going to save you. Theo, forget your instinct. Throw out the old wisdom. No more credit. Become creative. Become more generous in this crisis time. Make do with less. Take the loss. Pay back to the Earth some of your overdue debt, which has become unsustainable by now. Try not to whine when Life thins out the thicket of man. Revise your adolescent attitude toward death. Die and let die in due time. Tough advice! Yet it can be done. You can think of the Eskimo grandma who is said to have walked out of the igloo into lethal cold when absolutely not enough was left to feed them all." Ever since I was raised in wartime Europe, I have been modestly experimenting with living with a light backpack. I have found that living with essentials offers fewer tricks and more treats.

When I can better see why Life may have to betray our good old instinct in order to reorient some of our greed into new, more pressing chores, my grouchiness with this irksome phenomenon of Life will heal.

Here, a puzzle related to this point: I lay out food for Mona, our cat, that's full and fat, and not about to eat. Along comes another cat, and immediately Mona goes for the food. Tell me what the other-cat syndrome is about.

78. Don't blame the trigger of the gun.

Responsibility is an elusive beast to track down.

Every act has countless different shapes. According to what each of us recognizes clinging to that act, we quilt, each with our own bits and pieces of awareness, what may look to us like a master-piece of love, or a hell of a crime.

Take a terribly heavy act that wants to sink your mind in a sea of anger. Hold that kicking anger warm in your hands while you dive into that deep dark, looking for the complement of this limping act. Be patient—and more patient. Don't give up and spill your chance. Go deeper into time and further to your left and right. Send your questions for a walk-about to far-off people, places, and mountain villages in Pakistan. Remember: "There is no 'bad' that does not light a smile—somewhere." I bet you will finally breach into light with a sweet little catch for your angry, hungry mind. The law of likeness can lead a courageous seeker to such tasty finds.

An act is a story, a long, long story. Countless actors parade the stage to act out this story, hopelessly too many to count. With each of us allotted a unique set of blind spots, a man may only get to remember the glorious "beginning" of the story. Other times it is a trivial sentence in the "middle" of that fat story in Life's love affairs. Maybe I see only the radiant face of the receiver. Or I get to hear only the meager tail end of the story with the flushed out waste. To pinpoint an act to one woman or to one man, to a help or to a hurt? Ridiculous! To limit the water story to the rope that raises the bucket from the well—this fits the imagination of the cow.

Obviously, Life allows for very special chores, very special, very charged situations, where under enormous stress, clarity, vacuum or pressure, she compresses a dull lump of coal into a diamond. Or, under some rare hardship, Life hammers a slightly special lad into a prophet, a hero, a cataclysmic Genghis Khan, a Burning Man. Yes, the science of analogies hints to me that God can synthesize such extraordinary "gems" of consequences not only in the mineral and animal world, but also in the world of man.

"Whatever blunder, whatever frustration or goof creeps up on you, whatever happening wants to sink your boat, remember Theo: it also has another, completely impersonal, completely delightful aspect. It is one more revelation for you of how Life works." To know this can massage away half of a hurt. To know this might even make me love that blunder a tiny bit. When I can speak such words that unite, it makes my day!

I started here to make peace with some of my nagging, whining memories. They have been my revengeful children, for I never could love them. They are wasted rags of my awareness for I could not incorporate them into my quilt, my ugly ducklings so to speak. While angry with me, they keep on sabotaging me, pouring more gallons of stress into my heart. To make this peace is the creativity I need. The gist of it: "Theo, if nothing else, recycle the garbage that piled up in your mind and invent a new use for it."

Most outdoor civilizations have their version of this helpful archetypical proverb and soul catcher: *"no hay mal que por bien no venga."* Or, "no good deed goes unpunished," or "the yin and yang" personality theorem, or a "bad" man is in his next life allotted a "good" man's term. This above team of small, shining sentences has become the magnetic north that orients much of my thinking.

These simple, shining reminders have put my nifty
philosophical acrobatics in the shade. These simple finds
are the most nourishing loaf of wisdom that the inquisitive
lad in me has baked for me. The voluminous philosophical
back-and-forth is straw on my threshing floor.

79. The law of moderation—the mother that gave birth to the twins, aggression and compassion

Through all my veins, Life whispers: "Your killing and your taking, do it as you do your breathing in, do it with moderation.
Your caring, your comforting and your giving, do it as you do your
breathing out, do it with moderation. They are essential rhymes
that sustain the joys of Life. No motherly spring can happen without the spear of fall."

To visualize this advice, think of a happy trout that zips
around, devouring bunches of larvae, skaters, salmon eggs, mosquitoes and flies. Think also that the trout at the same time cooks
a tasty pot of two thousand eggs in her belly for its neighbors in
Lucky Creek. Soon she spawns: many fingerlings, so much food!
And she invites any able chiseler and nibbler to her feast, to dip
in beaks, claws, teeth, or fishing hooks into her heaped pot of
food. And she is moderate, she asks for just the two most creative
of her offspring to be spared by the team of sculptors and allowed
to mature, so they may hold this feast again in a slightly more
festive way. How generous of that brave mama trout to invite all
these artists to chisel, hammer, bite and claw away the least perfect in her work of art (now in progress for three billion years).
Mind, Life could have evolved an offspring that is poisonous for
all nibblers but their mom, but Life did not.

Here to "kill-and-take" is well matched with a hand heaped
with "gifts." Here Amazing Grace jubilates its alleluias with the

fullest sounds of lows and highs. No time is wasted with a boring Eden for simpletons, where the ass, the seagull, the lion, all have forever to eat hay.

> *Creative religions and creative science can make*
> *us see these larger rhymes of the Earth so we may*
> *not bog down in complaints but join Her Song*
> *of the Earth from the top of the roof.*

80. Eve's apple. We are not alone who have nibbled on that legendary apple in dreamland from long ago.

A canyon is calling to me, "Wisdom strolls far, far to the South to where it has never ventured before. Wisdom from the tropics goes exploring for knowledge cooked on the South Pole. There are hair-raising dangers, many mistakes, a maze of trails to nowhere, many graves!"

Knowledge is an adventurous little wart on what our souls know. Yet, as one dumb bone deformation has finally evolved into a useful wing, so, when we wrench wisdom apart, one lucky chunk of knowledge may become that successful wart that slowly, patiently, could take on a life of its own.

Ah, the wisdom to know what knowledge we should not try to know! Knowledge is the food of the mind. There is knowledge that is poisonous mushrooms, knowledge that are curses, that are formulas of herbicides that could instantly dry out every leaf on the Earth. There are thoughts that are quicksand and treadmills staking us to wear us out—knowledge that permanently can erect our penises and our guns. There are goofs, scares and moles growing in our soul that only in the most drunken intimacies want to be brought to light.

Yet what fun to bend a little The Law and play with this god-send toy of knowledge in our experimental gardens of consciousness. With our dime's worth of knowledge that our scientists wrestled from Life's jungle of secrets into the light and out front, we love to manipulate life's processes on these plots. And we sure are deadly fascinated with lighters and matches. We are such curious Curious Georges. Waves and more waves of devastation! Yet watch, trashing in our thousand and one errors, once in a great while a mischief-maker blesses Life with a worthwhile new addition.

A once-upon-a-time couple of solitary bees share a secret with me. Long ago we both stepped over our instinct to fall for the knowledge tree, and we have now an affair with her. A brew from the fruit of this hallucinogenic fruit tree put both of us on the fast track of evolution. Other species that stepped out of a paradisial stasis to socialize at much higher levels than us must have picked and eaten a whole basket of these potent apples. Think of the upheaval in the emerging consciousness of the bees when they brought to light the knowledge for upgrading their communication system, so that these highly social animals could start gossiping among their ranks. How they had to shake and shake that knowledge tree to get the tips on how to engineer their mind-boggling social skills, their new economic reckoning, the specialization of their workforce, the remodeling of their sex lives and their architecture, their air conditioning and their fantastic food processing which knows mysterious recipes that can give ten lifetimes to their queens, the use of the Doppler effect, the mathematics of their dancing, their "telephone" system, their identification humming and their singing, a sense of honor now so deeply inbred it needs no medals. They must have tasted fruits from mind-altering trees of which we have no idea. (Or was it the same rare fungus that triggered their Curious George gene into over-drive?) Yes, they do know about the story of original "sin," of leaving behind an old sweet home with sex in pairs, and living in paradisial stasis. Long before us, they took off on evolution's adventure trips and have learned to live creatively with this split between exuberance and nostalgia.

I swallow my human arrogance. And I look over my shoulder to peek at those busy little old-time socialists for advice. They can help me to invent a more cheerful story of this evolving natural phenomenon than the grim "Eve-nibbling-narcotic-fruits" story of shame and original sin, or the lost innocent wisdom of the ancient wise men, or of the yellow emperor from long ago our patriarchs have invented for us to further this ongoing creative nostalgia. These social little souls know about such growing pains.

Now, dear adventurer, would you venture to continue
this essay in a way that most warms your heart?

81. I am the crookedy grapevine. You are the clear wine.

Wisdom is a slowpoke. With zillions of Life's playmates to be questioned, before reacting to my inquiry, wisdom may take a hundred years to reply. Smart science with its technology is our revolt against this slowpoke. That old-timer is far too fussy for us, too darn careful in growing, too untidy and humpty dumpty, too weedy, too protective and motherly. When our minds are farmed, wisdom, this slowpoke, is our indiscriminate compassion, our turbulent and weedy emotional intelligence, our unpractical longings, our undisciplined, childlike asking and thinking, our untidy, unscientific learning that loves to be taught by the unscholarly way of metaphors.

Sometimes, Life processes the alchemist in a man—an immensely complex and impure man who patiently does science the long, poetic way, with his soul—to extract the scientist out of him. She may begin by luring a gifted man into a promising mine or a niche with a hall of fame. The grape is thoroughly cleansed and goes into the press. Later, Life decrees; here is your perfectly clear grape juice. Here is your clearheaded scientist, with no impurities or irrationalities, no side-glances, no sediments, mysteries, daydreaming, wild ghosts or weedy thoughts. May this pure juice swiftly ferment into a high-spirited vintage wine. This brewing is what an education in a high-class barrel can do. Later, Life may delegate such athletes in clear logic to science's Olympic Games, where highly structured and muscular knowledge competes. Life loves such dedicated athletes for her evolutionary games.

I also note that athletes in body or in mind gladly take great risks beyond health. These extremists are explorers. They do not mind the risk of getting lopsided or hurt when they squeeze into a niche to focus their life on some splinter skill. Not much inspiration here for harmonious, healthy living. It's their daring new way to have their "children" and their joys.

82. Does pornography deserve a more compassionate story than the one I obediently adopted from my upbringing? Likeness by likeness, I start here to compose my own.

This is a rough-ocean essay. Skip it, unless you enjoy riding it out.

Pornography has been a black sheep in my spring meadow, for it has been demonized in my young heart. Forgive me. It will be an awkward washing to get the dirty names off this poor kicking sheep, and welcome it to timidly join my flock of phenomena in Serenity Land.

Let me try. After all, Life has had this stand-in, which is so much in demand right now, in her emergency kit for a long time. And so, I infer, not for trivial reasons.

I learned this much: dark and somber acts, as somber shades of colors, may fall in step when I become creative and incorporate them into the larger canvas of Life than life on a farm.

All evolutionary ascents are littered with tears of nostalgia. And do not also the capacities have their seasons that come and go? A string of generations in Life's procession might be born into the springtime of a capacity. Exuberance, high-flying highs, luxurious aroma everywhere, glands cooking sweetly intoxicating hormones in us. Later generations may be born with that same once jubilant capacity, yet already wearing silently the colors of fall. In our own ascent into a higher socialization, dear abilities of yesterday may be laid off by evolution in some of us. Slowly, Life turns off the lights in them. On this journey of love, unfamiliar, young talents still in the making may become hotly needed items. And Life wakes them up feeding them energy bars.

Once, we digested hair and bones. We don't do that anymore and our appendix gets a little skinny and out of shape. Yet it still hangs on for now, and still gives us hell if not properly fed and loved. Once we took oxygen with gills. No longer. Worker honeybees love to produce honey and wax instead of having sex. The solitary bees from before frolicked in the sweet old world of sex for all. Anything evolution has up its sleeves must feel instinctively wrong. My instinct is guaranteed no innovator. That fundamentalist is the stout preacher of what has proven yesterday's best old hat.

My old self snorting, I watch Life exploring new ways for us to socialize and to love. I note, for instance, that she asks some of us the sacrifice to not have children and lighten our enormous population on Earth. Life may reorient their love into new highly specialized chores, like giving a society GPS orientation or radar eyes, or Greenpeace work. And some are chores that a noble individual on his own cannot do. I watch Life reorienting the old sweetly-intoxicating pollination game in them into a sweetly intoxicating glue for a new social bonding. I watch her gently calm, in more and more of us, this old talent of self-replication with solitary games as a substitute, in which only our imagination provides the partner. In this nostalgic social experiment, Life seems to lead us into a more tightly woven society, in which having children can no longer be our free-for-all. Probably our most dreamed-of natural act is under evolutionary attack. (In the U.S., only one in five children is now raised by its married parents.)

And for eons, have not our dreams, in emergency, been the safest, wisest, and most natural producers of pornography, safety valve, and sex relief? So much so that even the saintly St. Augustine thanked God for not being responsible and taken to court for his dreams. What a discreetly compassionate gift, that when in desperate loneliness, a woman or a man is helped to conjure up into her or his imagination the company they need ardently. Or should I see it as a crime to help a broken-leg man to a pair of crutches? And, yes, like any pain reliever, without a measure of self-discipline that liquor soon can turn into a tyrannical addiction.

You may recommend outright abstinence. Tell me, how to dam this roaring mountain stream that surges through a woman or a man, so that in spite of that dam, they can keep their inner forests watered and teaming with delights? Abstinence that does not form puss requires a creative mind. I have been trained in self-discipline, so I should know a little of what I talk about here.

Would you jump with me here into a daring likeness? Consider a woman or a man who, after a terrible happening, is not up to taking on the real confrontation and awesome results of a brave and ardent reconciliation, along with its many kinds of consequences. A church may invite that troubled soul to a way out, to come for relief to the silent window of a confessional. You can spill that burden with no consequences, guaranteed. Confessionals are "condoms" that can give such safe relief. Others might go cuddle into the couch of a disciple of Freud to do the same. I think also, for example, of our old battered wanderlust that mostly is now tied to a stake of a career, and how Miss Discovery

Channel can appease that lust, weaning a man gently of things he has to slowly leave behind.

I think of "nature porn"—we indulge in National Geographic, or "religion porn" in film documentaries, or "kill porn" in violent video games, where the laid-off hunter can get safely his fill. Our souls may also need their sports. Think of how Life, while socializing us ever more, in many of us delegates our old need to fight, defend, hunt, lie, or think to some agency or specialist. To soothe our personal loss, Life may give us ball games or online games of war craft as inoffensive substitutes for our retired needs. Pornography might also be such a sport.

Life is good. She gives us defused eroticism, to mannerly calm that explosive lust when a man is helplessly on fire, yet is not talented enough to reorient this mountain-moving inner power in a more poetic way.

Here I mind another biological aspect of this phenomenon. In over-crowdedness, the genetic police of a species might confuse and hamper sexuality to deviate it into all kinds of sweetly intoxicating dead-end streets. For many, pornography, with all its hilarious addictions, may have simply become the pill. Gifted people can reorient that zest in more creative ways. They become our pathfinders out of this traffic jam.

I realize that Life has let me get by with an old-fashioned chore, sweet to my old-fashioned heart. For forty-nine years, Clara has been loving this rascal here with his crooked love—without the need to exchange a mean word. That's forty-nine years living in a spring meadow for me. A monogamous life with five now grownup children surrounding and loving us—not much terror of change here, not much need for substitute, sacrifice, and ersatz. I must have something of a swan in me. I am stuck with fidelity.

In my trek-abouts I have also noticed that cultures that put a taboo on relief systems such as pornography are more hierarchical and more violent. Contented, relieved women and men make reluctant soldiers.

Here is a down-to-earth anecdote to the point. When fishing in the tropics I often run out at night with my panga to a shrimp boat to get bait for my long line gear when they pull up the nets at daybreak. The crewmen (young men, maybe a month at a time at sea) like to lament, "Oh, Chivil, you bring us oranges and baked treats. We can live without these goodies. We need women, women, badly, or at least girly magazines. We will pay you with the best of our blue shrimp. Our 'literature' on board is in rags from thumping through." And they are feverishly desperate about it.

These are some first hints that my brainstorming netted for me about how the relief Life sends our battered and endangered erotic needs may be seen in a brighter light. I still wonder how to make peace with this shadow. May the adventurous reader contribute and help me on.

83. Life is the storybook of happiness.

Life is a story of happiness, albeit written in a very large scale and for a soul large enough to decode that story. What is more, are we not all apprentices in the trade of producing this happiness?

For the wisdom to know that this is so, I rely on teaching stories, that I mostly subsistence hunt for, while bumming around in land which our educators blame for being way too rich and permissive in ideas to be served in school. The indoors has remained a cramped place for me to lay out and read that very large story.

The alphabet has far too few letters to catch that beast. In fact, the written language has become that permanent Berlin Wall that protects us from becoming in contact with the fleshy, messy, sensuous outside world.

Highly cultivated people and crops all went seriously to school, hence our outstanding smartness, our success in the halls of man, our skill at piling up the highest money and grain silos, our vulnerability in the wild, and our prodigious capacity to criticize.

There is a lesson the Jewish people are teaching me in this respect. Life has made an experiment with this brave people. It restricted many of them to work mainly indoors, in the arts, the media, the halls of the sciences, the intellectual and businesses and in the money fields. In this selective environment, the mindset of smart, highly cultured and widely read people prevails, with an exceptionally high IQ. Intellectual fitness prevails as well as a richly burdened soul, as some lovely outdoor talents had to be laid off. Here is perfect soil for analyzers, thinkers, and politicians. Here, also, the very large-scale social skill of the wide open, permissive land, with its healing gift of very large metaphors, has less of a chance to seep in and make tolerance grow. It creates an environment that is not the best at teaching success management.

Likewise, I consider my experience in Fiji where land possession at that time was reserved for natives only. I saw there the same reorientation happen among the many daring immigrants from India. No land possession by immigrants was allowed. Thanks to their superior skills in business, in the analytical thinking, reading, organization and politics that they had to acquire to survive, they are now respected rather than loved among the easygoing and amazingly generous native people. This selective climate for them favors characters of strictness, authority, and untempered success. Tolerance and generosity does less well, and is more a quality of people who live close to the land and continuously rub against all kinds of people, animals, and plants. Like it is for the sparrows, home sweet home for outdoor people is everywhere, with less need for special taboos, caps, garlands, and conditions.

Wisdom is, for me, a doctorate in the widest social skill. It rubs into my skin while I curiously walk about, away from highly structured people. Hence, my instinctive shyness when I am among athletes of smartness. Ah, but to meet people who do not write and read well and are not fluent talkers, people who learned their social intelligence from a biosphere so rich in social skills that if these skills were compressed into a book, that book would instantly burst into flames. When I catch a bad gloom, I head for this enthusiastic land. This motherly land counsels me, sways me, repairs my sick mood, gently massages my pissed-off mind, and all for free. Sacred books, heavy and flightless with words of sorrow and sad anger, are out of place in these festive scenes. This motherly land helps me to outfox my many negative assumptions, my prison guards, so to speak, that are out to give me hell when I am happy without some authority's permission.

Life is good. This unconditional faith has become the lightning rod for my delicate intellect. Struck by a cataclysmic happening or by a hurricane of a man, the labyrinth of my intellect is not toasted by such a high voltage attack. I am grounded in this huge belly of goodness. There are many items in Life's goodness too raw for my intellect to digest them. Without a way to defuse such raw godsends, I used to be helplessly stuck in the notion: there must be evil. And my intellect was mostly a somewhat grim and angry intellect. With this new faith, I am a little less of a grouch.

The other toolbox for tolerance that serves me well is a solid and objective knowledge, not only about man but also about Life.

84. It's the critter most awake that survives.

Pregnant with countless options, the young planet is in its restless sleep, still dreaming. All of a sudden, one of its zillion specks wakes up. It starts to dance around itself, drawing others into its circle. Don't ask me, ask the Creator why. Tiny crystals form. Precursor molecules awake to their surroundings and say, "Hello!" They form islands of cell communities. They awake to "love-the-next-such-community!" and then the not-so-next, and then the distant one too. Lichen starts to process granite. A sunflower starts necking with the sun—all this chatting and jabbering when the birds wake up. More and more evolutionary rings of growth. And now, look around; look at yourself to see what the miracle of awakening can do.

I watch myself composing what I see and what I do not see. While pulling in my three miles of long line gear, suddenly a big halibut jerks on the line. On genetic command, my awareness *instantly* contracts. Nothing but Theo fighting that big fish remains of him. This has become the totality of Theo. Here is egotism at its best. Here is a lesson on the importance of how I mix what I am aware of and what I cover up, according to my chores.

For a Sunday treat, a carpenter wakes up from his carpenter dream. Here is his luxury of an unfocused day. Astonished, he remembers the weekday carpenter in him with the carpenter-eyeglasses put, sifting for chunks of awareness useful for his working week. He remembers himself seeing on weekdays not that mighty tree but the nice pile of lumber, seven feet tall, that tree can give, and how he swiftly had figured out how many caskets and doors he can hammer together from this godly pile of boards—nothing more.

Today, for that Sunday feast, there is no carpenter dream. The Divine Shaker of the dreamers opened his eyes wide for a treat. Today he is a child of the Sun. With a sudden flash in his mental scene, he realizes, "But out of this green cluster of ideas in front of me, I can do much, much better than to compose a simple pile of boards." He sees a hundred different motives hanging in that tree. He sees the delicious shade, the bird-nests and the family of mosses settled there. He sees leaves breathing for him, roots drinking, branches dancing, ladybugs mating. He sees the whole motley assembly of tenants that moved up into this apartment house in green. The tree turns into one huge nest of delightful ideas. From that feast of ideas he composes an entire woodland scene. He sees Darwin's theorem enlarged, becoming a contest to find the fittest lovers settling in this tree. With such a wild, uncensored look, how could our Sunday-man be a good carpenter today? Here is his "wake up and see." Here starts his "know-your-self-in-all-your-immensity" every sacred book is talking about. Here is his "Become aware!"

I personally create all that I see, carefully calibrating what to sleep away and what to wake up to and take on. All this downpour of action out there! An umbrella, please! To be stark naked awake out in this downpour of love, what horrendous risks! Think of the daredevil swimmer who would refuse a kayak or a log to hold on to or a life jacket made of some credo so his mind wouldn't get all banged up. Fully awake and exposed, that daredevil would dive into the untamed whitewater of awareness with its boulders and falls. How not to go under in what all he hears, hits, meets and sees? Things start to happen terribly fast to him in that wide-open out there.

It may need a godsend or a willful detachment from "worldly" things, like having a wife, children, a profession, a doctorate, or a home in order for a special woman or man to enjoy the luxury of an uncommitted awareness—a mind with no walls, no roof, no titles. No wonder, the wise of East and West seem to have been mostly hermits, beggars, poets and other solitary outpost souls who are less bogged down in the nearsighted world of rice, sweet potatoes, sex, fish, carpentry and corn. Such poor-in-gadgets-rich-in-leisure women and men can afford to stay awake to the zillion things the world loves to grow yet does not sell in Wal-Mart stores.

Ah, the dark side of the savant! A man who keeps himself awake very selectively. A man invited to retreat into a promising cave to study very seriously the last details of that singular niche. Think of a Beethoven or a Marx lost on a walkabout in wide-open aboriginal land. The natives' merrily comment: "What ignorant, helpless men. Let's give these poor people a hand." It is said that when a prodigious expert grazes for ideas, he ties his awareness to a stake.

And so, to become an expert seems not the best path to become a tolerant man. Or, on a lower level, being bred to be a fine Holstein seems not to be the best way to become an all-weatherproof beast.

When we civilize a young lad, do we not manipulate the pattern of what he does and does not see? We tame his awareness. Sit down, concentrate, shortcut to a conclusion! The gist: erase ninety percent of his awareness and highbreed the precious part that can be sold in the Wal-Mart stores. When we highly breed animals and plants, do we not do the same to their genome?

Watch her: Whoa! Unbelievable! She jumps that fence.
She is going for a more exposed, more plentiful life.

85. The big firework—and what our creation myths make of it

This beautiful, lively Earth: composed of scars that healed! Zillions of offenses—and as many reconciliations. Breathe in this nourishing atmosphere that gives breath to all: the distillation of the countless burps, bubbles, fumes, and farts. The playful ocean: the sweat of the soil, the rock faces, the Amazons that all labor so hard. Look at this wondrous show of survival—of the wise plants, animals, and people that learned best how to spread compassion and to snare others into their compassion—all our sisters and brothers. Each life-form: a composition made of stabs and reunions that learned from these moaning and jubilating take and give games.

If I want to know about Life's politics, I study its history. This greatest work of remembrance is the original Book of Life. It is not written in words, as are our Creation Myths. The earthy, sexy

Book of Life is the source of our myths. There is no more direct way to hear what Life has to teach.

The Creator opened Her hand: "Here is your Big Bang, pregnant with uncountable options. And that firebird flew up and away producing and reproducing. Do you see it?" It's these slight variations in the tenseness of this Bang that are now evolving, circling, flying, blooming, thinking in an ever more complex web of interactions.

The story of that Big Firework is written in sediments, in the air trapped in the ice cores drilled from the South Pole, in the wanderings of the magnetic North. It is imprinted in the alignment of some minerals, and in the wanderings of the Tectonic Plates, in the movements of the firmaments, in the folding of the rock formations. It is found in a mineral's crystalogeny, in the calendar of the ice ages written in the ocean shorelines dancing up and down, and in the erratic boulders the glaciers left behind, in the biography of the very small particles, in the carbon dating, in the epic told by the Grand Canyon and the growth rings of stalagmites.

This epic of all epics is further written in fossils, in the family tree of DNA, in the footprints of Life's instincts and its many vestigial treasures left behind on its trail. That we, the men, have still also some sort of nipples is also one sentence in the divine comedy. Ninety-nine percent of the life-forms ever created are now extinct. They are embalmed in sediments. Yet, their nuggets of wisdom live on in our genes.

Following the footprints of Life, I came to think that the Creator avails himself of more voluminous workdays in His decoration of the universe than our little twenty-four hour sun-earth affair. Think for instant of the timetable of galaxies rhythmically turning around themselves. Take the present workday in which the animals are still being created. Don't be bashful. This is turning out to be a very long day, and with no repose yet in sight. Go into details. Visualize the story of how the horn of the rhino was composed—too long—too short—too black—too soft—and then, just right—for now. All in one second of that evolutionary working day. Think of our age-old arms-competition with the microbes and their relentless buildup of resistance to our antibiotics, and not even a lunch break yet for us in sight. Times and times before, the Creator hit Venus with an object so huge, it reversed this planet's rotation. And the planet is still figuring out what to do with all the new options.

The Earth is that great mysterious pagoda and labyrinthine museum. In spite of the pitfalls, a youngster may become a courageous Curious George and slowly grow out of his nursery rhymes and baby shoes. Continuously, we create new and updated creation myths. We add awe to our awe when in front of the mystery. That investigation makes our trust in the marvelous mystery grow. Stirring and cooking our creation myths, adding new ingredients and spices, they become a more nourishing soup for our confidence, so much so, that one bright morning, even the useless may proudly show us its use.

> *Crimes and ugly toads might have metamorphosed over-*
> *night in our minds into magicians that insist in the morn-*
> *ing, "Polish your vision and look again; we too, we are*
> *tools that do wonders in the Creator's hands."*

86. Are you the tough instructor who can teach me to outgrow our nice little dance floor and steps, and instead happily dance to the Song of the Earth?

Yesterday, down among a crowd of lamenters, I saw a bag lady being chased away from the dumpster that was her good luck for weeks, and I cussed the storeowner. I heard of a roadside bomb that brusquely silenced a jubilant boy and took him home—and I joined the wailing. The newsman told me of financiers who went berserk in the heat of Wall Street and became legalized world-class shoplifters and I balled my fist with the crowds.

Today it is Sunday; it is serenity time. Today, for a treat, I do not identify with the individual, do not join a crowd of applauders or fist-ballers, no listening to single players, no consoling, no complaining. Today I switch scale. I ask a whole country scene to be my drug dealer for that treat. I take off for Mt. Everclear and I paint on my canvas what I see. By and by, a grand mosaic is surrounding me, an entire valley, the vineyards with fat grapes, nifty sparrows stealing fruits, the first yellow leaves dancing to October winds, the thunderclouds hanging in the sky, and the village ladies gossiping, picking the fruits. I add the woodlands behind to that extended family picture many generations long, many species wide.

Seen from this Sunday-high, supercharged women and lightning men may fit in with other natural phenomena in the class of tsunamis, northern lights, thunderclouds, spring tides, eclipses of the sun. Today I listen to this chorus of lamenting, yelling, jubilating, bickering, and crookedly loving—and that identification hum makes my heart feel at home sweet home.

I join for a treat Life with her quiet, generous smile, doing her feasting, completely unconcerned about the neat little rows of morals our society planted in Theo's mind.

From up here, my tiny garden is barely visible yet safely nested in Life's great wild work of art. Life sure uses some unapproved recipes when she cooks my joys and my tears. Up here she metamorphoses some of my whining into cheers. Up here a scenic view may come over me so tipsily high, some of my needs to criticize distill into awe and joy.

And when a funeral party passes by, I may also think of a woodland scene in fall with the aroma of brewery and its splendid color display—and the funeral grief becomes a little less of a grief. My messy, unscientific investigating up here has privileged access to my vast subconscious knowing.

Oh! I should shut up and hide, when this sense of wholeness comes over me. The weekday folks tend to scold me for being heartless, when I fly high into this expanded mood. Once above their morals' curtain and their dear routine, I see bunches of reasons why I should not be sad. Yet, they demand that I be sad. But tell me: how can Theo take himself to court, if he has no higher viewpoint than Theo?

When I fly this highflying plane, full of highflying thoughts, I also worry, "How do I safely land this thing?"

On such vacations, I treat myself to that grand, heart-joining show. Here all these bunches of selfish genes blend and join, pulling on my sleeves and telling me, "Look well from up here. See, we do not fend only for ourselves but, very mannerly, with the fittest of social skills, together we all contribute to the Song of the Earth, each with its own variations of ups and downs." On these days, reserved for the heart, I am invited to scoot a little closer to the Creator's lookout and join in with his: "How pleased I am with what I see!"

> Don't get nervous when I sneak away for a minute to these lighthearted respites. I will soon be out of this wine. I will again be back among the crowd of moaners in no time.

87. The Buddhist Stanza: Fundamental Wisdom of the Middle Way

Biology's Stanza: The Law of Moderation

In the camp of man there is lately so much taking—and so little giving.

Above the faculties of medicine, energy, genetics, reproduction, before all above our ethical haggling in these domains, the one luminous question lightens up all over our morning sky: "How many more advantages should we pile up on the side of man? How much is too much?" It is true, also a boat with an overload of advantages can sink.

Take a deep breath, Theo. This answer needs a paradigm shift to a compassion that ignores all our many dear little -isms.

Columbia, the tallest Sitka spruce in Deep Inlet, told me, "We, the families of the plants and the animals homesteading here in and around Deep Inlet, we tremble in terror of your globalized, applied sciences. Your sciences are turning away from enlightenment to instead scheme weapons of mass destruction so to expand even more your advantages when you colonize the kingdoms of the other animals and the plants. Our flyers, our tunnelers and wrigglers, all the photo-synthesizers, the unborn creatures, including the unborn generations of man, even Ms. Cow, we are all up in arms, flippers, paws, branches, muzzles, in solitary protest. Your cold, egotistic sciences have become for us the most catastrophic happening on Earth. Your applied sciences lost all table manners. Some of your 'autistic' particle physicians for example are so deadly fascinated with using monstrous power, they stay up nights to fuse the nitrogen atoms so mankind may become the ultimate dictator of the Earth with a zillion of manpower to your command. And, unbelievably, we must watch your honored lifesaving and reproduction enhancing businesses pour even more buckets full of people into the terrible flood you have become.

"We ask your upcoming scientists not to give mankind even more firing power, more life extensions, more pensioners, more megawatts and 'cures,' more papers published in *Nature* or *Science* about how to serve you even more plates of advantages. With so many wonderful teaching stories we act out on the shaded side of your souls that can heal the grudges you have with Life, may your new scientists bless you with insights on how you are well taken care of while you treat all the family members of life as neighbors."

To validate their claim, I judged their quality of life and counted their numbers and their elbow room. And I must give Columbia a little credit. How much energy should the rosebush invest to grow more thorns? How much for the rhino to grow a larger horn? How much more dancing around the clinical medicine should we do and load our children down with more pensioners? Life could have evolved an eye that could kill just by looking at a pathogen, or a skin that paralyzes any intruder in no time. Why did it not?

When I was young, in wartime Europe, I heard it sung from across the Rhine, "One nation over all!" Now I hear that refrain again: "The empire of man over all." No, we will not on our own be able to get ourselves out of this celebrated traffic jam we have squeezed ourselves into. We have to trust Life, now that we forced Her to use her genetic medical chest and trigger the cure for us. To be grateful for her cure, I will have to weather my mind and let her go wild. For what I start to see of that cure breaks the frame of my learned morals and will make my domesticated mind helplessly bleed.

Life is a very ingenious boat bobbing on the cosmic sea loaded with gadgets of which we have no idea. I note, if a load shifts dangerously to one side, that boat does not sink. She has ways to bring that lost son, or that misplaced load, back home to the center again. Or, after having duly recorded the lesson, She dumps that experiment overboard and uses the priceless lesson to start experimenting how to fill the niche with a more balanced act.

After this entree laced with medicine, here is a yummy dessert. In our time, in which many of Life's mysteries are so generously revealed to us, to have the valor to take on, one by one, and incorporate into our mind-scape these iconoclastic revelations, can become our most enlightening, most amusing soul-adventure yet. No other species has ever been gifted with a survival test that stretches and stretches her soul to lose or win so much. To become aware that we are a wonderful toenail somewhere on the body of Life and so mysteriously being well taken care of, this step into a brighter light, this sweet trust in Life, is the sweetest, safest anesthetic yet. Clouds of fears will simply dissipate. Truly, a mind-blowing expansion of consciousness is reaching out toward us. The enough-is-enough principle now insists on being discovered by our scientists' commune.

Ah! After this long ice age in my soul, if I can touch you, if you can touch me, warm me. We can sing together, write, talk and massage our battered love for Blue Blossom Land in our mind into greening again. Spring is here! Free, not inmates of humanism anymore!

88. Goodness is each man's personal jigsaw puzzle.

There are zillions of different pieces in Life's jigsaw puzzle. Each woman and man and critter is a proud holder of a few. Each of us in the morning fumbling through his wake up routine is fingering his unique little pile of pieces, fitting and again fitting, trying to figure out one more happy day, before heading for the "battle grounds." After a hundredth time fitting and trying, don't give up, Theo, and throw that stubborn, unfit piece to the dogs or on the pile of evil. You are frustrated about not understanding each other or that darn whatever? Quick! Grab that gift circling you. You are close to pay dirt. It's a chance to a handshake as short as the spark of a flint.

Take a hay meadow in spring. It's made up of a thousand different piles of such pieces. A thousand different kinds of goodness bring out their different flowers; each shade of red or blue is of a different, customized recipe for being good, each kind of heart is gifted with a different set of blind spots and window views. The spruce has a different red rule booklet of what is proper than what the elm tree is told about the right way to live. For fault of other "enemies," a male grizzly is told to sometimes kill a grizzly cub, and thereby keep their population in tune. This has become goodness in Grizzly land. We choose another goodness to keep our population from becoming monstrously big. And it seems we do not do so well.

Think here of the shepherd, the sheepdog and the sheep. Think of our leaders with their cadre of diplomats, spies, marines, sharp shooters and their other special troops of "sheep dogs." And think of the huge, shy populace that huddles under the umbrella that our professional killers, demonizers, and foreign aid teams provide for us. The same goodness for all? Ridiculous.

Think of a stern winter-man whom Life puts to laying bare and tilling the soil while the seeds are curling up in sleeping bags. Think of an exuberant spring-blossom woman who wakes up again these seeds in that well tilled, well fertilized, well soaked soil, eager for all kinds of love affairs. The same sweet feelings for both? Ridiculous! Now, isn't that a comfy rest stop of a thought for a mind rolling in broken ideas or in broken glass?

There are so many chores in Life's enterprise. Each jobholder is imprinted with a different set of morals to do what others cannot do. Did you ever ask yourself who is doing on your behalf the lying and killing, the logging, the night watching, and the demonizing of your opponents, the messy crude oil pumping, while you are safely stretched out, nicely fed and watching TV at home sweet home?

Givers of birth are being instructed in different classrooms with soundproof walls than the classrooms for providers, sharp-shooters and undertakers, so as not to confuse these differentiated souls. Some would die if they kill. Others would truly die if they did not kill.

Raw goodness still on the hoof and kicking is all around me—blinding brilliance everywhere. Samples of a mind-boggling generosity wherever I look. But I do not have the right stomach for most of it. I want goodness simplified, cultivated in a garden plot, cooked or barbecued at home to my taste so that my delicate mind can digest it. I am such a fussy soul on high heels.

Yet what would I have done for my growth had my sense of goodness no rings of growth, had I made my mind not a little more omnivorous, had I never made peace with one of my shadows?

Once in a while the fog breaks and a star peeks through—and another and another one—and the Big Dipper tells me, "North is over there!" Once in a while a most joyful "aha!" so happily resounds in me and tickles my heart much longer than do my licks on a chocolate ice cream cone.

There are many people who need an unbreakable routine. Are we not in terror when a crack appears in our overcast sky and the North Star peeks out where we presumed to be the South, when a goodness steps out where there should definitely be none, when our orientation—or a moral—is suddenly turned upside down? It's the same old terror of the chick about to hatch.

89. Under the makeup, I have found the beauty for grownups—and I am restoring it.

Finished with this soul dress-up! No more need for this makeup to catch the eyes of surface schemers. The parade to present us as the darlings of Life or of some little god, for which soul beauticians have dressed me up, this ruse has caused much arrogance, loneliness, and confusion in my soul. No more sweating under such a stressful mask.

The difference between a soul of a raven and my soul is that mine went to the beauty salon for all kinds of nifty soul lifts and cosmetics and the raven did not. Read our western mythology and you might give me a little credence.

It is the dress that makes the bishop, the mask that makes the shaman, the mythology that tattoos our front with "you are

Life's chosen one" that graduate us to the Masters of Life. Think also of the celebrated Parisienne who takes off her eyelashes, her fingernails, her paint job and breast supports before she huddles into her bed, alone.

And is it not also such long-term cover-ups that make our heroes and our saints? Ah, if we could listen in on the gossip on the other side of our garden fence. Over there, our heroes and saints might be a little less celebrated. In the court of the Earth some of these very "good" folks might even have a case of favoritism waiting for them. Our "bad-men" might even be a little thanked for their help when meeting them later again way up the hill.

Yesterday evening, anchored in Kelp Bay, I watched from close by a sea otter mom tenderly grooming her pup. To be still so loving and nurturing in this tough environment after a million years, Ms. Otter wins my love and makes me think. We are barely a few thousand years into our declaration that "we are the grandest," and look how we are messing up our homeland and our love.

This cherished illusion of grandeur has proven a fruitful ruse of Life. It sure made of us the most willing martyrs for Her evolutionary mischief.

Son, be a friendly visitor. Leave your medals and guns at home.

90. With the comfy belief in evil, my intellect has become lazy.

Each man is a small earth on Earth. Each heart holds an enormous inner heat contained by a delicate web of love. What happens on a larger scale to the Earth, happens to a man. Sometimes, the raw inner magma erupts, producing cataclysmic changes of climate and mental scenery. Fault lines break open in our love and our dear routine lies in pieces. Is it an act of God?

Here I stand. On one side are the believers in evil—the largest religious congregation ever, so numerous, so powerful, with every easy commonsense logic on their side. This enormously practical belief releases us from the arduous task that itches every soul: to make peace with its shadow. It gives us the license to condemn.

On the other side: the motley little gang of draft dodgers who resist submitting to this helpful commonsense doctrine—and at great risk. These brave rebels do not go for: "Dammit!" They are explorers. For them, the belief in evil is a totalitarian mental tool. This tool does not listen. It condemns without appeal. That notion of evil aborts any dialogue that is pregnant with painful new insights. It allows the mind to swiftly put many mysterious living processes in jail for life. It puts our morals in jail. The notion of evil is a very effective mental Ritalin and Aspirin. It is a godsend for unadventurous minds. Dismissing something as evil is the cheapest intellectual way to deal with a painful happening. It is the pill against growing pain.

This is going to be a difficult thought to follow through. Hold on.

Think of a man staggered in a terrible drought of kindness that dried and shriveled his onion of love, ring by ring, down to its last and most primitive layer. With a careless, tiny spark, or wink of an eye, an absentminded woman ignites that man full of tinder into an uncontrollable and terribly destructive wildfire. Imagine the catastrophe in a helpless man, when his rushing glands completely sweep him finally away with no foothold left to give him strength—or a woman stranded in a desert so brutally dry that she must steal water at gunpoint.

It is an enormous, nearly monstrous leap of the faith in the goodness of Life to even consider that a rapist's act, for example, might also be a natural disaster or an act of God. This is a leap with practically no foothold in sight. Only a woman or man who divested her or his soul of all the exclusive add-ons and exemption myths, only such wild souls remain open to hints from likenesses in Life that such natural disasters or hormonal wildfires can happen also among man as an act of God. Tearing up their license to condemn is their crime. They may see evil as a sad, sad lack of empathy—the affliction of a deep inner blindness. This leap of faith is the price a woman or man pays when choosing the steep, lonely road up toward serenity land.

And while the crowd whips that man on fire with nettles, a young woman goes over to that man on fire with a bucket of water and touches and sings that hurting man into love again. She repeats the marvelous Mongolian legend of the "Weeping Camel." In it, a mama camel—after a terrible birthing—can only kick and bite, and refuses to love and nurse. A young village woman goes over to this kicking, burned-out mama camel and caresses her, and with the help of the local violinist sings her into tears, love, and milk again.

How to talk about the consequences of a terrible drought in kindness and love? I have never had to live through one.

When out of town, beating waves or bushes, I hear Life or God clearly say through any act or critter: "Theo, I am here! Theo, stick to these 'ruinous' hints that whatever we are, whoever we are, we might all be innocent and blameless. Never mind the outrage among all of your parasitic little ghosts like guilt, regret, blame, free will or 'dammit' who might threaten to move out." I note that Life moves on a wide front of options when it goes on the warpath of evolution.

If Life had stuck to our tender little morals, it might still be algae all over.

91. The expert syndrome

The general practitioner is recruited.

When my life is turned into a monoculture, will not many species of talents in me cry for help and end up on the list of endangered species?

Each gene, each cell in me is a ghost, a little mama burning to nurture me, keeping me healthy, whole and in sweet company. This is her joy. If put away in a closet, she finds a way to pester me to be heard. The ghosts of my sperms that dream of eggs, yet end up in some you-name-what. The ghost of your leg that dreams of walking about, yet is glued to a gas pedal. The ghost of my thinking is a mustang. It burns to roam the vast horizon, yet tied to a stake to practice some expertise, it soon turns into a cranky farm mare. The ghost of my biological clock wants to harmonize my body functions. I impose an unruly schedule—it gets pissed off and rebels. The ghost of a woman's reproductive anatomy we chemically sabotaged into confusion with the pill knows: this is no time for fertile intercourse, and refuses to do its job. So it demands a new, timelier way to be creative and to love. In a love-forsaken toddler, billions of cells, meant to become friendly mirror neurons to later touch and mirror the pains, needs, and the joys in a partner's heart, are mercilessly drafted for pure defense. Soon they render that tender lover entirely to thorn. Love affairs will not grow well in this expert in thorns. And what does the merchant do who wants the biggest, shiniest, most expensive chrysanthemum flowers on the market? He mutilates each plant, twists off all its flower buds but one.

The weekday job of the expert is to butcher the beast and lecture about the qualities of the ribs, the tongue, the hind quarters, the lung. For sheer fame, scientists now release on the market enormously explosive knowledge whose fallout can put the fallout of the nuclear technology into the shade. To avoid becoming mildewed in their niche, experts badly need their Sunday time, so they may not become a mental hospital for their talents that are left to starve behind. Ask a celebrity, ask a woman on an assembly line. They know about being broken-hearted. Highly skilled people, whether on the assembly line of some knowledge or of some shoe-wear, may have to divorce many mistresses of their heart. Many talents laid off soon cry out loud, "Let us live, let us in on the sweet joys of love. We want to be seen and heard. Use us or lose us! Without some kindhearted reorientation, our revenge syndrome will take you down." A madhouse of family quarrels. A madhouse of anxiety and stress. Lucky you, with a bent for creativity who can respond and compensate.

Theo is a beehive. May unemployment among my bees remain low. In my beehive, may the workers I need to reorient or condemn to rocking chairs be few. May there be in my life bearable stress and nostalgia. May my fishing and my loving become elegant. May my inner music remain a harmonious working hum.

92. The prodigious genetic variability, the main attribute of wilderness, is Life's greatest tool for adaptation. Should we declare war on this outrageous profusion of options?

As a wild soul, so a wild stretch of land, they are bags of immensely diverse capacities. Not being practical—that is their "crime."

It was decreed by the priests of the internationals, proselytizing the belief in one single global economy: to produce profit, the peoples, the plants, and the animals are all way too crookedly diverse for our enterprise. How to fit a hundred wildly exuberant puppies under our one single hat? And so they founded the greatest corporation in proselytization ever. The airwaves, the halls of PR experts, the conference rooms in the chic hotels filled with their earth-flattening message: "small and local is humpty-dumpty and wasteful." And from this simplistic dogma of economics a tide of simplifications now rises and rises, surging into every heart, nook, and cranny of China, of Ladakh, of Hotland and Iceland. Look, this brute tide of kickass culture uproots anything dreaming, creeping, breathing, or crawling without a passport to the commodity market and their money fields. Alarmed, we now notice: oh! But this program to straighten out the curly, crooked love of our dear and so permissive hearts and Earth is terribly successful!

Look at our banquet of languages, skin colors, handshakes, of ways to worship and courtship, to dress and cook fish and all the exotic positions to make love. That exuberant bundle of delights is disappearing in the trashcan! One kind of money, of pants, of Russet Burbank french-fries and soft drinks fitting all. High on that anesthetic simplicity, the baggage of our diverse religious feelings and historic awareness is left behind in this exodus. Truly, our souls are being trashed. With this radical simplification of our souls, Madam Economy, mother of all prostitution, gets more busloads of customers. This standing in line for the madam's handouts now discreetly compromises my fitness to bring forth and take care of my unique love-brand called Theo.

We sure have become fine indoor players. Our sense of beauty and of goodness has become elitist and choosy. We have become creative at lavishly embellishing our indoor world. We retreat into things manmade, standardized, man-controlled and alphabetized. The sight of a cockroach has become a storm. No wasting time to just ponder about the happenings on a single flower stem that nonetheless beats the complexity of our latest fighter jets by a thousandfold.

Are we joining Life's social experiment with the termites that turned these munchers so exclusive and so fragile, they now need to dwell continuously in enormous sealed-off housing complexes, no longer fit to ever again peek into the songful, colorful, sunny outside? Termites must now build protective mud tunnels to wherever they go.

And so our daily packs get less stuffed with adventures and more with safety equipment. What yesterday was lighthearted luxury, today is five heavy pounds of "The Law." Are we becoming the little emperors of the Earth bundled up in ever more survival suits and safety measures?

To realize that single, "global village" of man, the rowdy circus of our 4,000 rather independent tribes and cultures needs to be melted down. Sweet old family life, one of the last and sweetest goodies from our bygone wildlife, must be melted down into one single pot of production power. Home-raised children and chickens become a danger for "sanitary" reasons.

Now we start to note it: that meltdown, dressed in beautiful words, spreads a toxic mental environment that literally sickens billions of our hearts—hearts stressed out from muffled yet rightful local voices still pleading yet already bagged for the city dump. Think of the "better" Earth of our modern economists as a fantastic, worldwide birdcage for a simplified mankind that lives together with a few darling plants and animals in one posh, exclusive club, a rare symbiosis of man, cow, pig, internet, pets and corn. Tell me, is this the sanitized and practical living your big, adventurous soul dreams about?

The sweet elitist myth of the "global village" is a wolfish idea in sheep clothes. That camouflaged beast wants a local culture served for lunch at every stockholders' meeting. And remember what such a simplification brought in the 1840s to the Irish people and their one highly cultivated potato variety, with which they developed a highly practical symbiosis for two. The potato blight came—and apart from emigration, only one exit door—closed by that blight. And what do we learn? Globalization makes our wealth in cultures and options for survival so darn vulnerable.

Have you also rediscovered that there is a more fun
way to walk a life than the practical way?

93. What yesterday was right, today is a mistake. Each new insight leaves behind a garbage can full of mistakes.

Thanks over and over for all the joy the mistakes I made have given me. These side-steps and tentative connections have been my stepladder to find out who I am. May I be given a long life to make many more mistakes. May they be sparkling new mistakes, so, in the morning, I do not have to lament, "Darn, do I have to chew on this again?"

What I thought is a cat is not a cat. What yesterday was a myth pointing the way, today may be a road-sign pointing to a dead-end street. Where yesterday I would attempt a good deed, I may now happily resist intervening. Yesterday, I could convince you and, like any preacher, beam in victory. Today, no victory! Today I might want to listen to you and enjoy your own song so excitingly different from mine, as I listen to the birds, each twittering its very own morning-glory song. Today reconciliation sings sweeter in me than victory. I used to enjoy being nice to you. Not anymore. I am learning to do better. I can endure your whining. I can be brave and become your sharpening stone.

I packed away from a ruin some old bricks, and *oops!* Instead of stealing bricks, I ended up stealing myself a lesson. I had to have a very humbling talk with the angry caretaker who found out—and Butchy and I became friends. I twisted my ankle between the tussocks and I learned to peel my eyes. I tried to bend her thinking my way, and all I did was step on her toes and heart. That started talk of things I never heard before. He shouted at me and I shouted back. We exploded into an idiotic shouting spree. Later I learned that I can do better than to be an echo. I bit into an apple-like thing and darn, I blistered my tongue. With such a fine learning process at hand, I start to be a little grateful for such lessons, and less regretful. Today is a sweet day, for Theo pokes fun at Theo: how come, you "grandee," that yesterday you could not see it— and missed out connecting with this marvelous string of ideas?

Ah, the mischievous smile of the trickster in me when I found out that I didn't have it right, that further up there is another more scenic viewpoint where I can assemble a bigger "right." New, freshly baked adventures can start. Overcoming a mistake, and another mistake, I assemble and reassemble my patchwork of insights. I quilt together those darn mysteries of Life. I demolish my yesterday and reassemble it into a roomier today. Yesterday, he thought of you like this, and he made a gesture with his hands of pushing you away. Today, after listening to another chapter of your story, he took you in his arms. So, it is when you prove me wrong and you light in me that sunlit *ahhhh* where our profit starts.

Fishing for forty-six years, I have been providing the daily food for maybe seventy people for these years. Yesterday it was right that I felt pride. Today the ocean tells me that to keep on fishing the same old way with the same old pride is a mistake.

The history of Life is a history of mistakes and extinctions— and, of course, of the precious residues distilled out of these mistakes and extinctions. Look at you and me. Think of an onion. After each onion ring: done with it, never again. Think of our hammering with a rock, long ago, many smashed fingers! And look, a handle could be added to that rock; never bloody fingers again! Think of the blessing that genetics can make out of mistakes. It's because of this brave experimenting that Life stood up from a soup of mud to become that fantastic circus that performs now around us.

How could we regret making mistakes? How could we
repent at having learned? I start to like this happy song:
"I-was-wrong!" May we shout it loud and with pride.

94. The merry explorer of Life's working

A beehive, with which I had a stingy run-in, had some advice for
an apprentice in serenity like me: "Theo, serenity has nothing to do
with being a universally likeable lad, has nothing to do with how
many friends or opponents you surround yourself with. Serenity is a
handshake with the mountain you are about to climb, a handshake
with a man that steps into your life who is on a high or a low you
barely know, a handshake that takes entirely place in Theo's heart.
You make a peace agreement with the steep canyon you are about
to descend in order to meet the secrets it has stashed away. It is your
thumbs up for us, the bee people, and for our different needs than
yours, like using stingers instead of AK-47s to defend ourselves. It
is a thankful 'yes' to an invitation to learn from someone with the
need for a different size of soul and shoes than you. It is your 'yes' to
meet your 'ouches' as your teachers too."

Now, could you tell me why the Earth is graffitied all over
with so many keep-off signs? Certainly not to keep us off the
premises. But maybe to lead us to enter the guesthouse through
the door and not through the sewer pipe. I am still learning that
there is kindness that must touch me with thorns, warning me,
"Sorry: not here—try there, no need to break down walls!"

No candies and ten-cent talk for us. May we twine together a
long rope for our buckets to reach down into our deeper well when
we meet to bring up these intimacies, these peace agreements,
these handshakes, these thank-yous, these goodies for the heart.

95. Western culture had turned into my most successful drug dealer.

With a string of mantras, the present idealistic culture of make-believe kindled my imagination and my expectations into a fantastic high. It sold me a sweet delusion of grandeur and omnipotence with no success management attached. Few politicians avoid this narcissistic high. This drunken imagination made me believe that we can squeeze a gallon of juice out of one orange, squeeze out of the Earth a living standard for all seven billion people on it that equals our own binge-living, that we can live forever on the goodness of an eternal spring.

We sure have embarked on this wonderfully inventive folly with great energy. To keep getting our way, in the United States we now bulldoze into the living Earth with a continuous thirty kilowatts per man. That is three hundred times our body's physical strength (2,500 calories per day). And we are begging our gods for more energy, more, more, more. This is technology, the art to evermore bend the Earth our way. How physical we have become! When Life talks back to us, we simply step on the gas. This is believing that goodness is a one-sided sword, that "good" deeds and credit cards are not debts. We insist on keeping up a sustainable growth of our advantages after our economy surpassed its point of sustenance maybe fifty years ago. Figures tell us that we would need five planet Earths to sustain the dear affluenza we now enjoy, and keep in balance with the animals and plants that supply our joys.

When I get out from under our sweetly intoxicating media cloud, fresh air, fresh thoughts! I detox. I sober up from this high. I find my strength to start to deconstruct the bubble of luxurious thoughts and possessions I have become. A pill of solitude helps me on.

96. At the junction, here is the entry to the speedway for hard smartness. There starts the curly trail preferred by compassion.

I watch the emotional dance between the mama and her baby. A nourishing conversation is going back and forth. These are the moments, when the neural road system of this little lover is talked over and laid out. In these far reaching moments, her later relationships are engraved. One session of sweet, time-less nursing, tickle-tickles and lovely burps: billions of neurons arranging themselves into a trail net toward the fun of being cared for and to care, toward the world that rewards intima-cies, cooperation, trust, and social skill. Here, old conventional wisdom is the builder of the mental pathways. In this gener-ous, peaceful home sweet home, some of the neurons remain free to mirror the feelings of other people and of ravens and of meadows too. That's how compassion is engraved into this little "open sesame."

In this shielded environment, there is no urgent need to invent, to defend, to adapt, to rebel, or to grow thorns. Instead of being primed for shocking novelty, a mindset that is not geared for innovation may prevail. This is also the soil out of which the less adaptable fundamentalist may grow.

What if an infant is being efficiently raised in some very hygienic, licensed care and feed center and misses out on that leisurely, sweaty, non-paying, emotional mama-baby conversa-tion and dance? Her first cascades of neurons may well arrange themselves differently, to face a hyper-world in a rush, a world of strangers and of mistrust, of having to avoid and be nice, a world of aggressive competition in efficiency, inventiveness, and of structured love for pay. A world where barely a "yes" is heard and barely any doors are kept unlocked. In such a life situation, a young intellect might not be guided down the avenue for deep social intelligence and for old wisdom, but onto a street for hard smartness, hard self-defense and hard cash, which are the needs for that tightly structured world. Here smartness tediously figures out the lock-combination of the sinking *Titanic*'s vault while others light-footed run for the few remaining dinghies. Here there is little time for luxuries, like building a road system in the mind for reading the emotions and needs of other people. A love to explore love in unconventional and new ways might prevail. The ruses of brutally successful business might prevail. A "think-big-money-kick-ass" mentality might prevail. In such an outbreak of smartness, people everywhere starve for kindness. Like a hostile environment, laced with our deadly antibiotics stimulates microbes to become creative and concoct a new resistance and immunity, this frost bitten environment may also stimulate adaptive creativity in a gifted young mind.

In outright hostile environment, like cold, egotistic parents, many neurons in a young child are drafted to become soldier-neurons: trench digging, barbed wire, deceiving techniques, an army of defenses. Here, again, few neurons are delegated to perceive and process the other's needs and feelings. Indeed, a mind might turn entirely to thorn. Such gifted soldiers can step on your toes and "luckily" have no mechanism to know your hurt. There were cultures that put a taboo on hugging their children and lo, highly hierarchical, highly violent societies came of that taboo. (e.g. the Spartans). Happy children do not later make good soldiers.

How we connect and chat with all nature has unimaginable consequences. In his first encounter with the world, a youngster's whole neural road system for later seems to be laid out according to what kind of environment touches him and teaches him the dance of love. His childhood memories might so well remain his most trusted guides for life, for better or for worse. Those initial tiny neural trails, when later trotted into highways, are as hard to change as what started as a trickle of melt-water and dug itself deep into a canyon-land. Only adventurers keep the plasticity of their mind into adulthood.

My relationships are my soil. All my everything
grows, or does not grow out of this soil.

97. Theo, be kind with your precious capacity to become sad. Don't throw this gift away. It is one of your magic remedies.

When a black event is about to drown me in blind anger, when down under in that blind rage I find again the way to reconcile with that menacing event and surface into sadness, breath is here! The wound can mature. Pus is ejected. Light and sight is here! I start to revive and to put feelers out again.

When anger starts to cry with tears in its eyes, this is the magic happening. This is when the tulip bulb frozen in the winter ground remembers spring. Sadness is pregnant with deep, healthy, wrenching longings. It crumbles barricades and walls. It unties my anger's knot. It grows the scab on my wound. It mobilizes the troops of my heart. Love with tears in its eyes talks lovingly of love. Promising questions cry in me for the Mother of all answers—and the mama's breast starts to swell with milk, squirting those answers toward me. Sadness, that most fertile soil, cries out for joy. And the spirit of the Earth is listening. Even our cat Dusty hears Clara's tears. No water hole can resist a longing seed. The capacity to be sad is as great a gift as ecstasy. Both are the gift that a woman or a man can draw from their deep well. Tears can melt a snowed-in heart. Tears are the privilege of those who are not stone-walled by egotism.

No water hole can resist a longing seed. The capacity to be sad is as great a gift as ecstasy.

They are a language more persuasive than my philosophical bla-bla-blas Deep sadness and deep joy may be sisters after all. In goes a lemon, out comes the lemonade.

Sadness makes me so, so alert and open-eyed. In strictly regimented fields of rationality, sadness is the unappreciated wetland, teeming with bundles of endangered delights. In sadness, we do amazingly fruitful things. The one thing we do not do? We do not lie. In its warmth, iced anger starts to drip away. If anything can, sadness will find the trail back to the sunflower field.

98. Our species is flying away on evolution's roller coaster.

My loud mind is the scholarly manuscript lately typed by mankind. My quieter mind, from deep down in my rootstock, is an archeological site of immense wealth that looters of our economy now dynamite, scavenging for marketable chunks of treasures they bring to light. The result is many chunks of broken ideas.

In this brute mining, souls are hacked in two by the sword of dualism. This enormously fruitful tool of evolution, which can also split one species and diversify it into many, makes us gallop after our wildest dream. Nothing seems meant to be restored to past wisdom. All these precious fragments are meant to be continuously re-engineered into a beauty beyond our horizon. This is creativity. So, Theo, don't ask just your memory. In an ever new world it's old hat. The approach with what was to what is, is inadequate. Have a conversation with Life on the go.

Should I beg in some *padre nostrum* to be relieved of the temptations, of the duels between my strict, old instinct and the explorations my new conscious reasoning enjoys messing with? No, no, and no! These notorious tugs-of-war between what's old hat and the games of my playful imagination, are they not the playground of Life's messy creativity?

Life has always watched our strict, static morals with their thousand and one "don'ts" with an amused smile, saying, "You can have your little safety rules for your little herd, but I am no lullaby. I claim some of you for my experiments, so you may never have to yawn: 'Oh, this again!'"

Never before in our history has Life lined us up for so many adventures. We are now in front of a hundred Grand Canyons that we have to cross with our antiquated wagons, which we must now re-engineer so we can keep on enjoying our journey to who-knows-where. We have to come to terms with the fact that our scourging crowdedness the celebrated medical industry has produced on the planet is now discreetly producing its antidote, triggering among us an I-give-a damn and dumbness, many kinds of brakes for that fat success. We are asked to invent for "death" a more friendly personality, so that we can defuse our population bomb with less pain. We must face that the exaggerated physical energy with which we bulldoze now through Life leaves a colossal wake of friction that upsets the climate and the fertility of the Earth.

Yesterday we took a walkabout around our homes. Today we ride a high-speed train to nobody-knows-where. We are a cataclysmic happening. There is no precedent, no old culture we can imitate. So much for our nostalgia for a dear, lost home. Evolution is a mustang on the run—and I am riding it. Cemeteries are the proper places for homes. I am meant to live in the saddle, ready for any of the freshly wrapped gifts I am presented each morning, never quite sure what kind of explosive love I may find.

What drug, what bone game or mind game, what neurochemical, what psychedelic food, what new cascade in our neurons is it, that has in the last ten thousand years made our species behave as if we were omnipotent, all knowing and recklessly daring? A ten thousand year high related, maybe, to some opiate concocted by our genes in response to our stress from working overexcitedly against our dear, old hearts? I know of no other wriggle of Life that

I know of no other wriggle of Life that works as hard as we do to make illusions come true.

274

works as hard as we do to make illusions come true. And, yes, our hearts stagger from adaption pains.

When Life tiptoes in the dark, uncharted jungle of options, looking for new tricks and additions, when Life recruits volunteers for its pricy evolution, it whispers a delusion of being God-like into our ears. And it seduces us, "Go teach Life a lesson!" And why not? After Life sifted through uncountable uncountables of options, there are still countless options left begging to be explored. And I bet that our amazing addiction to playing with extremes makes evolution rub now its hands with an incredulous too-good-to-be-true!

I am from a species of traditionally rather solitary queens and kings living on a shoestring. Seen in evolutionary time, what other highly social species did in eons, we are now plunged into doing overnight. Hence the furious reshuffling of our sex lives, of our priorities, of our thinking, and the explosion of consciousness. Our system of mental regurgitation of knowledge is culminating in the internet. With no shame, technology now puts an immense wealth of secret personal knowledge on the market. An autonomous mind of a society, outside the individual, seems to form.

A man and a woman reproduce together. We dance to that most vitalizing and intoxicating soul song of the wild. This is Independence Day for a woman and a man. Reproductive science is envious and claims, "We can do better!" It catches and tames this jubilant capacity and passes it on to the technological society for managing and marketing that "beast." So, as we buy our cars, we now start to also buy our children—an in vitro lovemaking here, a joist for their education there, a support beam for their health, a sitter for some of their morning hours, later a couple of entertainment hours a day from War Craft or the Disney Channel, a drug to manipulate hormones shifting puberty's arrival—many kinds of counselors. Society is molding and managing that little lad. Clinical medicine comes of age. It openly becomes the undertaking of society to farm its individuals. People still desperately hang on to their eroticism as one of the last legacies of their wildness. It's society versus the individual. Yet in handling its new-found strength, our brave new society is still more inexperienced than ants that fell into a sugar bowl.

Feverish from all the anxiety, we are becoming the terrific ground breakers, forest breakers, ice breakers, relationship breakers, heart breakers, DNA breakers, autonomous man and woman breakers, family breakers, subatomic particle breakers, Amazon breakers, and climate breakers. Consider that each man in the U.S. has now become empowered with continuous thirty kilowatts, his footstep three hundred times his body's physical strength; every puff and whack of this harnessed energy is being used to break up and reshuffle the kingdoms of the streams, of the animals, of the plants—to make them serve breakfast exclusively for man. The energy of each of us, clean or not, renewable or not, leaves a thundering, continuous thirty kilowatt wake behind.

How many spiritual solutions did we replace with newly harnessed raw power in order to become so fast, so tremendously physical, and leave these enormous footprints? Why didn't Darwin simply remind us: "It all is a love contest." Will we ultimately do better than the ants, the cockroaches, the oceans, the winds?

Most of us are still quite useless for the "real" thing. We are made too solid. We are mostly a mimicry of altruistic kindness. Yet I note that when Life in its giddy playfulness turns creative, it often starts with faking. These elaborate pretensions of ours to be altruistic may be nature's toolbox for training us to do the "real" thing. While pretending to be of a brave new society, we are like little boys with wooden rifles ordered to play soldiers. Marching together, the soldiers pretend to be united. In games, children pretend to be fathers and mothers. Fresh from the jungle, we fake loving our neighbors.

Pretending is life's training center and beauty salon. Fake being a runner. And lo, you may end up a runner. Fake being a Christian. And lo, you may end up physically and mentally a Christian. The taste to reorient our aggression seeps in. We are the first instant in a social experiment. Evolution is endlessly wounding and healing us.

How to avoid crash landing on such an evolutionary roller coaster? So many new memories that could not yet settle deep into biological genetics are still just loosely written down in our culture, like focusing our awareness and acquiring expertise and knowledge. Enormously time-consuming, our finds need to be verbally and electronically transferred from generation to generation. So much springtime has to play dead in school while a young mind gets its "haircut." We drag our feet. And for good reason. Who dreams of being retired in his role to walk his very own road as queen or king with few other decision makers commanding her left and right?

The adoration of the past, of the good bygone or golden times indoctrinated by most cultures, still always tempts me to look backward. One thing I know. This adoration is the choice liquor of sedentary minds unable to quickly invent new saddles to ride galloping evolutions to ever new and more fantastic ways of living life. This adoration must be the wrinkles of old age.

Beyond the myths we have composed to see ourselves as the darlings of the Creation, I am shown that the work of Life is not to bring forth and to please nice people. These myths, though, might be a ruse of Life. They entice us to be endlessly a little angry with the Creator. They whip us on to be the Earth's most furious doers and inventors. Selfish capitalism with its license for unlimited egotism is an enormously successful catalyst for inventiveness. We are a species of very avid apprentices and so may be forgiven for still hammering our fingers instead of the nails. After all, every addition to our evolution has been done "wrong" a million times before that addition has been approved—for the time being. I speak here about the playground of transgressions and creative mistakes. I speak here about Life's annoyingly creative irregularity in rhythms, truths and rhymes. I speak here of Life's need to sometimes choose a courageous woman or a man who can violate an old outworn social norm and can take a beating for doing so.

And now we have to arm our intellect with some brand new immunities. Wild horses from yesterday with their enormous love and vitality break up when caught in the maze of our gated communities, while lame stable mares do not.

It might be our most creative grandchildren, who can arm themselves with a daring clarity, and a pocket full of serenity, who can survive shooting through this cascade of evolution, navigating these white waters without being sunk by stress and friction. Think of a breakthrough in our very natural religious feelings.

I wonder aloud, "Theo, on the very day you are no longer a creator in the Game of Evolution, you start to become a loser. Hence your secret fear of galloping science and being overrun by it and composted. Are you to remain lifelong cradled in your warm little logic, a chick in terror of hatching? Are you meant to be adventurous and do your space jumps outside the safety net of good old common sense?"

I am still learning to balance on the tightrope between making a racket and adapting. If we only did what comes naturally to us, would we not still be worms munching through mud? My task in this tremendous physical and mental weather front I am sailing through, is to create one more happy story out of this storm. To create this story, I have to shed my old skin. Like nifty Ms. Snake, my old mythology, my yesterday's heroes, my old successes, ah, and some of my old good deeds, which have outlived their purpose, have to go. My old snake skin is strangling me.

Poetry can arrange for the soft landing of such loaded paradigm shifts. Science has a reputation for crash landing extreme novelties into our souls.

*What a waste of a man's life to be born and to be buried
again with the same big armful of what he hated and with the
same little armful of what he loved when he was a boy.*

99. A pirate story

Ride with me through this cascade of thoughts. A hunch tells me that there is a prize waiting for us. Stay with me.

Do you know why a pirate puts a black patch on one of his eyes? It's because he does not want to be bothered to see with his other eye what's going on in the heart of those poor souls whose ship he puts into the crosshair of his guns. When I take sides, I also become a pirate. I put a black patch on one of my eyes. Half my sight gets conveniently blacked out. I stop being an apprentice in the workshop of Life. I join the huge crowd of bashers of God. I give up walking in the moccasins of my enemy for two weeks. I refuse to visit that "bad" man's scenic point of view, see *his* gorgeous ears of corn, listen to *her* good news and *her* dreams. Walking in her slippers could ruin my dear old point of view.

Watch the waves of mad applause surging in a packed stadium. A sea of mass-drunken howlers! Waves of triumph first from this and then from the opposite side, surge through these two sameness drunken crowds—two breeds of pirates, each with the opposite eye patched, each crowd with an opposite notion of what's good news. Taking sides is enormously contagious—a sea of tears here, a firework of joy there—and for the same action! Sometimes, that division takes nothing more than a red ribbon or the color of the skin. It's a neurologically induced neglect of personal courage. No wonder I get an itchy feeling of wasting myself when I am simply part of a crowd. A crowd is such superglue.

I run alone. I think on my own. Nobody is on my side, hypnotizing me to fall in step and to sway with him—or to join her yawn. No temptation here to become one more happy inmate of a milling, mental crowd, drunk on some sameness brew. In short, I mount the courage to break and rise above the most fundamental propaganda and demonizing law—the one-sided attitude one must take toward every question one deals with. And then it might happen that I do not even take sides for Theo. And for a treat, I renounce being a pirate—no need to patch one eye, no need to permanently think "provide, provide." I mount the courage to ride this flying mustang of my soul on the scary edge of seeing it both ways. Things become more exciting than for a Marlboro-man up here. I start to pile up that magic wealth the *Forbes* magazine knows little about. On this scenic ridge, insights from left and right can connect and ignite me into that joyous ahhh! No victims, no winners. My wealth of insights piles up that needs no maintenance and does not offend.

Yesterday, riding on that scary ridge, out of the blue, a voice rose in me, "From now on, there will be only one kind of news—only good news for you—if you give me your hand. From now on, wherever you are, you are in a classroom. All news will be revelations. Fox News, Al Jazeera News, the Raven's and the Irish Meadows' news. All happenings will be revelations on your safari through the unimaginable treasures of Life. All becomes news from the working of the Creator's mind, whether your senses like it or not." My old notions fret and kick, "No, no and no. Bullshit!" That notion of only good news sinks me in a sea of confusion!

While fishing alone with the seasons in the North and the tropical Pacific, this simple faith that all is ultimately good news starts to lick on, and to leak in and surge over my safe little commonsense island from all around. This good faith pats my shoulder when I am hopelessly pulled down into a bashing spree against her, him or it. This faith saves me from wasting myself in mental lawsuits. Many profoundly useless questions evaporate in this mental climate change.

Out here, where my dear ocean is testing me, it would be dangerous to have that patch on one of my eyes. Here a clear non-critical perception is what I need. I listen to and follow the ocean's doctrine. I do my practice. On the sea I am less drunk with some freewill-brew. And testing me the ocean does. Ten days ago I had the most difficult home-coming yet in my forty-six years on the sea. With such towering seas and howling winds, the mast broken and on one side the stabilizer gone, I barely managed to let me be hurled around Cape Georgiana into Salisbury Sound. With all the mistakes I made, I still wonder how I passed my test.

> *In the cosmos, Life is the best news. How could*
> *its revelations be anything but good news?*
>
> *What a gift to be alive!*

100. A naked mind shivers out in the cold

To be safe from the naked, brutally beautiful world of the four seasons, those of us with a creative bent quietly nail together our own custom made mental home sweet home—and we love to add new balconies to it. Others with less religious feelings like it simple. They buy an iPod and switch to rap-music, march music, great symphony music, to feel swayed and comfy at home. Others buy into a mental home sweet home constructed with mythical stories, or with age-old sacred thoughts of poetic prophets. Others prefer freshly baked scientific theorems to provide that mental comfort. Outdoor minds need a very baggy mental survival suit so no seam will crack when they must jump a norm, a creek or a barbed fence made of safety morals. Very timid indoor minds may like to dwell year-round in a kind of tightly woven beaver's winter den to feel safe from confusion.

Each chooses his personal magic brew of sounds, of thoughts or visualizations to keep afloat on the wild sea of questions, according to the walk of his timid or curious soul. The religious imagination of a person says much about the richness and the daring of her mind.

When I talk and walk naked as I please, no, I am not pleasing. I am shocking. I pass signs of "no trespassing." I wake up minds that are sleeping. Naked minds and naked bodies have learned to blush with shame for they are compelled to wear clothing. An extra-extra large credo, please, to accommodate the gesticulating mind of Theo. People who have no religious feelings can forget about how to clothe these feelings.

This much I have learned: a religion that does not breathe and grow every day soon blisters a mind that loves to gesticulate and reach for the moon. Ask a snake how it feels not to periodically shed its skin.

I am thinking here about the natural instinct for religion, about each mind's need for a personal safety net of helpful theorems made of custom made illusions. I am thinking of shelters that keep a mind safely bobbing on the sea of confusion. A little fur for the little soul, a big fur coat for a big bear of a soul that is ready to leave home.

Theo, if you burn to ridicule a person's religion, first go spend a winter without a parka with the Inuit people.

101. In the Court of the Earth, does the parliament of the birds have legal standing?

Consider what I have overheard at the parliament of the local birds. In their long agenda, a sticky proposition by the wader birds was presently discussed. Their motion: "We ask the Court of the Earth to take action so the huge tribe of man does not squeeze us further out of our good wetlands and keep on soiling our air. We find it misguided that mankind still bestows medals of honor on their scientists who dream up for their agriculture even deadlier weapons of mass destruction in order to colonize what little we, the no-farm animals and plants, have left of our homesteads. Don't they realize how overweight they already are?! We propose that the earthquakes, the floods and man's own self-deconstructing neurochemicals be called on for help. May Life let their stupefying smartness ultimately choose for them their misleaders in order to march some of their flooding troops into whatever. Before all, we propose that our neighbors, the nifty little pathogens, should be asked for help to brake man's runaway population and their blind technology with no table manners, so that these rioters may find the way home and to the center. Any diet that slims mankind's huge masses and aggression is welcome. And we promise to honor Life's moderators and slayers of excesses for their good work with a cross of merit made with the humming-birds' feathers of the most radiant blues and reds."

Even the field starlings and the town square pigeons didn't make a fuss about this request. Truly there was not a single bird present that didn't feel menaced by drunken man's lopsided technology madly intent on making the Earth a one-species affair.

The delegates from the swallow clans cut short the roar of applause with a petition of their own: "We want the Court of the Earth to rehabilitate mankind's chauvinistic spokesmen for some god who still preaches an agenda of 'Mankind Over All' and have these misleaders do community work service for the wader birds who have suffered so much from their affliction of arrogance. In this way, may the birds' Great Commonwealth with all Life rub up a little on these self-proclaimed speakers for God. We also propose that these prophets' haughty sacred books that deny us equal standing in the Creation be collected and reprinted with the Good News."

And the Blue Heron, the assembly clerk, reminded the delegates that another hundred complex cases against mankind and their war crimes against the other animals and plants are waiting to be decided in that Court. And as you may see, that Court reacts. The Court starts to confuse the gene expressions in mankind's children so they may trip over each others' toes when they keep on fighting their apartheid wars.

102. The kite that proudly severed its ground line to celebrate Independence Day

Visualize for a moment the Earth as The Great Market Place. Try to write a thesis on what merchandise for instance the leaf cutter ants have been trading on that grand open market, in order to be still successfully around haggling for homestead and food for the last forty million years, and with no pending bankruptcy to worry about.

Ah, if we could never, never forget when reading, seeing, conversing, fishing, haggling, hiking and jailing that every person, every critter, any anything is a master in some field, and that we barely can imagine what old friends we all really are. How many times we have already met! How many times all our families of genes have gossiped with each other, traded and made gifts! And how we all got so quite similar in habits, organizations and rules over the last billion years so to still keep on celebrating our festive stay on this Earth.

We all slowly, humbly have learned that the Earth is far too dangerous a place to let go of interspecies compassion. This compassion is the only lifeline that guarantees us death if we let it go. The notion of independence is a kite that proudly serves its ground line, free to swivel in its lofty independence around itself, free to tumble and crash land who knows where.

Now, with one glimpse of light in the heart, with one fleeting glance at this incredibly wondrous mosaic of Life, how could I still expect that one person, one lifetime, one anything will ultimately be judged by itself? That would be such an underestimation, nearly a blasphemy of the incredibly complex interconnectedness of Life's web. Such a blind man's plot could only hatch in a joy forsaken nook of some dark, dark underworld.

No, there's no need to ever play with the idea that we may be the inventors of compassion. It is the first, oldest invention and law of Life. And what do we do with this wild, outrageously generous compassion? We try to tame that divine "internet" like we tamed the cow. We sling a tie up rope around its neck to monopolize this fountain of love for us.

Theo, stop this judging unless you can crowd all critters that ever lived into one jury box. And we, the tribe of man, we are such a minute part in that jury box.

An ovation, please, for all the poetic scientists and other great spies upon Life's wondrous, totally compassionate workings!

103. To be brave and endure—or to kill the heart's growing pains?

For body aches we may go to the drug store. For desperately needed forgetfulness some of us may visit a contact of a drug lord. Refined people may inhale a refined mini-beauty served by one of our aesthetic art works to get oblivious for a treat of the big brother love with which Life manhandles us out of door.

There is art that is a painkiller made of harmonious sounds and rhymes, art that is thought compositions, philosophical concoctions, splendid displays of colors or simple *pum pum pums* that parade for me in entrancing union. Like all pain relievers, they should be taken with caution, because pains are messengers.

"Theo, remember this warning, when you get addicted on dreaming sweet little feelings while you sway for example in the arms of mama Beethoven. Remember this warning when you are in some tiny, manmade cubical featuring one of the tiny imitation worlds and mind sweeteners. We create them to soothe our heart's growing pains. Remember, your mind becomes braver when fed on organic food served in the wide open classroom of Life's four seasons."

Please, be frugal when you charm me with these miniature art works and other pain soothers. Our dear works of fake clarity can give the logician in me anesthetic relief when he is dead tired and blistered from faithfully hammering together my Great Work of Art. That Great Hammock I knot together is the relationship I tie with Clara and with all people. It is the mysterious union with the green rowdy world I build in my heart. For this only your art that evokes my ovation for brave Life at large will help me on.

I have noticed that people who are not addicted to those arty heart-pain relievers are more tolerant and more forgiving people. Whether he is bringing rain or shine, they do not shoot their mailman.

104. When Life plays with extremes

Moderate compassion, spread evenly, engenders moderately avid hunters on the one side, and on the other side it gives us healthy and caring mothers. Extremely focused compassion engenders on its dark, shaded side extremely cold cruelty and the most vivid color displays of fall. Gold medal winners produce, in the shaded side of their heart, the saddest losers. The highest waters cause the deepest waterfalls. Summer fields with the sweetest honey bring plagues of wasps and armies of killer bees. Fat prosperity produces ghettos outside of town. Man's enormous prosperity makes the wild animals live miserably in "shanty towns." The lushest vegetation prepares the deepest layer of decay and compost. A high tide of charity work makes for an obese population that is led to the center again with a low tide in loving. The brilliant Nobel Prize winners tend to be in their dark side Life's problem children. Ever smiling sunshine cooks the hurricanes.

Those who love little know little sadness and have few tears. The deepest loving tenderness comes from the pounding of calamities and wars. Long, well-behaved niceness leaves much unspent tinder. It prepares the hottest forest fires and the meanest explosions of temper.

Life's daring playfulness with extremes, like her symbiosis between extremely cold hearted cruelty and extreme hot hearted compassion, these mystery-plays still give goose bumps to my tender heart. Yet people long before us recognized these mind-boggling symbioses and battled in their brave hearts to integrate these rascals into a very large goodness fitting Life at large.

Ask around. Is the feast of evolution fueled by smiling wisdom or by brave unhappiness, foolishness, broken windows, legs, genes, walls, and hearts? The common folks, a little too fragile for such safaris, we may want to keep on exiling in our minds these extremists into some silent pit of evil, or seat them apart in some saintly heaven. People meant to live in peace are not drafted to become such outstanding acrobats and lovers in our circus.

No other species has to balance through Life between such loaded extremes. We walk the scariest sky rope, always compensating a terribly effective spring-man with the terribly effective fall-man. We are "privileged" to be apprentices in the most risky classroom.

Four thousand years ago, the Chinese knew and taught how Life passionately lures its explorers into the extremes, and how with its complementariness it leads us, from such outings, back home toward the middle way again. Theo, take off your blinders—face and embrace this healing law of compensation in all its un-forgiveness. Look at how our fuzzy manmade goodness, when we overload it with sweetener, must make others later bitterly cry.

This primordial law of compensation is dear to Life. It underwrites
Life's harmony. This law is so simple and so unforgivingly clear,
it scares the heck out of the shameless good-doer I learned to be.

105. The art of conversation

Can you spare a dime of love for a bad listener whose mind is running wild?

Dear adventurer, hold your raw gem of an insight tightly to your heart, long and long. Be a miser. Chisel and sculpt that raw hunch so long, it can finally burst into a feast of light and colors. Think of how long the pregnancy of a diamond lasts.

> *Dear adventurer, hold your raw gem of an insight tightly to your heart, long and long.*

When I am in labor with a ripe idea you touch in me, how can I have a conversation with you while this wild mustang is stabled in my mind? That horse is feverish and ready to run, run, and run past all traffic signs when you touch me and let that horse out. No, there is no way to remain a good listener. I have to give a "lecture" and I cannot even walk straight at the same time, or be polite. How can you walk nicely and talk the fine line when you are passionately in love? You can't. You forget the safe walking. I have to pour out these thoughts that I hacked out of my inner wildlife-refuge, getting up in the middle of the black night, writing them, barefooted, with no pants on, no light.

Nice people can converse politely and artfully, nodding here, shutting up there, consciously intervening, so each gets her turn, structuring, weaving in the rest stops in small talk, bridling that possessive, unbridled need to pour it out and give birth to that child, whole and right now when ripe. Nice artful conversation violates the needs of a woman giving birth.

When so carried away it's up to you to mount me, lead me back to the pasture, make sure my worst and my best does not come out, make sure you get a nice Starbucks talk. Or? Or you take a deep breath and opt for going on a safari and just watch and listen to a birthing mind go wild. Here there are things so deeply felt, they can only be said without elegance.

In the present epidemic of instant food and instant communication, how to carry the pregnancy of a thought patiently to its full term?

106. The gift of vulnerability

Be brave, Theo, think of a snake that periodically sheds its skin, remaining vulnerable. Tender again, receptive again to infectious ideas and the risk of new birth pains. Confusion of yesterday's dear common sense! Blood may be spilled. This is how Mrs. Snake laboriously bleeds a new ring of growth.

Ah, the exuberant feeling of being an open house. Prospects of new insights that come to stay! Here certainty is not a welcomed guest. Righteous knowledge would spoil the ambiance with intolerance. I become an invitation to other organisms to be givers and takers, to be artists who chisel on me, bestowing upon me gifts of their ideas and genetic memories. I welcome in teachers and quality controllers Life is sending me. Every growing person and critter must remain an open wound for life. Other ideas, persons and critters must continuously try to fill this wound so all together we may grow. When Theo is finally sealed in a coffin, that wondrous wound is healed and sealed. And he will leave you an invitation to a thanksgiving party. Look at the harvest; five beautiful, loving children are now following Clara and Theo.

I push my capacity to tolerate pain. I dare to handle your wild questions and hot, freshly baked doubts. Whether with meanness or kindness, you help me to stretch and crack open my old, tight little theorems. That's how Life grafts gifts and more gifts onto me. That's how Life laughs off my terror of change. You tell me of a pitch-dark event. In its rawness that puzzling act may still be completely indigestible to my tender, little self. So I barf it back out. That's what the unappreciated talent of hate is about. Yet Life must love this rascal of an event for a reason. It lures me to more and more scenic points of view. And in a clear moment of "Ahh—I see," Life adds that new ingredient to Theo. And now look and smell! What before gave Theo the creeps, smells now like pecan pie. Another growth ring takes shape. From cow dung, the gold of buttercups has emerged.

A critter may risk losing its bank account, but it will never risk losing its gift of playing with sickness and other vulnerabilities. Consider here that the virus genomes provide the greatest source of gene diversity. Every animal and plant makes darn sure that it can get hurt, can be eaten, and yes, that it can rot and turn itself into one great give away. Look at the tiger, the butterfly, the thorn bush, the moss. Each watches its vulnerability and its armaments, its rate of reproduction and its capacity to die and be digested, making sure there is always room for fellow species to also happily live. All of Life's associates watch that they never, never become accident proof, "sin" proof, fool proof, sick proof, rot proof, mutation proof, or break-a-promise proof. They make darn sure that their genetics and morals remain vulnerable to changes, ever ready to adapt, change course—and overcome.

Think of all your hidden talents you kept off your premises, of all your missing corners begging to be filled, of your empty plug-ins dreaming of plugs. Continuously Life wears new wounds and holes into your heart, genes, and shoes in order to continuously fill you with news.

Why does a diamond have a hundred enemies and barely a friend? Because that stone is so frigging hard and invulnerable, no criticism, no oxidation and cracks, no soft roots, no needs, no sickness, no confusion or learning is able to penetrate. Nothing can crack its perfect surface, break in and make Life happen. What loving love would lean her warm face against this perfect, totally impotent stone? Diamonds do not make good soil.

Invulnerability is the guesthouse with the hardest beds. It is a heart that is stainless and guaranteed to still be lifeless after a hundred years. Theo, don't be a diamond. Turn into a ripe mango. Overnight the whole town will want to make love with you and move in. Next morning, discover what such a hothouse for love can do.

Call it kindness, compassion, vulnerability, innocence—no, these godsends are not some nice little human charity just recently invented. They are the rope that keeps the raft of Life tied together and floating. Find in it the mysterious capacity of the wolf to enter into the needs, the feelings, and the fears of the caribou and to let that animal do the same to him, so in a joint venture they can create a pleasing and harmonious togetherness. They entered that life spirit that knows that you are me and I am you.

The capacity to be intimate with Life, is that not the highest social skill? To be well connected with all of us joyful suckers and givers, is that not the cash in hand needed to win Life's survival games?

107. My humanistic education left my mind with indigestion.

I was a hurting belly, constipated with assumptions that I could neither throw up nor digest. For example, any great, wild thought I kept on tracking down, the prudent assumption—we, mankind, we are the exemption, we are the chosen, cornered them in a dark alley fenced with no exit signs. Not anymore. These writings here have become my sweat lodge. I sweat out these assumptions. I cleanse my mind. I formulate my wild ghosts of thoughts full of adventure dreams. I give them names. I bring them out of my underworld into the sunlight. I pet them. I make peace with some of my shadows. I do my adult work. I become a mountain sheep that out climbs the shepherd. Doing so together with you, we can tease and laugh together a little more when next time we meet. We can rub a finger full of that sweet serenity lotion under each others' skin. Yesterday's grim man or woman in us will get less of a chance.

Whoever wrestles with inconvenient truth will not come down with mental indigestion. A chimney sweeper, please, for a congested mind!

108. Life thrives on side effects

Theo, don't get too worked up about the immediately obvious effects of what you do when you follow what your inner voice is telling you to do. The obvious results are not so important. The immediate smell of what you squeeze out is not so important. Above all, it's the marvels Life does with the zillion little side effects of your acts that compose the tasty feast of Life.

Ah, to remain receptive to the whole chorus of the needs and the gifts of our dear Earth, to remain open to every troublemaker out there winking: "Dance with me!" It is these zillion unnoticed side-glances of our souls that compose our larger social skills and the great net of feedback loops. And there are way, way more ingredients that sneak into our dear tasty life than we have on our welcome-list

Think beyond the big, loud beat of your heart. Think what wonderful work the thousand miles of your tiny capillaries and what the billions of your cells can discreetly do with this initial thump of a heart. Think of the boss of a logging camp who with his foul talk makes his loggers fume and go on strike. Now unfocus and with a side-glance see a whole woodland scene that he made burst into a smile. Think of the robberies the feckless financiers recently bestowed upon our economy and the subsequent media gloom. Unfocus now and check out the sidelines—fewer cars, less heavy industry belching, less extravagant traveling, less luxo-chic that pisses away our resources, and more time to scratch our heads, ask a neighbor for a hand and reflect. And listen: Do you also hear the Earth smiling all over and applauding at this good news?

Today on a walk along the Indian River, I rested and opened wide my arms, calming my endlessly jabbering thinking. Knots of my scheming opened up. Joyfully the chorus of conversations from the greens all around started flowing through me. I was the raindrop that fell into the pond. I became partner of a bigger story than Theo. This clinic out here has good medicine for me.

109. Can you help me to bring this winter thought out into the warmth of May?

Socrates produced and gave away knowledge that did not sell. That was his "crime."

University corporations produce now much knowledge that is highly profitable for our species alone, some carcinogenic to the living Earth, other more explosive than our love affair with nuclear power. They produce knowledge that sells. They do not commit Socrates' "crime." Look around in the family of Life on Earth. Book a window seat for your next flight. Find out whether my hunch is not a little right. Do not some gifts of our sciences cause symptoms of cancer on the lovely face of the Earth?

Take the endeavors of our celebrated stem cell research or our reproduction enhancement science, like surrogate pregnancy. For what? For making a profit helping our obese species to become more obese, or to let a spent individual drag on a mostly painful while longer while aborting children?

Science has become our most potent mind-altering drug. Sciences' gifts are a most difficult test for our compassion: do we love or do we whore with what science is giving us?

How much is enough for a science to tilt the advantages our way? Tell me: how much is enough? For all other species, do not some of our sciences' endeavors look now like Earth crimes?

Here is a subject an enlightened university can research.
May our children become springtime scientists with hearts
of poets, who turn our suspicious winter-hearts toward
serenity, confidence, curious walkabouts, and joy.

110. When Theo smokes the peace-pipe with Theo.

Theo, have you done well today in the contest to make peace with your shadow? Did you hang one more lamp in your mind? The rocks of pain you swallowed, mistaking them for yummy food, the menacing pictures and idea you obediently gulped down, like regret, blame and evil, intimidating you now from the shaded side of your heart, did you drag today one of these items into the sunlit landscape and make it confess that it was just an illusion meant to keep little children out of harm? Did you make Theo admit that, as with Galileo's hecklers, it was your terror of change that had fits again in front of one more piercing revelation of how unnervingly wonderful Life does Her work? Or when you thought you were "shipwrecked," did you tell yourself out loud that this panic happened while you were dreaming, that while awake your heart could have easily told you that you were well and safe on dry land and in no danger of shipwrecking but invited to learn and to frolic?

Think about the landmines like guilt some patriarch buried in your heart, meant to keep you safely inside the fence with his flock. Did you defuse one of these fence-keepers so to become an adult and stand on your own? Did you ask a starving little "I-hate-this" over for coffee and pie—and hear it out?

Yes, today you were brave. You let go one of your convenient, long-held assumptions—the belief that you must play safe. With one firm handshake, done entirely in your mind, you welcomed one of your dangerous talents for grownups. You welcomed your gift of brave, critical thinking that was kept safely out of reach for little Teddy. And then there's Ricardo, your neighbor, who periodically asks you to loan him a twenty or a fifty (which he does not pay back) to nurse his craving for cigarettes. Can you welcome this colorful man into your heart and have fun with one more of God's clowns?

This sweet peacemaking is what the "step-out-of-your-placenta" can do. Oh yes, out there my loving must become a little more omnivorous to survive.

111. The placebo effect, and its dark side, the painebo effect

There are many ways to heal or to hurt. There are the sunny thought pictures we create meant to massage and to heal. Other thought pictures are meant to sabotage her peace, or corner him in shame. There are positive feel-good stories that are kites making us fly. There are negative myths and stories that curse and drill holes in our self-esteem and make us sink or submit to some "savior." Enchanting words can make a man's penis rise. Mean words can make that marvelous tool go lame.

There are words that are bouquets of lights a man brings into her heart. Other stories are a hundred pounds of rocks of blame and regret that an enemy sneaks into her backpack of love;

ballast meant to sink her pride, wear him down, and make of him a grateful follower. There are illusions that are landmines a shepherd builds into the hearts of his flock meant to go off when one of his flock oversteps his rules and follows her own road to merry land.

We can conjure up benevolent thought pictures in a mind that can do even more wonders than to make that penis erect. We can infect a mind with painful thoughts that are phantoms of fear made to rape his heart. Others use their power of intent to light a campfire in a shivering heart.

Think of a country that demonizes its neighbor with waves and more waves of ill-will, millions of hate missiles home in, obscuring that neighbor's sky with fear. And then bring to mind a gathering place of pilgrims swarming with intents of goodwill— a sea of exuberance. Think of what the healing power of such a huge goodwill massage can do. Others drag along their pain made of all needless regrets from their past and from all the worthless worries for their future that comes from a tragic loss of trust in Life. These stowaway pains can tie a once ecstatic child mind into a maddening tangle of fishing hooks.

Each single look, welcome or mean, alters the chemistry of the receiver's body and mind. Such is the power of intent.

For more details, ask the advertising and the demonizing industry. They are experts in placebo and painebo effects.

112. With so many new gifts of handicaps, how creative we lately have become.

Are we not all gifted with some personal handicap that gives each of us a chance to grow a curl, a twist, a mole all of our own? Rivers dearly love their personal boulders in their flow, so each river may jubilate with its very personal song. Do these custom-made handicaps not make us people all thrilled that we each have our own way to quilt our love? How exciting! Did you notice how these special gifts tickle our creativity?

Practical people may spend gallons of sweat to weed out these unappreciated nuggets of "surprise-surprise." Creative people learn to treasure their handicaps. They make peace with these rascal gifts.

So many varieties among our creative too-little, too-much, and out-of-step! In fact, we are knee deep and all confused in a flood of too many marvels that are born with the help of our many handicaps.

113. It's payback time for a species that got carried away in its advantage grab. This is the story overpopulation and overconsumption is telling me.

The Earth is a bank. In springtime everything alive stands in line for a loan—to buy a new dress, to sing, to make love and seeds, to soon jubilate in summer clothes with all kinds of things to do that are summer fun. Come fall, some loans come due. Did anybody hear Ms. Oak and Sir Badger complain about it? Actually, some add a little genetic extra when paying back their loans to the Earth and enrich Her love-affair with another trick. Lately a little too much "good" has happened to us. We have been indulging in a summer we extended to ten months.

In fact, never before have we piled up in front of a deeper canyon, scratching our heads. Is it that darn, smart kind of science we perfected for the last two hundred years which taught us to mine our future, that brought us to the brink of this menacing open pit? Never before has mankind piled up so many bad debts on to Life's economy. And notice: people the world over start now to worry whom Life will lay off if mankind should go bankrupt. Yes, also species can go bankrupt and be forced to restructure in a leaner way. Around here where I live in Alaska, there are no wolves left for the deer to pay their dues, so the winter must help the deer out with a periodic winter kill. It's high time our money farmers start to pay back for services rendered by the soil so the soil is ready for a new crop. No, our credit crisis is not a financial crisis. It is about all we owe to the oceans, the forests, the aquifers and wild waters, the elbow room of the lemurs and the resources of the soil. Economists with tiny eyes have not yet added these debts to their equations.

No, our credit crisis is not a financial crisis. It is about all we owe to the oceans, the forests, the aquifers and wild waters, the elbow room of the lemurs and the resources of the soil.

By our deeper, wilder nature, our compassion is a loving vagabond. That lovebird flies on long and wide errands—at times way beyond the camp of man—to hand out her pay checks and favors. These favors sometimes do not seem to serve us, but she gives them away for the love of Life. Because she knows of vital needs of Life's enterprise we do not know. Other times, she orders our deeper compassion to just rest, resisting intervention, when misery nibbles for example on a logging commune that is on strike. Next week she gets a thanks-for-the-help letter from a stand of mahogany trees that has feared for its life for years. There is no way to know to which of Life's construction sites Life's winds will now cast our compassion to pay our debts. For we sure run up a debt, each time we cut a tree or hook a fish.

Our patriarchs did with our wildly permissive compassion what the Incas did with the wild corn. The Incas proselytized, tamed, and rationalized the corn so to become good corn, corn that serves the table of man alone. To be good to the coons, the parrots, the corn borers, the fungi, the sundry marauders of the hills that wear no shoes, and only a few bushels of kernels for us? No, and no, our "wise" men rebelled. What a waste of compassion. Hand all of it to us! And so, our patriarchs invented a smart way to make mankind rich, richer, and a little too fat. They declared a leash-law for our compassion.

When a population enlarges itself beyond its means, do you think it helps to keep saving and enlarging the menaced overload of that sinking "boat" with more infusions of food? Or should Life be called in to pay back some of the debt load by trimming and restructuring that ailing human enterprise? Should we learn from our new breed of forest firefighters and let some fires, diseases, and setbacks take their course? Or should we maintain the status quo of again and again swiftly extinguishing them and amass an even tenser, untested population that becomes a thicket of tinder headed for the critical mass to be finally ignited and helplessly devour itself?

Did you notice that with an absolute authority Life now starts to contradict that wisdom of our old preachers and their darn neighborly love? She does not let us heap more fuel and urgency into the great fire on Earth we lately have become. Reversing our morals, She sabotages our unstoppable success. She calls the dark side of our elitist goodness into action. With drastic fall strategies, Life turns around our runaway summertime. She amends the leash-law that our smart culture put on our love.

In that scourging overpopulation and overconsumption: fewer sunny days! She prescribes a diet of "bad" weather to take its turn. At mealtime, the masses start to burn their extra fat fighting each other to get a bite while the huge hungry crowd is bearing teeth milling around the "carcass." Mannerly sharing becomes a luxury in such overcharged times. A neuropathway system of naked egotism, even self-destruction, may be triggered into action. Every day a new kind of futile litigation. Agronomists with undernourished minds "bless" us with wonder-pesticides (organic phosphates) that also discreetly burn off seven points of our childrens' IQ. Life gives us her own kind of exercise machine to make us again lean. In such a cramped place, a mind may turn entirely thorn, or a man boxes himself in a money-armor from head to toe. In short, after feasting on a fattening compassion, a diet of losing weight is served.

But note: we are not alone with such sacrifices. In a tense raven population, for example, these wise birds might wait seven years for the privilege to breed. When estates are readily available, they do it in their third year. Some species of fish even change their gender to bring their reproduction rates back into harmony again.

Now when I see somebody totally possessed by that spirit of fall, I know in my innermost heart that this bundle of "bad news" may make the payments some full time "good doers" left unpaid. Luckily, for his work of compensation, that "downer" seems also rewarded with a kind of joy I do not know. His chore? With the coldness or the infertility of his heart, that cold man is asked to run into the tremendous fire on Earth that we have become, and cool it down. We can see him as a martyr if that helps—a dizzily high goodness in action, especially for a mind that may only see one generation high. Outstanding goodness is hammered down, deep meanness is uplifted to The Center again. "No good deed goes unpunished," as the Chinese say. Our ship is helped in this way, so that it does not skip into thin air, or sink from overloading.

And now, dear adventurer, remember when as a child your mom opened the door—and there was the lit up Christmas tree with piles of unexpected gifts underneath. To let go of our dear exemption myths, to let go of our belief that our grandiose goodness is a free-for-all, this is the opening of that door and of our eyes. And what a pile of gift boxes you see! And each box is a wrapped secret of how to completely redeem one more grouch, a hate, a fear, a crime or complaint when Life corrects itself with a telling smile: "Look what wonderful things my law of compensation can do with your meanness and your waste, and the icebergs in your soul. There is no need to shipwreck on dry land."

One thing becomes clear. It takes courage to think wild.

114. In this time of obsessive hygiene, safety and perfection— I crave imperfection.

Don't be a diamond! That expert in symmetry and purity makes poor soil. Turn into dirt, invite in lots of impurities, cracks, question marks and footholds. Add a little anger, rot, and dung to the menu. Life loves to settle where such rich menus are served.

Don't bore me with a nice face with no wrinkles, no scars. Give me a weathered, life-beaten face to look into, a rich, beat-up face-scape, carved and hammered by many, many stories, by many hardships, and by the banquets that alleviated these hardships. Show me a face a hundred times broken and healed again, still glowing with unbroken trust: "Life, what a bargain!" Let me walk into a face that is scarred with exaggerations and deprivations, a face as richly scarred as the face of the Earth.

I am a hungry lion—and a little skinny. When I meet a feast of vitality framed in a face with adventure scars, I get glued to that feast with a hungry envy that comes close to inspiration. I get excited and antsy for a wild ride, as I did in the presence of the storytellers on Marrakesh's square.

Show me a face a hundred times broken and healed again, still glowing with unbroken trust: "Life, what a bargain!"

I dream of politic speakers who, overruled by an inner sorrow, may break down into tears, of painted walls that become again a guesthouse for all kinds of fungi, spiders, cracks, and colors, of walls that tell me stories. I dream of a concert pianist, who, overwhelmed by a love in danger, all of a sudden breaks up her performance and adds her sorrow to her playing. In a world that remains for us ninety-nine percent a mystery, I am soul-brother to the messy scientists who are not obsessed with fake clarity. I long for a judge who sometimes gets a little drunk and rowdy. In the character of a perfect host, I wish for cracks and holes and overdone personalities that give her flavor. It warms my heart when you stutter, telling me truths that nobody wants to hear. I prefer my tax accountant to have a little garden soil under her fingernails. In my home town, I wish for blackouts with their eloquent silence and healing power of the night. Let me step up a staircase with its steps worn down into gentle curves by a million footprints that carried each imprinter's story up and down. I desperately look for dandelions and daisies in the city lawn. Sometimes it takes a fart to make my polished face come alive. In the jungle of life, do you think that a wheel should be perfectly round and egocentric? Or should it be of a more compassionate form, with humps and flats to accommodate the wonderfully humpty-dumpty world? Geometric forms are hurtful, round wheels and straight lines leave wounds; a "straight" man and a straight bed are not accommodating.

Left to myself, I can be a miser. Clara is my left hand. Clara is my generosity; she cannot sell but only give away. She cannot work for pay, but only volunteer. She cannot lie. Clara's unsustainable generosity is my cure. United, we scoot a little closer to that legendary perfection which cannot be told. The baby cries. The breasts overflow. Here are imperfections that are easily rhymed. Like faults in a rock formation, faults in a person have deep meaning. They fulfill special needs. That's where the precious stones assemble, or the rare and sometimes precious characteristics of a special man or woman can form. That is where the boobies can nestle their nests. That is where the cracks and the footholds are that I use to climb up to her.

When I upset you, it's because I still have my secrets. Don't cuss or ignore these dark, unappreciated pits in my character offhand. They lead to one of the secret treasure caves we have sadly learned to fear or ignore. Get to be friends with my secrets. When shared, they become the strings we use to knot that hammock for two in which we later swing, comfy, back and forth. Is it not our imperfections that help us to get mad at each other, break up and open up? We react. When so cracked open, these fault lines make us spill and talk deep unspoken truths. We get the chance to reconcile. We get the chance to make much more of an offense than to simply make good again or cheaply say: "I am sorry!" Is it not in such courageous healing that we grow the deeper blood vessels into each other that make our relationship grow? Is it not for these short and long-comings we search each other out to become friends, and to become whole?

Think also of the present epidemic of physical allergies. Here, in an overdone hygiene, does not an untrained immune system detect danger where there is none but deep wisdom acting? Take a highly hygienic, highly humanistic mindscape. Our untrained mental immune system develops allergies that fight healthy long-range wisdom with hates, phobias, and rushes of anxieties and fears.

Theo, don't worry if you don't get it right the first time—or the tenth time. Your homework is to contribute missteps, many missteps. We all learn from them and together we might ultimately get it a little righter. Those mischief-makers open their hand: "Here is your photosynthesis, here is your pearl!"

Don't worry if you don't get it right the first time—or the tenth time. Your homework is to contribute missteps, many missteps.

Here a helpful observation to the point: in the wild out of doors, the makeup of our soul gets hammered, and peels off. We are animated to be more honest. Maximum honesty is a quality of the wild. That wild lust out there to shoulder that extra load of vitality rubs under our skin. We become more truthful. And we cannot help but become catalysts for each other a little more. In this rich and impure environment, we start to weave our thoughts in a way we might not dare while sleepwalking in town. In town, self-denial and mannerly lying are the mental lubricants we are soaking in. Not much contact there. Go, find out with your partner in which environment you rub against each other and get to know each other more. Go take him off-road.

A song bird from my inner wildlife refuge sings to me, "How do you want the world to be different from what it is? Do you want more dams, more pesticides, prisons, asphalt and toxins, more fences, flatter mountains and flatter hearts, a tamer mustang? Do you want the lively, permissive Earth to be wrapped in one huge condom? Remember: thanks to Life's creative ability to live happily with anxiety, misspellings, and doubts, it never had to lock itself up in a perfection that ends with a yawning merry-go-round."

These stories here are for people on the move with a continual unfolding of vistas. There is no way to guess the result, and so the result is of no importance. People eager to settle down on perfectly cooked and rounded conclusions are not invited to this outdoor storytelling.

115. My Test

Now I am given the test. Did I learn to celebrate the goodness that Life is teaching me? Last fall, out of a blue sky, Clara, my wife and soul mate, who made my life beautiful for fifty years, was diagnosed with ALS (Lou Gehrig's disease), a fatal nerve disease. This is the woman who among her zillion works embroidered my bedsheets for the boat with her secret love signs, so I know that I am not alone when I am alone at sea. Clara needs me now more than ever. So my best is for her, while she is still with us. No writing for me now. So, can I accept this difficult gift without complaint, sprout some goodies out of my sadness, and not end up an old grouch?

I dedicate this collection of "try-me-outs" to Clara, my wife and soul mate who inspired and made my life beautiful for fifty years.

Marie Claire Grutter passed away on Sept. 2, 2011 with her husband Theo and her children. She died from ALS (Lou Gehrig's Disease) at 73. Clara was born in Anderlues, Belgium, and grew up on a farm. She began playing piano at 7 and shortly thereafter studied it full time, to become a concert pianist. When she was 16 she moved to Paris to continue her studies where she met Theo, who had moved to Paris from Basel, Switzerland, and they decided to go together on a lifelong trip in 1963.

The couple moved to New York City briefly, and after a few years of traveling settled in Sitka, Alaska in 1966 in the summers and San Blas, Mexico in the winters. Clara raised their five children, and took them on many hikes and camping trips near where Theo fished for salmon during the summer. She home-schooled them in Mexico, after they spent the mornings at the local school.

Clara and Theo spent every November traveling and hiking in exotic places such as Borneo, Papa New Guinea, Ethiopia, Sikim, Cuba, Honduras, the tribal areas of Pakistan, and dozens of other countries.

Clara loved to garden and especially to dance. As her children got older she began playing piano again and went on as many hikes as the weather permitted. Hikers recount how they often encountered her hiking, alone, in the middle of nowhere with just a granola bar and bear spray in her backpack. She loved to accompany her son Fabian goat hunting, and rode her bike everywhere.

Marie Claire Grutter is survived by her husband Theo; her children Lexa of Brisbane, Australia, Gila of Astoria, Ore., Pia of Bellingham, Wash. and Ivan and Fabian, both of Sitka; and her grandchildren Tehsa, Tirsa, Rowan, and Anik.

~

Did you ever hear the right arm say to the left arm: "Thank you" or "I love you?" In our 50 years, Clara never felt the need to say: "Theo, I love you" for her acts told it a million times. Does not such wonderful simplicity come over us when two start to become one?

About the Author

Theo Grutter is a big, friendly bear of an unpretentious, spontaneous outdoorsman. Born and educated mostly in Switzerland to enter the corporate world, he soon discovered that this life wasn't for him. He moved to Paris and married Clara, a concert pianist. They landed in New York to search for a lifestyle more to their liking in which to raise a family, which soon grew to include five children. They lived in many places, finally settling in a small Mexican Pacific coast fishing village in winter and traveling up to Sitka, Alaska in the summers, where Theo still fishes as a solitary commercial fisherman. Theo and Clara took yearly walkabouts in many exotic countries of the world, with Theo ever observing, learning, and writing about how life works on Earth.

Also by Theo Grutter:

Dancing with Mosquitoes: To Liberate the Mind from Humanism